WRITING & GRAMMAR

9

second edition

for Christian Schools

TEACHER'S EDITION

Dana Denise Gage

Denise L. Patton

Elizabeth Rose

Dawn L. Watkins

Bob Jones University Press, Greenville, South Carolina 29614

NOTE:
The fact that materials produced by other publishers may be referred to in this volume does not constitute an endorsement by Bob Jones University Press of the content or theological position of materials produced by such publishers. The position of Bob Jones University Press, and of the University itself, is well known. Any references and ancillary materials are listed as an aid to the student or the teacher and in an attempt to maintain the accepted academic standards of the publishing industry.

WRITING AND GRAMMAR 9 for Christian Schools® Teacher's Edition, Book 2
Second Edition

Coordinating Authors
Dana Denise Gage, M.A.
Denise L. Patton
Elizabeth Rose, M.Ed.
Dawn L. Watkins, M.Ed., M.A.

Contributing Authors
Alicia M. Bernson, M.A.
Eileen M. Berry, M.A.
Sarah Miller, M.A.
Kimberly Y. Stegall, M.Ed.

Melanie N. Suydam
Danielle J. Sweede
Denise C. Zutter, M.Ed.

Consultants
June W. Cates
Grace Collins Hargis, Ph.D.
  *Chairman of the Departments of
  Linguistics and English Education,
  Bob Jones University*
Coart Ramey, M.A.
Steven N. Skaggs
  *Product Development Coordinator,
  Secondary Level,
  Bob Jones University Press*

Editor
Shelby J. Morris

Compositor
Kelley Moore

Cover Design
Elly Kalagayan
Duane A. Nichols

Designer
Duane A. Nichols

Photo Acquisition
Cindy Mauk

Illustrators
Timothy Banks
Paula Cheadle
Johanna Ehnis
Justin Gerard
Cory Godbey
Preston Gravely Jr.
Dyke Habegger
Jeremy Jantz
Stefanie Kubina
John Muessen
Scotty Pruitt
John Roberts
Lynda Slattery
Del Thompson
Sanela Tutaris

Produced in cooperation with the Bob Jones University Division of English Language and Literature of the College of Arts and Science, the School of Education, and Bob Jones Academy.

for Christian Schools is a registered trademark of Bob Jones University Press.

© 2001 Bob Jones University Press
Greenville, South Carolina 29614
First Edition © 1985 Bob Jones University Press

ISBN 1-57924-528-5

15 14 13 12 11 10 9 8 7 6 5 4 3 2 1

Table of Contents

To the Teacher

The reproducible blackline masters in this volume supplement Book 1 of the Teacher's Edition for *WRITING AND GRAMMAR 9 for Christian Schools,* Second Edition. Each blackline master serves a specific purpose. Since every teaching situation is different, these blackline masters are provided to help you adapt to your students' needs.

Pretests

Pretests are diagnostic tools for Chapters 1-12. Evaluating your students' skill levels prior to teaching will allow you to tailor your lessons to the needs of your students.

Teaching Helps

Teaching Helps accompany specific grammar, usage, and reference lessons. Some are designed to be used as overhead transparencies; some are designed to be used as student worksheets.

ESL Worksheets

ESL Worksheets accompany specific grammar and usage lessons. These worksheets give ESL students (those who speak English as a second language) extra help and practice with difficult concepts.

Concept Reinforcements

Concept Reinforcements accompany specific grammar and usage lessons. These worksheets provide students with extra review of the skills taught in the student text. Each set of fifteen questions is divided into three sections, with each group of five questions being more challenging than the one before.

Writing Worksheets

Writing Worksheets accompany specific writing assignments in the student text. These worksheets guide students through the steps of the writing process.

Writing Rubrics

Writing Rubrics accompany each specific writing assignment in the student text. The rubrics inform the students of your expectations and give you a method for evaluating fairly yet quickly. The grids allow objective and balanced scoring, and the space at the bottom that begins with the prompt "Overall, this writing . . ." provides room for personalized instruction. Each rubric can be used by students as a revision checklist or by you as an evaluation tool. (See "To the Teacher: Grading Writing Assignments" in Book 1 for further help.)

Chapter 1 Pretest: Sentences

I. Four Kinds of Sentences

Identify each sentence as *declarative, exclamatory, imperative,* or *interrogative.* Place the appropriate punctuation mark at the end of each sentence.

_____ 1. Many interesting salvation stories are found in the Book of Acts

_____ 2. Wow! God works in such miraculous ways

_____ 3. Have you accepted Christ as Savior

_____ 4. Christ tells us to give the salvation message to all people

_____ 5. Obey His commandment to witness throughout the whole world

II. Subjects and Predicates

Draw a vertical line between the complete subject and the complete predicate of each sentence.

6. Paul and his companions looked for a place of worship in Philippi.

7. They found a group of women by a river outside the city.

8. One woman, Lydia, knew about God but did not know Him personally.

9. The salvation message was given by Paul and his companions that morning by the river.

10. Lydia believed and was saved.

III. Inverted Order and Imperative Sentences

In each sentence underline the simple subject once and the simple predicate twice. If the subject is understood, write the understood *You* to the left of the number.

11. Have you heard about the salvation story of Saul?

12. There are so many interesting circumstances in that story.

13. Did Saul murder many Christians?

14. Present at the trial of Stephen was Saul.

15. Read in the Book of Acts about the rest of the story.

IV. Sentence Patterns

Label the sentence pattern in each sentence *S-InV*, *S-TrV-DO*, *S-TrV-IO-DO*, *S-LV-PN*, or *S-LV-PA*. Above each word of the sentence pattern write its label.

16. Cornelius was a centurion of the Italian band.

17. He was devout.

18. One day God sent him a vision.

19. God had answered his prayers.

20. Cornelius's men went to Joppa.

V. Phrases and Clauses

Label each italicized group of words *P* (phrase), *IC* (independent clause), or *DC* (dependent clause).

_____ 21. Peter was staying in Joppa *with a tanner named Simon.*

_____ 22. *In the middle of the day,* Peter went onto the housetop to pray.

_____ 23. *When he was on the housetop,* he fell into a trance.

_____ 24. A great sheet *that was filled with animals* was lowered before him.

_____ 25. *God told Peter to eat the meat.*

VI. Sentence Problems

Label each word group *S* (sentence), *F* (fragment), *FS* (fused sentence), or *CS* (comma splice).

_____ 26. Peter, thinking about the vision's meaning.

_____ 27. Peter heard the message from Cornelius's men, he went with them to Cornelius's house.

_____ 28. Cornelius had called his relatives together he called his close friends too.

_____ 29. Peter preached Christ, the Holy Ghost came upon those who were present.

_____ 30. God is no respecter of persons.

Chapter 2 Pretest: Nouns

I. Plural Nouns
In the blank write the plural form of the noun.

_____ 1. toll bridge

_____ 2. tomato

_____ 3. *m*

_____ 4. half

_____ 5. flagpole

_____ 6. business

_____ 7. child

_____ 8. sister-in-law

_____ 9. country

_____ 10. car wash

II. Possessive Nouns
In the blank write the correct possessive form of the noun in parentheses.

_____ 11. <u>?</u> geography teacher told him that France is the biggest country in Europe. *(Duane)*

_____ 12. My <u>?</u> pen pal lives in Nice, the fifth largest city in France. *(cousin)*

_____ 13. Aimee took her <u>?</u> camera with her when she visited France. *(parents)*

_____ 14. She saw <u>?</u> home, the Palace of Versailles. *(Louis XIV)*

_____ 15. To climb to the top of Mont Blanc has been my <u>?</u> lifelong dream. *(friend)*

III. Common and Proper Nouns
Underline each noun. Above each noun, label it *C* (common) or *P* (proper).

16. The Edict of Nantes gave religious freedom to French Huguenots.

17. Joan of Arc was a heroine of the Hundred Years' War.

18. The first king of France was Hugh Capet.

19. Those who supported the monarchy during the French Revolution were sent to the guillotine.

20. The Arc de Triomphe commemorates a conquest of Napoleon .

IV. Count and Noncount Nouns

In the blank write *count* or *noncount* for each italicized word.

_____ 21. France possesses eight island *territories*.

_____ 22. France produces more *barley* than the United States does.

_____ 23. The *scenery* in France is beautiful.

_____ 24 The Loire River is France's longest *river*.

_____ 25. The French Riviera is a favorite *place* to vacation in Europe.

V. Collective and Compound Nouns

Underline the compound nouns once and the collective nouns twice.

26. The Normans were a Viking group that invaded the region known today as Normandy.

27. Charles Martel led the French army at the Battle of Tours in 732.

28. Alsace is a region of France that is rich in farmland.

29. The Bourbon family reigned in France from 1589 to 1792 and from 1814 to 1830.

30. France is the world's second largest producer of sugar beets.

VI. Noun Functions

Label the function of each italicized noun *S* (subject), *DO* (direct object), *IO* (indirect object), *OP* (object of the preposition), *PN* (predicate noun), *App (*appositive), or *NA* (noun of direct address).

_____ 31. The Tuileries Palace is located next to the Louvre in *Paris*.

_____ 32. Louis XVI, the *"Sun King,"* reigned from 1661 to 1715.

_____ 33. Pierre-Auguste Renoir was a famous French impressionistic *painter*.

_____ 34. The British gave *Napoleon* the epithet "Corsican Ogre."

_____ 35. The Pyrenees Mountains separate France from *Spain*.

_____ 36. Claude Debussy, a French *composer*, demonstrated his musical talent at a young age.

_____ 37. *Guy de Maupassant* was a writer who was a contemporary of Debussy.

_____ 38. The ancient Greeks established *Marseilles*, France's oldest and largest city.

_____ 39. Mont-Saint-Michel is a *fortress* that was constructed by Philip II.

_____ 40. *Marcia*, what is the name of the river that flows through Paris?

Name_____

Chapter 3 Pretest: Pronouns

I. Pronouns and Antecedents

Underline each pronoun and write its antecedent in the blank.

_____ 1. Many people are very conscious of the style of clothes they wear.

_____ 2. The clothes a person wears can often give him authority.

_____ 3. A businessman often wears a suit so that he can look professional.

_____ 4. A teacher dresses in such a way that she will not appear intimidating to students.

_____ 5. Claudia, do you prefer to wear comfortable clothing?

II. Pronoun Case and Function

Underline the correct pronoun from the choices in parentheses. In the blank, label the function of the pronoun *S* (subject), *DO* (direct object), *OP* (object of the preposition), *IO* (indirect object), *PN* (predicate noun), or *App* (appositive).

_____ 6. The clothing styles of people from foreign lands fascinate my cousin and *(I, me)*.

_____ 7. *(We, Us)* two have purchased many items of clothing from different countries.

_____ 8. When I was in Japan, I bought *(she, her)* a beautiful green kimono.

_____ 9. Last summer *(she, her)* and her husband visited Mexico and brought me back a sombrero.

_____ 10. My father said that he will buy a dirndl dress for *(I, me)* when he goes to Germany this April.

_____ 11. My brother already owns some lederhosen. He bought *(they, them)* in Bavaria.

_____ 12. Grateful recipients of two lovely silk sarongs were *(my mother and I, me and my mother)*.

_____ 13. When Deborah went to Russia, she purchased fur caps for her uncles, Richard and *(he, him)*.

_____ 14. The sari that my cousin bought in India looks very attractive on *(she, her)*.

_____ 15. Jack gave *(we, us)* girls berets that he found at a boutique in Paris.

III. Case, Person, and Gender of Personal Pronouns

Identify the correct case, person, or gender of each italicized personal pronoun. In the blank write the letter that corresponds to the correct answer.

_____ 16. A waitress sometimes wears a hairnet to keep *her* hair pulled back.
 A. subjective
 B. objective
 C. possessive

_____ 17. Do construction workers always wear hardhats when *they* are at work?
   A. first person
   B. second person
   C. third person

_____ 18. Whenever *he* rides his motorcycle, Brad always wears a helmet.
   A. masculine
   B. feminine
   C. neuter

_____ 19. Did Kirsten wear a veil when *she* got married?
   A. subjective
   B. objective
   C. possessive

_____ 20. Did *you* know that a milliner is a person who styles hats?
   A. first person
   B. second person
   C. third person

IV. Demonstrative and Interrogative Pronouns

Underline the demonstrative and interrogative pronouns. Label each underlined pronoun *D* (demonstrative) or *I* (interrogative).

_____ 21. What is the traditional dress of Scotland?

_____ 22. The customary clothing is this: the kilt and the plaid.

_____ 23. Are these always worn together?

_____ 24. When did the Scots first start wearing kilts?

_____ 25. To whom should I address other questions concerning traditional dress?

V. Reflexive and Intensive Pronouns

Underline the reflexive and intensive pronouns. Label each underlined pronoun *R* (reflexive) or *I* (intensive).

_____ 26. I myself did not know that the first sweaters were worn before and after sporting events to keep athletes warm.

_____ 27. Since wool sweaters can be itchy, Ryan himself prefers to wear cotton sweaters.

_____ 28. My mother crocheted herself an angora sweater.

_____ 29. The pattern on the sweater itself is very interesting.

_____ 30. Joy and Ellen purchased new cardigans for themselves.

VI. Indefinite and Relative Pronouns

Underline the indefinite pronouns once and the relative pronouns twice.

31. Anne-Marie's ski vest, which is filled with down, is one of her warmest items of clothing.

32. My aunt, who is always prepared for inclement weather, carries a plastic poncho in her purse.

33. Moths have eaten through some of the jackets that are in the closet.

34. Dad has worn the same wool overcoat for years. It's hard to believe all of its buttons are still intact.

35. Several have told Alec to buy a jacket that has a hood.

VII. Correcting Unclear Reference

Rewrite each sentence to make the pronoun reference clear.

36. As soon as Kim tied Margaret's scarf, she was ready to go to the opera.

   _____

   _____

37. Ruffs were pleated collars worn in the sixteenth and seventeenth centuries that were popular.

   _____

   _____

38. The two storeowners had filled their small shop with all sorts of neckwear. Scarfs were displayed on racks, and ties were arranged on round tables. In addition, a number of colorful cravats graced the shelves on the wall. Overall, they had given it a pleasant atmosphere.

   _____

   _____

   _____

39. Mr. Cline told Stephen that his tie was very colorful.

   _____

   _____

40. They say that styles have changed drastically throughout the years.

   _____

   _____

Chapter 4 Pretest: Verbs

I. Recognizing the Complete Verb

Underline the complete verb in each sentence. Underline each auxiliary twice. Do not underline interrupting adverbs.

1. Insects are a part of God's marvelous creation.

2. My brother is keeping an insect collection.

3. All of his insects are displayed in a glass case.

4. I like the butterflies the best.

5. Do you own a butterfly net?

II. Sentence Patterns

Label the sentence pattern in each sentence *S-InV, S-TrV-DO, S-TrV-IO-DO, S-LV-PN,* or *S-LV-PA*. Above each word of the sentence pattern write its label.

6. A butterfly begins as an egg.

7. Then it becomes a caterpillar.

8. The third stage of a butterfly's life cycle is the pupating stage.

9. The caterpillar forms a chrysalis.

10. The adult butterfly emerges from its chrysalis.

11. Many moths look similar to butterflies.

12. Their life cycle is the same as the butterfly's.

13. The moth spins itself a cocoon.

14. Many moths produce silk.

15. Butterfly watching can be an enjoyable pastime.

III. Verb Tenses

In the blank, label the tense of the italicized verb *present, past, future, present perfect, past perfect,* or *future perfect*. Not all answers will be used.

_____ 16. Butterflies and moths *feed* themselves through their proboscises.

_____ 17. A monarch butterfly *had trapped* itself between the window and the screen.

_____ 18. Quincy *bought* a mesh-screened cage to house his butterfly caterpillars.

_____ 19. If Felicia catches one more butterfly, she *will have caught* twenty-three specimens.

_____ 20. I hope that she *will remember* to show her collection to me.

In the blank, label the tense of the italicized verb *present progressive, past progressive, future progressive, present perfect progressive, past perfect progressive,* or *future perfect progressive.* Not all answers will be used.

_____ 21. I *am planning* an insect collection for my biology class.

_____ 22. I *will be working* on it all semester long.

_____ 23. I *have been catching* every insect that I see.

_____ 24. Yesterday I *was sitting* on the porch, and I noticed a Japanese beetle.

_____ 25. I *had been reading* a book about insects, so I was able to identify the beetle.

IV. Other Uses for Auxiliaries

Underline the complete verb. If the sentence contains *do* or *will* as an auxiliary, label the auxiliary according to its use: *E* (emphasis), *Q* (question), or *N* (negative).

_____ 26. Some people do not know the difference between an insect and an arachnid.

_____ 27. Did the book discuss their differences?

_____ 28. Yes, arachnids do not have only six legs; instead, they have eight legs.

_____ 29. Many insects do have two sets of wings.

_____ 30. Will some insects open and close their wings several times before flight?

V. Active and Passive Voice

Underline the complete verb and label it *A* (active) or *P* (passive).

_____ 31. Cockroaches are considered household pests.

_____ 32. Dogs and cats are common flea hosts.

_____ 33. The Asian carpenter bee is known as the world's largest bee.

_____ 34. Wasps often kill grubs.

_____ 35. Some mosquitoes have spread diseases among humans.

VI. Mood

In the blank, label the mood of the italicized verb *indicative* or *imperative.*

_____ 36. *Mount* the insects in your collection with a straight pin.

_____ 37. The bee *stung* me on my right hand.

_____ 38. Please *get* me the fly swatter.

_____ 39. Mr. Eckard *says* that ladybugs are helpful insects.

_____ 40. Linda, *help* me catch this lacewing.

Name_____

Chapter 5 Pretest: Adjectives and Adverbs

I. Adjectives

Underline the adjectives. Write *PA* over each predicate adjective. Draw an arrow from each other adjective to the noun or pronoun it modifies.

1. It is hard to believe that people lived without many of the household items that we enjoy today.

2. A refrigerator, an electric stove, and a dishwasher are several items that a person may use daily.

3. All of my kitchen appliances are Kenmore appliances.

4. Which brand do you prefer?

5. Ours are General Electric appliances.

6. That mixer is efficient because it has six different speeds.

7. I like to use the blender to make ice-cream shakes.

8. The toaster, handy and compact, toasts bagels and bread.

9. Microwaves are especially popular.

10. We still own the same microwave that we purchased in 1994.

II. Adverbs

Underline the adverbs. Draw an arrow from each adverb to the word it modifies.

11. The vacuum cleaner quickly removed the dirt on the floor.

12. A vacuum cleaner that has a rather long hose is much simpler to use.

13. Change the bag on your vacuum regularly.

14. I can easily reach difficult places with the attachments on my vacuum.

15. I often use the vacuum to clean my car.

III. Comparisons

Underline the correct adjective or adverb from the choices in parentheses.

16. Of all of the stoves we have owned, I think our electric stove is the *(better, best)*.

17. Compared with our old refrigerator, our new one is *(wide, wider)*.

18. The microwave heats food *(quickly, more quickly)* than the oven does.

19. The electric can opener is a *(more efficient, most efficient)* alternative to the hand-held variety.

20. The coffeemaker should be placed *(closer, closest)* to the sink than where it is now.

IV. Using Modifiers Correctly

Underline the correct word from the choices in parentheses.

21. I think it would be *(difficult, difficultly)* to wash all of one's clothes by hand.

22. Clothing that is stained *(bad, badly)* can easily be washed in a washing machine.

23. If you overload the washing machine, it will not work *(good, well)*.

24. When the washing machine is overloaded, it often sounds very *(strange, strangely)*.

25. Our washing machine may be old, but it still does a *(good, well)* job.

26. The dryer is a machine that dries clothing *(quick, quickly)*.

27. One should not put *(anything, nothing)* in the dryer that is likely to shrink.

28. When I took my clothes out of the dryer, they felt *(warm, warmly)*.

29. After you unload the dryer, look *(careful, carefully)* to make sure that you have not left any items inside.

30. Those who have had a *(bad, badly)* experience at a Laundromat are thankful if they own their own machines at home.

V. Problems with Modifier Positions

Rewrite the following sentences, correcting any problems with modifier positions.

31. Our dishwasher only has two racks.

   _____

32. All dishwasher racks are not arranged the same way.

   _____

33. People who wash their dishes thoroughly rinse them before placing them in the dishwasher.

   _____

34. Adrienne even washes her fine china in the dishwasher.

   _____

35. A person who has washed dishes frequently realizes how helpful a dishwasher can be.

   _____

Name _____

Chapter 6 Pretest: Prepositions, Conjunctions, and Interjections

I. Prepositional Phrases

Place parentheses around each prepositional phrase. Underline the object of the preposition.

1. Geneva says she wants a new watch for her birthday.
2. The watch with the iridescent face has no numbers on it.
3. Before this week, I had never worn a watch.
4. Now I am never late to school.
5. Instead of a wristwatch, Zane carries a pocket watch.

II. Functions of Prepositional Phrases

Place parentheses around each prepositional phrase. Label the prepositional phrase *Adj* (adjectival) or *Adv* (adverbial). Draw an arrow from each phrase to the word it modifies.

_____ 6. Jared's signal watch beeps on the hour.

_____ 7. Last week it beeped during the church service.

_____ 8. The jewelry store around the corner sells both costly and inexpensive watches.

_____ 9. The watches in the glass case are very expensive.

_____ 10. Mr. Hobi times our sprints with his stopwatch.

III. Using Prepositions Correctly

Underline the correct preposition from the choices in parentheses.

11. *(Among, Between)* all the clocks in the Schneiders' house, the clock in the hall chimes the loudest.
12. The movers carried the grandfather clock *(in, into)* the living room.
13. They placed it *(beside, besides)* the grandmother clock.
14. *(Beside, Besides)* long-case clocks, there are also table clocks.
15. Monique placed her new mantle clock *(between, among)* the two candlesticks.

Label each italicized word *Prep* (preposition) or *Adv* (adverb).

_____ 16. When the alarm clock went *off,* I accidentally pressed the snooze button.

_____ 17. I then woke *up* an hour late.

_____ 18. When I walked *into* the office, my supervisor gave me a stern look.

_____ 19. I explained *to* him what had happened, and then he started to laugh.

_____ 20. He said that my being late was all right as long as I did not get *behind* in my work.

Pretests **13**

Correct each misplaced prepositional phrase by rewriting the sentence correctly in the blank. If the sentence is correct, write _C_ in the blank.

21. The cuckoo pops out every half-hour in the cuckoo clock.

    _____

22. From the Black Forest, Sven bought a cuckoo clock made of wood.

    _____

23. Many colleges and universities have a clock tower on their campuses.

    _____

24. In her rose garden, Great-grandmother told us that she wanted a sundial.

    _____

25. Weight-driven clocks have a weight from the drum of the clock that hangs.

    _____

IV. Conjunctions

Underline the conjunctions in the following sentences. In the blank, label the conjunctions _coordinating, correlative,_ or _subordinating._

_____ 26. Both "How Soon Hath Time" and "On Time" are poems by John Milton.

_____ 27. Mallory has two watches, but only one tells the correct time.

_____ 28. In early days, people used water clocks and hourglasses to keep track of time.

_____ 29. Water clocks were used not only for tracking the time during the day but also for timing the duration of speeches in Roman courts of law.

_____ 30. The early hourglasses held either sand or mercury.

_____ 31. Today some people use hourglasses for kitchen timers or game timers.

_____ 32. Before these devices were created, people kept time by relying on the length of their shadows.

_____ 33. The first mechanical clocks had neither pendulums nor hands.

_____ 34. Although these clocks lacked certain mechanisms, they did have a bell to announce the hour.

_____ 35. Many improvements had to be made to the early clocks because they were often inaccurate.

V. Interjections

Underline each interjection in the following sentences.

36. Could you wind the clock downstairs, please?

37. Wow! I can't believe how old your antique clock is.

38. Hey, do you know of a good jeweler who could fix my watch?

39. As a matter of fact, yes, Mr. Kuntz just repaired my watch last week.

40. Well, could you tell me where his store is located?

Chapter 7 Pretest: Verbals

I. Participles

Underline the participles. Draw an arrow from each underlined participle to the noun it modifies.

1. Many biblical characters are developing characters.

2. Jacob and Esau are two brothers who had a maturing relationship with each other.

3. Jacob and Esau were both favored sons.

4. Esau was a cunning hunter.

5. Esau became a deceived brother.

II. Participial Phrases

Underline the participial phrases. Draw an arrow from each underlined phrase to the noun it modifies. In the blank, label each underlined participial phrase *present* or *past*.

_____ 6. Tired from work in the field, Esau asked Jacob for some food.

_____ 7. Taking advantage of his brother's ravenous state, Jacob gave Esau pottage.

_____ 8. Esau, swearing that he would keep his promise, sold his birthright to Jacob.

_____ 9. Blinded by old age, Isaac was also deceived by Jacob.

_____ 10. Dressing Jacob in Esau's clothing, Rebekah helped Jacob to trick his father.

III. Gerunds and Gerund Phrases

Underline the gerunds. Place parentheses around the gerund phrases. In the blank, label the gerund or gerund phrase *S* (subject), *DO* (direct object), *IO* (indirect object), *OP* (object of the preposition), or *PN* (predicate noun).

_____ 11. Jacob was also able to fool his father by offering him savory meat.

_____ 12. As a result of his deceitfulness, Jacob received the blessing from his father.

_____ 13. Esau wanted the birthright, but his weeping could not change what had already transpired.

_____ 14. Serving Jacob in the future became Esau's lot in life.

_____ 15. Since Jacob received what Esau wanted, Esau entertained the thought of killing his brother.

_____ 16. Rebekah knew that Esau's plan was murdering Jacob.

_____ 17. She said that Jacob's best escape would be running away.

_____ 18. Jacob's fleeing led him to his mother's brother, Laban.

_____ 19. Jacob gave working for Laban his utmost attention because he loved Rachel so much.

_____ 20. After these years, Jacob received a calling from the Lord.

IV. Infinitives and Infinitive Phrases

Underline the infinitives. Place parentheses around the infinitive phrases. In the blank, label the function of each infinitive *N* (noun), *Adj* (adjective), or *Adv* (adverb).

_____ 21. To return home was God's command to Jacob.

_____ 22. Jacob obeyed God and decided to leave Laban's house.

_____ 23. To get to his homeland, Jacob traveled through Esau's territory.

_____ 24. Jacob sent messengers to speak with Esau.

_____ 25. Although God had promised him prosperity, Jacob felt that overwhelming Esau with gifts was the thing to do now.

_____ 26. To give Esau a gift of cattle was Jacob's plan of appeasing Esau.

_____ 27. Jacob's efforts to satisfy his brother worked better than he had expected.

_____ 28. Esau ran to greet Jacob.

_____ 29. Then he wanted to know about Jacob's family.

_____ 30. Jacob's family came before Esau to bow before him.

V. Participles, Gerunds, and Infinitives

Underline the verbals (not the entire phrases). In the blank, label each verbal *P* (participle), *G* (gerund), or *I* (infinitive). If the verbal is a modifier, draw an arrow from the verbal to the word it modifies.

_____ 31. Jacob decided to obey God no matter what the cost.

_____ 32. Although Jacob was God's chosen man, he demonstrated humility before his brother.

_____ 33. One way that Jacob showed his humility was his bowing before Esau.

_____ 34. Jacob no longer sought to scheme for Esau's ill.

_____ 35. Jacob's offering Esau a gift showed that he had changed in his relationship with Esau.

_____ 36. Esau's tears were no longer for sorrowing .

_____ 37. On the contrary, he cried to express his joy.

_____ 38. Esau was not greedy to take Jacob's gifts.

_____ 39. Esau's surprising response shows that God can change a bitter heart.

_____ 40. The reconciliation of these estranged brothers demonstrates that all things are possible with God.

Chapter 8 Pretest: Clauses

I. Phrases and Clauses

Label each italicized group of words *P* (phrase), *IC* (independent clause), or *DC* (dependent clause).

_____ 1. *Although numerous trees fill the world,* they are very different from one another.

_____ 2. The majority of trees fall into one *of two categories.*

_____ 3. *These two categories are broadleaf trees and needleleaf trees.*

_____ 4. Other trees *that do not fit* into these classifications are palms, ginkgoes, and cycads.

_____ 5. *Broadleaf trees produce vibrantly colored leaves* in the fall.

II. Using Independent and Dependent Clauses

Label each sentence *S* (simple), *Cd* (compound), *Cx* (complex), or *Cd-Cx* (compound-complex).

_____ 6. In the winter, broadleaf trees are characterized by their bare branches.

_____ 7. In the spring, broadleaf trees produce flowers that grow into fruit.

_____ 8. The birch and the beech are two broadleaf trees.

_____ 9. The birch has papery bark, and the beech has papery leaves.

_____ 10. Actually, there is a particular type of birch that is called the paper birch.

_____ 11. The paper birch is also known as the canoe birch or the white birch.

_____ 12. The paper birch got its name because its bark has the consistency of paper, and the canoe birch received its name because the Indians made canoes out of its bark.

_____ 13. The white birch grows in North America, whereas the European white birch grows in the northern part of Europe.

_____ 14. People use the wood of yellow birches and sweet birches to make furniture, and they use the wood of gray birches to manufacture spools.

_____ 15. The river birch grows in a moist climate, and it has a bark that can turn from salmon pink to almost black.

III. Adjective Clauses

In the blank write the word(s) modified by the italicized adjective clause.

_____ 16. The yellow birch, *which is also called the silver birch,* can reach a height of fifty to seventy-five feet.

_____ 17. Robert Frost, *who was a New England poet,* wrote a poem entitled "Birches."

_____ 18. Frost describes the birches as trees *that have been bent.*

_____ 19. Frost offers two reasons *that the trees are curved.*

_____ 20. Either the ice storm has bowed them, or they have been bent by a boy *whose hobby is birch swinging.*

IV. Adverb Clauses

In the blank write the word(s) modified by the italicized adverb clause.

_____ 21. *Although many trees are classified differently,* they often grow beside one another.

_____ 22. Palm trees exist *where the environment is warm.*

_____ 23. *Even though the majority of palms have one trunk,* some possess several trunks growing from the same roots.

_____ 24. Reina always collects coconuts *whenever she visits her aunt in Hawaii.*

_____ 25. *After she obtains several coconuts,* she carries them back to her aunt's house.

Place parentheses around the dependent clauses. In the blank, label each clause *Adj* (adjective) or *Adv* (adverb).

_____ 26. Palms are trees that provide many benefits.

_____ 27. Chairs and baskets that are woven are often made of palm leaves.

_____ 28. Raffia, which is commonly used in decorating, comes from the Madagascar palm.

_____ 29. I often use raffia when I need to tie a package.

_____ 30. Palm Springs is a city in California where palm trees line the streets.

_____ 31. Palm Sunday occurred before Christ was crucified.

_____ 32. Palm Sunday commemorates the day when people placed palm branches on the ground before Jesus' entry into Jerusalem.

_____ 33. When they placed the palm branches on the ground, they cried, "Hosanna!"

_____ 34. Although some palms produce poisonous seeds, most produce nontoxic seeds.

_____ 35. After we had bored holes into the coconuts, we drank the milk inside.

Name_____

Chapter 9 Pretest: Agreement

I. Subjects and Predicates
Underline the simple subject in each sentence. Underline the verb that agrees with the subject.

1. Scientific studies *(has taught, have taught)* us many fascinating things.

2. How does a person *(solve, solves)* a scientific problem?

3. Scientists *(follow, follows)* the scientific method.

4. First, a scientist *(establish, establishes)* a problem.

5. Preliminary research *(is, are)* profitable for the scientist who is trying to establish a problem.

II. Compound Subjects
Underline the verb that agrees with the subject.

6. Latasha or Kami *(knows, know)* where to get the best information for the science project.

7. Neither Tyler nor Jerome *(has started, have started)* his scientific research.

8. Both Helen and Melita *(is, are)* responsible for observing and recording the data.

9. Our biology teacher and our chemistry teacher *(is conducting, are conducting)* experiments in the lab.

10. Either Mr. McCarnan or Mrs. Holmes *(works, work)* at the Center of Science and Industry.

III. Finding the Subject
Underline the simple subject in each sentence. Underline the correct verb from the choices in parentheses.

11. Here *(is, are)* a section of our book that talks about heredity.

12. Cells *(is, are)* one thing that we will study in this chapter.

13. One function of cells *(is, are)* respiration.

14. There *(is, are)* also other important roles for cells in the body.

15. The genes, not the nucleus, *(is, are)* the "blueprints" of the cell.

16. Cell division *(is, are)* the formation of two cells from one cell.

17. The process of mitosis *(is, are)* the replication of genes from the parent cell to the two new daughter cells.

18. What *(is, are)* the four phases of mitosis?

19. The first of these phases *(is, are)* prophase.

20. Prophase, metaphase, and anaphase, but not telophase, *(is, are)* stages of mitosis in which the cell has a spindle.

IV. Indefinite Pronouns and Problem Nouns as Subjects
Underline the verb that agrees with the subject.

21. Genetics *(is, are)* the study of heredity.

22. "Where did you get your curly hair and gray eyes?" *(is, are)* a question that people often ask Tiffany.

23. "Gregor Mendel's Findings" *(is, are)* the title of one of the sections in the genetics chapter in our book.

24. Most of the students in the class *(enjoys, enjoy)* Punnett squares.

25. Each *(works, work)* out the combinations on his own.

26. Then the class *(divides, divide)* into groups to compare results.

27. Charles's group *(is, are)* discussing their results with each other.

28. Today the news *(is, are)* featuring an article about modern genetics.

29. Many of us students *(plans, plan)* to read the article.

30. "Be sure to take good notes and study hard for your test" *(is, are)* the advice that Mrs. Klinger gave us before we left biology class.

V. Number and Gender with Noun Antecedents
In the blank write an appropriate personal pronoun to complete the sentence.

_____ 31. Hemophilia is often called "the disease of royalty," and _?_ is also called "the bleeder's disease."

_____ 32. Although Queen Victoria did not have this disease, she passed it along to _?_ offspring.

_____ 33. Alice and Beatrice, Victoria's daughters, carried the hemophilic gene; consequently, _?_ had children and grandchildren who were hemophiliacs.

_____ 34. A *carrier* is a person who carries a gene for a trait; however, _?_ does not show the trait.

_____ 35. Alexis, a great-grandson of Victoria, was also a hemophiliac. _?_ was heir to the Russian throne.

VI. Compound Antecedents
Underline the correct pronoun from the choices in parentheses.

36. Both dominant and recessive traits reveal *(itself, themselves)* in a person's biological makeup.

37. Neither Shelley nor Marienne can roll *(her, their)* tongue.

38. Valerie or her two sisters will carry *(her, their)* father's gene for colorblindness.

39. Hank and Patrick have arched feet like both of *(his, their)* parents.

40. Neither Jessica's uncles nor her father has a cleft in *(his, their)* chin.

VII. Indefinite Pronouns as Antecedents

If the italicized pronoun does not agree with its antecedent, write the correct pronoun in the blank. If the sentence does not contain an agreement error, write _C_ in the blank.

_____ 41. Both of my aunts have dimples in *her* right cheeks.

_____ 42. Each of Emil's brothers has *their* father's nose.

_____ 43. Neither of my nieces has *their* mother's straight hair.

_____ 44. All the members of the Merrill family have *their* grandfather's hazel eyes.

_____ 45. One of the girls in my youth group has a widow's peak in *their* hairline.

_____ 46. Some of the other girls wish that *they* had one as well.

_____ 47. Not everyone appreciates the traits God has given *them*.

_____ 48. Quite often only a few are thankful to God for the traits He has given *him*.

_____ 49. However, no one should be disappointed with the way God has made *him*.

_____ 50. God always designs someone so that *they* can glorify Him.

Name_____

Chapter 10 Pretest: Spelling and Troublesome Words

I. Spelling

Underline any misspelled words and write the corrections in the blank. If the sentence is correct, write *C* in the blank.

1. I would never think of skiping breakfast on a Sunday morning.

   _____

2. Mother always prepares our family a bountyful breakfast.

   _____

3. This morning she cooked pancakes, bacon, eggs, and fried potatoes.

   _____

4. Mom's hearty breakfasts are a favorite part of my deit.

   _____

5. After breakfast Dad, the leader of our home, directs us in our family devotions.

   _____

6. I forgot to bring my Bible to the table, so I had to retreive it from my bedroom.

   _____

7. Today we discussed practicing holyness in our dayly lifes .

   _____

8. Some think that only those who have committed heinous crimes need to be deterred from sin.

   _____

9. However, in God's eyes sins such as conciet and laziness are just as wicked as theivery or lying.

   _____

10. Nevertheless, Christ's death on the cross made atonment for all sin.

    _____

II. Troublesome Verbs

Underline the correct verb from the choices in parentheses.

11. My family always *(sits, sets)* on the fourth row at church.

12. Whenever I see a hymnal *(lying, laying)* on the floor, I place it in the hymn rack.

13. The music director always has us *(rise, raise)* to our feet for the third hymn.

14. I asked Father if I *(may, can)* hold my own hymnal.

15. I think I *(shall, will)* never lose my love for singing hymns in church.

III. Other Troublesome Words

Underline the correct word from the choices in parentheses.

16. For the past several months, our pastor has been preaching about prophets and their *(prophecies, prophesies)*.

17. He has preached on Jonah, Amos, Obadiah, *(etc., and others)*.

18. Last week his message was entitled, "*(Prophecy, Prophesy)* the Truth!"

19. This message contained *(fewer, less)* points *(than, then)* his previous sermons, so I have been able to remember his points quite easily throughout the week.

20. What he said has *(affected, effected)* my thinking, and I have been looking for opportunities to witness to my unsaved neighbors.

21. I am *(real, really)* glad that I was able to talk to my unsaved friend Stacey yesterday.

22. She doesn't have a Bible, so I *(lent, loaned)* her one of mine.

23. I told her that she may *(borrow, loan)* it for as long as she likes.

24. I was able to share with her that Christ *(Hisself, Himself)* gave His life for her.

25. I was able to tell her that she needs to *(accept, except)* Christ as her personal Savior.

IV. Homonyms

Underline the correct word from the choices in parentheses.

26. After I shared the gospel with Stacey, I told her that I would *(pray, prey)* for her.

27. It is sobering to think of all the people that Satan *(prays, preys)* upon.

28. However, it is comforting to know that God will never *(desert, dessert)* His children.

29. Christians can always go to God's Word for *(council, counsel)*.

30. I am going to use my new *(stationary, stationery)* to write some letters to my unsaved relatives.

31. My unsaved uncle lives in St. Paul, the *(capital, capitol)* of Minnesota.

32. He is a man of good *(principals, principles)*; however, he still needs Christ to save him.

33. Christians should remember to pray for the many unsaved legislators at the *(capitol, Capitol)*.

34. We should also keep in mind the unsaved persons who serve on our local city *(council, counsel)*.

35. Hard-hearted people often seem to be *(stationary, stationery)* in their beliefs, but we Christians need to remember that God is in control of people's hearts.

V. Possessive Pronouns v. Contractions

Underline the correct word from the choices in parentheses.

36. *(Its, It's)* a humbling experience to witness to someone *(whose, who's)* making fun of you.

37. However, *(they're, there)* not really scorning you.

38. *(Their, They're)* scorn is actually mocking *(your, you're)* God.

39. *(Your, You're)* not going to allow another person's behavior to keep you from witnessing, are you?

40. Remember that *(theirs, there's)* always the chance that a seed will be planted in that unsaved person's life.

Chapter 11 Pretest: Capitalization

I. Proper Nouns: Personal Names, Religions, Nationalities

Underline any word that is an example of a capitalization error and write the correction in the blank. If the sentence is correct, write *C* in the blank.

1. Last semester my brother Jeff took a poetry class with dr. Joachim r. Langenscheidt.

    _____

2. Although he was austrian, Dr. Langenscheidt spoke impeccable English.

    _____

3. On the first day of class, he shared how he had come to know the redeemer.

    _____

4. He grew up in a catholic home, but he came to Christ after reading a german new testament that his aunt Ingrid had given him.

    _____

5. Dr. Langenscheidt told Jeff's class that he has always had a love for poetry.

    _____

6. As he read more of the bible, he realized that God had filled his Word with books of poetry.

    _____

7. Dr. Langenscheidt always begins his poetry class by teaching from the proverbs.

    _____

8. Although he does put an emphasis on old testament poetry, he also teaches other types of poetry.

    _____

9. Jeff really enjoyed learning about the differences between elizabethan and petrarchan sonnets.

    _____

10. Jeff told me that his favorite poem was one in which John Milton addresses Time.

    _____

II. Proper Nouns: Place Names, Transportation, Astronomical Terms

Underline any word that is an example of a capitalization error and write the correction in the blank. If the sentence is correct, write *C* in the blank.

11. Although I really wanted to go to Australia, I plan to spend my summer vacation in the midwest.

    _____

12. Justine promised to take me sailing on lake Michigan.

    _____

13. She also said that we need to visit chicago and green bay.

    _____

14. When we are in Ohio, she said that we could take a boat ride on the *goodtime II*.

    _____

15. If we take the ride at night, perhaps we'll be able to spot ursa major.

    _____

16. I've always wanted to see saturn's rings, but I don't think that we'll be able to see them without a telescope.

    _____

17. Justine's dad said that he would take us to a train museum that displays models of old trains.

    _____

18. The Museum is located downtown on 1400 main street.

    _____

19. Her dad's favorite train is named *royal blue*.

    _____

20. Before I return to the South, I want to visit the great plains and the ozark plateau.

    _____

III. Proper Nouns: Businesses and Organizations, Cultural and Historical Terms

In the blank write the letter of the choice that is capitalized correctly.

_____ 21. A. Oxford University
                B. a Grocery store
                C. february

_____ 22. A. the Cia
          B. the American cancer society
          C. Pepsi

_____ 23. A. The Language Club
          B. Senior class field trip
          C. Bull Moose Party

_____ 24. A. Tower of London
          B. winter Festival
          C. Castle drawbridge

_____ 25. A. Presidents' day
          B. Valentine's Day
          C. fourth of July

_____ 26. A. Pulitzer Prize
          B. statue of liberty
          C. Industrial revolution

_____ 27. A. world war I
          B. april showers
          C. Empire State Building

_____ 28. A. Trade school
          B. Saturday at the zoo
          C. declaration of independence

_____ 29. A. Phi beta kappa
          B. Football team
          C. Boston Red Sox

_____ 30. A. Program for Better literacy
          B. Federal Deposit Insurance Corporation
          C. national guard

IV. Titles and First Words

In the blank write the letter of the choice that is capitalized correctly.

_____ 31. A. My dad delivers our local newspaper, the _Plain Dealer._
          B. Edmund Waller wrote the poem "Of the last verses of the Book."
          C. Miss Green subscribes to _Good housekeeping_ magazine.

_____ 32. A. chapter 21
          B. Act III
          C. "The Sands of time are Sinking"

_____ 33. A. Monet's painting _The Road Bridge at Argenteuil_
          B. Literature
          C. _Good morning America_

_____ 34. A. "Are you going to lunch?" Asked Sheila. "I don't think so," replied Brooke.
　　　　 B. "Let's go to supper," suggested Sheila, "and then we can talk."
　　　　 C. Brooke replied, "well, I believe I'll have time to do that."

_____ 35. A. My heart is like a singing bird whose nest is in a watered shoot;
　　　　　　 my heart is like an apple tree whose boughs are bent with thickest fruit;
　　　　 B. My heart is like a singing bird whose nest is in a watered shoot;
　　　　　　 My heart is like an apple tree whose boughs are bent with thickest fruit;
　　　　 C. my heart is like a singing bird whose nest is in a watered shoot;
　　　　　　 my heart is like an apple tree whose boughs are bent with thickest fruit;
　　　　　　 (from "A Birthday" by Christina Rossetti)

_____ 36. A. The geese fly in a v-formation.
　　　　 B. Did Blythe make a b+ in Science 101?
　　　　 C. The first note I learned to identify on the piano was middle C.

_____ 37. A. Dear Pastor Ashbrook and church family,
　　　　 B. Sincerely yours,
　　　　 C. your loving son,

_____ 38. A.
　　　　　　　 I. Gathering the materials
　　　　　　 II. Wrapping the gift
　　　　　　 III. Decorating the wrapped box
　　　　 B.
　　　　　　　 I. Gathering the Materials
　　　　　　 II. Wrapping the Gift
　　　　　　 III. Decorating the Wrapped Box
　　　　 C.
　　　　　　　 I. Gathering the Materials
　　　　　　 II. Wrapping the Gift
　　　　　　 III. Decorating the wrapped Box

_____ 39. A. Did Beethoven write the "moonlight sonata"?
　　　　 B. Have you read _Pride and Prejudice?_
　　　　 C. I love to study Fine Arts.

_____ 40. A. Grandma always reminds me, "call me when you get home."
　　　　 B. Who will defend us, o prince?
　　　　 C. Do you think that I will be invited to the Spanish party?

Chapter 12 Pretest: Punctuation

I. End Marks and Special Uses of Periods

Identify the sentence or address that is punctuated correctly. In the blank write the letter that corresponds to the correct answer.

_____ 1. A. I met with the pastor on Tuesday at 11:00 A.M.
B. I met with the pastor on Tuesday at 11:00 AM.

_____ 2. A. He asked me whether I had ever memorized any verses from the Epistle to the Philippians?
B. He asked me whether I had ever memorized any verses from the Epistle to the Philippians.

_____ 3. During our interview he gave me three things to remember:
A. 1. Be a servant.
   2. Be content.
   3. Rejoice in the Lord.
B. 1 Be a servant.
   2 Be content.
   3 Rejoice in the Lord.

_____ 4. A. He said I may send any further questions to him at the following address:
Rev. James Smythe, P.O. Box 11, Willoughby, OH 44094.
B. He said I may send any further questions to him at the following address:
Rev James Smythe, PO Box 11, Willoughby, OH 44094.

_____ 5. A. Did you know that the apostle Paul wrote Philippians around A.D. 60?
B. Did you know that the apostle Paul wrote Philippians around AD 60.

II. Commas in a Series and After Introductory Elements

Identify the sentence that is punctuated correctly. In the blank write the letter that corresponds to the correct answer.

_____ 6. A. Paul addresses the Epistle to the Philippians to the saints, bishops and deacons at Philippi.
B. Paul addresses the Epistle to the Philippians to the saints, bishops, and deacons at Philippi.

_____ 7. A. In the opening verses he expresses his earnest, joyful prayer for them.
B. In the opening verses he expresses his earnest joyful prayer for them.

_____ 8. A. Paul says that he longs after the Philippians, and he prays that their love would abound.
B. Paul says that he longs after the Philippians and he prays that their love would abound.

_____ 9. A. In verse 12, Paul explains why God has allowed him to be in prison.
B. In verse 12 Paul explains why God has allowed him to be in prison.

_____ 10. A. First he says that all those in the palace know about his bonds for Christ.
Second he says that others outside the palace also know about his bonds for Christ.
Finally he says that other Christians are bolder to speak for Christ.
B. First, he says that all those in the palace know about his bonds for Christ.
Second, he says that others outside the palace also know about his bonds for Christ.
Finally, he says that other Christians are bolder to speak for Christ.

III. Commas to Set Off Certain Sentence Elements and Incorrect Commas

Identify the sentence that is punctuated correctly. In the blank write the letter that corresponds to the correct answer.

_____ 11. A. Paul says that some people preached Christ with contention, not with sincerity.
B. Paul says that some people preached Christ with contention not with sincerity.

_____ 12. A. Yes, there were others who did preach Christ out of love.
B. Yes there were others who did preach Christ out of love.

_____ 13. A. Chapter 2 which tells of Christ's humility is one of my favorite chapters.
B. Chapter 2, which tells of Christ's humility, is one of my favorite chapters.

_____ 14. A. A person who humbles himself acts in a Christlike manner.
B. A person, who humbles himself, acts in a Christlike manner.

_____ 15. A. Paul hopes that Timothy will be able to visit the Philippians, and, he also says that he himself would like to see them.
B. Paul hopes that Timothy will be able to visit the Philippians, and he also says that he himself would like to see them.

IV. Commas with Quotations, Dates, and Addresses and Commas in Letters

Insert any missing commas in the following sentences. If the sentence is correct, write _C_ in the blank.

_____ 16. "In the second chapter of Philippians" said Merle "Paul talks about Epaphroditus."

_____ 17. "Does Paul mention why Epaphroditus was sick?" asked Nadine.

_____ 18. I hope to have all of Philippians memorized by my next birthday, May 7 2002.

_____ 19. Please send the commentary on Philippians to my new address: 872 Bank Street Painesville Ohio 44077.

_____ 20. Pastor West always closes his letters in the following manner: "In Christ Rev. Scott West."

V. Semicolons and Colons

Insert any missing semicolons or colons in the following sentences.

21. The first part of Philippians 2 discusses Christ's humility and exaltation the first part of Philippians 3 discusses Paul's credentials.

22. Paul warns the Philippians to beware of the following dogs, evil workers, and the concision.

23. Paul was of the people of Israel Paul was of the tribe of Benjamin.

24. Philippians 3 14 has been my life verse since I was ten.

25. One theme that appears to be repeated throughout Philippians is this likemindedness.

VI. Quotation Marks, Italics, and Ellipses

Identify the punctuation mark missing from each sentence. In the blank write the letter that corresponds to the correct answer. (If necessary, you may use your Bible to answer these questions.)

> A. quotation marks
> B. italics
> C. ellipses

_____ 26. The word joy is repeated throughout the Epistle to the Philippians.

_____ 27. How many times does Paul use this word throughout the book? asked A. J.

_____ 28. Peg said, "I believe it appears um, actually, I'm not certain how many times, but"

_____ 29. "I'd like to hear what songs you'd like to sing, said Ryan. Perhaps we could sing a hymn."

_____ 30. Irene suggested, "Why don't we sing Joyful, Joyful, We Adore Thee?"

_____ 31. Have you ever read the book Be Joyful?

_____ 32. Philippians 4:7 says, "And the peace of God shall keep your hearts and minds through Christ Jesus."

_____ 33. In its last issue, New Testament News carried a ten-page article on the Epistle to the Philippians.

_____ 34. The article was entitled Philippians: A Prison Epistle.

_____ 35. Cole's painting, The Rejoicing Christian, is a magnificent piece of art.

VII. Apostrophes, Hyphens, Dashes, and Parentheses

Identify the punctuation mark missing from each sentence. In the blank write the letter that corresponds to the correct answer.

> A. apostrophe
> B. hyphen
> C. dash
> D. parentheses

_____ 36. This morning I read Philippians 4:113.

_____ 37. At the beginning of Philippians 4, Paul requests that two women Euodias and Syntyche be likeminded.

_____ 38. The next verse talks about Clement do you think that Euodias and Syntyche heeded Paul's exhortation?

_____ 39. Paul rejoices in the Lord for the Philippians generosity.

_____ 40. Im so glad that Ive been able to read this book of the Bible.

Teaching Help 1: Sentences

Join the clauses from the right column to the clauses in the left column by using an appropriate conjunction from the middle column. Some combinations may be written as two separate sentences, and the same conjunction may be used more than once. Remember to use the proper punctuation when combining the clauses.

Early fans were made of palm leaves		the lorgnette fan even had an eyeglass
	but	
People used fans to cool themselves		in China both men and women carried fans
Some painters included fans in their paintings	yet	by the Victorian period fans had radii of more than twenty inches
A "broken" fan resembles a leaf		people often carried them as part of their attire
The Japanese invented the folding fan in A.D. 700	so	the Portuguese brought the folding fan to Europe
Many people associate fans with women		a banner fan looks like a flag
	however	
In the early 1800s fans had about an eight-inch radius		Anthony Van Dyck painted ostrich-feather fans in some of his paintings
Fans were an important accessory	or	they used fans to chase away flies
Fan handles were often fashioned from ivory or tortoise shell	and	later fans were made of ostrich or peacock feathers
Some fans incorporated very interesting features		some were crafted from bone or sandalwood

1. _____

2. _____

3. _____
_____

4. _____

5. _____

6. _____

7. _____
_____

8. _____

9. _____
_____

10. _____

Teaching Help 2A: Forms and Kinds of Nouns

Fill in the blanks with the correct answer to each question. Then find each answer in the scrambled letters below.

_____ 1. What kind of noun names a specific person, place, thing, or idea?

_____ 2. What kind of noun names a group?

_____ 3. What kind of noun combines two or more words?

_____ 4. What is the plural form of *pastry?*

_____ 5. What is the plural form of *echo?*

_____ 6. What is the plural form of *auto?*

_____ 7. What is the plural form of *knife?*

_____ 8. What is the plural form of *criterion?*

_____ 9. What is the plural form of *species?*

_____ 10. What is the plural form of *beach?*

```
T B M I C W S A S H R T D E E T S S
E E T E S H C T O G S C G N O E E C
A A D R P I S B S A P N S I O N I C
S C O N O E M A D L A O A T D N E E
H H O O H F L E H E S M U N E E I M
E S P C O U N T V S T A E R O T E O
O C A A T A R I B S R E C H O E S O
C E N S A O T N N T I E C E C C M A
B U E H I C W O T M E T S I O H N H
O I E T E M I D B A S O E E M S X S
L P W L N R A K C C T O F I M E L P
E S L A E A T N N U R B Y D O C O E
L O T T E R D R A I W I S A N H A C
C T I E E C F G R K V S T H F O R I
X R A P A S T R Y S R E D E E S A E
C A O H E A D L E L H S S T R H T S
O R A B K N I F E S I H E E S I D S
P C O M P O U N D S H O E X F W A E
```

Teaching Help 2B: Nouns

Answer the following questions about the paragraph below.

_____ 1. What noun is a subject in sentence 5?

_____ 2. What noun is a predicate noun in sentence 2?

_____ 3. What noun is a direct object in sentence 10?

_____ 4. What noun is an indirect object in sentence 9?

_____ 5. What noun is the object of the preposition in sentence 1?

_____ 6. What noun is a noun of direct address in sentence 1?

_____ 7. What noun is an appositive in sentence 4?

_____ 8. What possessive noun appears in sentence 7?

_____ 9. What compound noun appears in sentence 3?

_____ 10. What proper noun appears in sentence 6?

[1] Benjamin, did you see the starfish my brother found at the ocean? [2] I think it's a fascinating creature. [3] As he was walking along the shore, he found the starfish between some rocks. [4] Justin, my brother, told me that starfish are sometimes called sea stars. [5] Both names are appropriate, I think. [6] I asked Justin if all starfish have five appendages, and Justin said that some starfish have more than forty! [7] I noticed that Justin's starfish was missing an arm, but Justin said that the starfish would grow another arm to replace it. [8] Isn't that amazing! [9] I wanted to give the starfish a name, but Justin said that we should return the starfish to the ocean. [10] Perhaps we'll find some more sea creatures tomorrow.

Teaching Help 3: Pronouns

In the blank write the pronoun that completes each sentence correctly. Choose the pronoun from the list below.

I	she
me	her
we	they
us	them
who	himself
whom	themselves
he	
him	

_____ 1. _?_ girls were admiring the artwork around your house.

_____ 2. _?_ painted that portrait in your hallway?

_____ 3. It has captured the attention of Katarina and _?_.

_____ 4. Charles Willson Peale painted that picture. His family and _?_ were well-known American painters.

_____ 5. From _?_ did his family learn to draw?

_____ 6. Many of them learned from Charles Willson Peale _?_.

_____ 7. Raphaelle and Rembrandt Peale were two of his sons. Do you think he named _?_ after the famous artists?

_____ 8. Raphaelle and Rembrandt Peale _?_ became prominent artists.

_____ 9. Still life and portrait painters were _?_.

_____ 10. Sarah Miriam Peale was Charles Willson Peale's niece. Some have named _?_ as the first female American portrait painter.

Teaching Help 4: Verbs

Answer the following questions. Then use your answers to complete the crossword puzzle.

Across

_____ 6. An _?_ helps the main verb.

_____ 9. _?_ verbs do not have a complement.

_____ 11. The verb *will read* is in what tense?

_____ 12. A declarative sentence is written in the _?_ mood.

_____ 13. In _?_ voice the subject receives the action of the verb.

Down

_____ 1. In _?_ voice the subject is the doer of the action.

_____ 2. The auxiliary *do* creates _?_, makes a sentence negative, or forms a question.

_____ 3. To form the present perfect tense, use *have* or _?_.

_____ 4. A state-of-being verb is a _?_ verb.

_____ 5. _?_ verbs have direct objects.

_____ 7. _?_ verbs show continuous action.

_____ 8. _?_ tense verbs express completion of an action.

_____ 10. The _?_ mood is used for commands and requests.

Teaching Help 5A: Adjectives and Adverbs

Fill in appropriate modifiers to complete the paragraph.

As Colin and I approached the _____, _____ house, we heard
                                    (adjective)   *(adjective)*

a _____ noise behind us. At first we were _____ frightened, but we
        (adjective)   *(adverb)*

_____ discovered that the sound we heard was only a _____ cat. We
        (adverb)   *(adjective)*

continued to walk _____ towards the _____ door and then
                            (adverb)   *(adjective)*

_____ stepped onto the _____ steps. Trying the door handle, we
        (adverb)   *(adjective)*

discovered that the knob was _____, but we were still able to open the door
                                        (adjective)

_____ easily. As we entered the house, we _____ noticed that there were
        (adverb)   *(adverb)*

cobwebs everywhere. It was obvious that this house had been deserted for _____ years.
                                                                                    (adjective)

Colin found a broom in a _____ closet, and he started brushing away the cobwebs.
                                (adjective)

Although the house was _____ and _____, we figured that it wouldn't
                                (adjective)   *(adjective)*

take long to clean it up. After we explored the rest of the house, we _____ decided that
                                                                                (adverb)

this place would be the _____ spot for our _____ club.
                                (adjective)   *(adjective)*

Teaching Help 5B: Adjectives and Adverbs

Choose the correct modifier from the choices in parentheses.

1. The sky looks *(ominous, ominously)*.

2. Dark clouds appear *(quick, quickly)*.

3. We look *(expectant, expectantly)* at the sky.

4. The distant thunder sounds *(loud, loudly)*.

5. We remain *(safe, safely)* in our house.

6. We needed the rain *(bad, badly)*.

7. It has watered our lawn *(good, well)*.

8. Now the air smells *(fresh, freshly)*.

9. The sunshine feels *(good, well)*.

10. We hope that the weather will stay *(warm, warmly)*.

Teaching Help 6A: Prepositions

Rewrite the scrambled sentences. In each rewritten sentence place parentheses around each prepositional phrase and underline each object of the preposition.

1. botanical garden visited on a I Saturday. _____

2. I stayed The weather the shade in was very warm whenever so I could. _____

3. the tall trees was cool under It the shade of. _____

4. a stone bridge I walked hanging from it ivy over that had. _____

5. winding stream a Beneath was the bridge. _____

6. everyone of Melinda took by standing a photograph the fountains. _____

7. walking exotic plants among enjoyed I the. _____

8. gardens explored until We the 4:00 P.M. _____

9. learned I greenhouse inside that some were edible of the plants the. _____

10. worn out Melinda our tour after I and were. _____

Teaching Help 6B: Conjunctions

Rewrite the following paragraph by adding appropriate coordinating and correlative conjunctions. Use a variety of conjunctions.

Peacocks belong to the pheasant family. The male is called a peacock. The female is called a peahen. The peacock is a peafowl. The peahen is a peafowl. The Indian peacock is a species of peafowl. The Javanese peacock is a species of peafowl. Indian peafowl live in India. Indian peafowl live in Sri Lanka. A Congo peacock feather was found in 1913. The Congo peacock was not discovered until 1936. A male peafowl possesses a train. He also possesses a head ornament. The female does not have a train. She does not have a head ornament. Some peacocks are wild. Some peacocks are tame. Wild peacocks inhabit open forests during the day. They roost in trees at night. Peacocks are mentioned in an ancient Greek play. They are also mentioned in the Bible.

_____

_____

_____

_____

_____

_____

_____

_____

_____

_____

_____

_____

_____

_____

_____

_____

Teaching Help 7A: Participles and Gerunds

Use the following phrases to form a sentence with a gerund and a sentence with a participle.

1. growing sunflowers

   A. participle:_____

   B. gerund:_____

2. running water

   A. participle:_____

   B. gerund:_____

3. cooking vegetables

   A. participle:_____

   B. gerund:_____

4. dripping ice cream

   A. participle:_____

   B. gerund:_____

5. training employees

   A. participle:_____

   B. gerund:_____

Teaching Help 7B: Infinitives

Place parentheses around each infinitive in Philip P. Bliss's hymn "Dare to Be a Daniel."

Standing by a purpose true,

Heeding God's command,

Honor them, the faithful few!

All hail to Daniel's Band!

Chorus:

Dare to be a Daniel,

Dare to stand alone!

Dare to have a purpose firm!

Dare to make it known!

Many mighty men are lost,

Daring not to stand,

Who for God had been a host,

By joining Daniel's Band!

Many giants, great and tall,

Stalking thro' the land,

Headlong to the earth would fall,

If met by Daniel's Band!

Hold the gospel banner high!

On to vict'ry grand!

Satan and his host defy,

And shout for Daniel's Band!

Teaching Help 8: Clauses

Identify the sentence type. In the blank write the letter that corresponds to the correct answer.

_____ 1. Lord Baden-Powell was a British soldier who started the Boy Scouts in 1908.
   A. simple
   B. complex

_____ 2. He wrote *Aids to Scouting,* and he also wrote *Scouting for Boys.*
   A. compound
   B. complex

_____ 3. The Wolf Cubs, which are also known as the Cub Scouts, were also founded by Lord Baden-Powell.
   A. complex
   B. compound-complex

_____ 4. Boys who belong to the Cub Scouts are under the age of eleven, and boys who belong to the Boy Scouts are eleven years old or older.
   A. compound
   B. compound-complex

_____ 5. The left-hand handshake and the fleur-de-lis badge are symbols associated with the Boy Scouts.
   A. simple
   B. compound

_____ 6. The Girl Guides, which were begun by Baden-Powell and his sister Agnes, were founded in 1910; in America they became known as the Girl Scouts in 1912.
   A. compound
   B. compound-complex

_____ 7. Juliette Low is the one who started the first Girl Scout troop in America.
   A. simple
   B. complex

_____ 8. She had already organized troops in England and Scotland.
   A. simple
   B. compound

_____ 9. Daisies, Brownies, and Juniors are troops for younger girls, and Cadettes and Seniors are troops designed for older girls.
   A. compound
   B. compound-complex

_____ 10. Boy Scouts and Girl Scouts learn about good citizenship and good conduct.
   A. simple
   B. compound

For each *A* or *B* you chose above choose the corresponding letter below. For example, if you chose *A* for question 1, write *W* in the blank. If you chose *B*, write *B* in the blank. If your answers are correct, you will form the motto of the Boy Scouts.

1. A=W, B=B	5. A=E, B=G	8. A=R, B=O
2. A=E, B=Y	6. A=S, B=P	9. A=E, B=W
3. A=P, B=A	7. A=H, B=A	10. A=D, B=I
4. A=T, B=R		

____ ____   ____ ____ ____ ____   ____ ____ ____ ____

Teaching Help 9: Indefinite Pronouns and Subject-Verb Agreement

To complete the Bible verse underline the correct verb from the choices in parentheses.

1. All the words of my mouth *(is, are)* in righteousness; there *(is, are)* nothing froward or perverse in them. (Prov. 8:8)

2. *(Is, Are)* any thing too hard for the Lord? (Gen. 18:14)

3. There *(is, are)* none that doeth good, no, not one. (Rom. 3:12)

4. Some *(trusts, trust)* in chariots, and some in horses: but we will remember the name of the Lord our God. (Ps. 20:7)

5. Divers weights, and divers measures, both of them *(is, are)* alike abomination to the Lord. (Prov. 20:10)

6. None of these things *(moves, move)* me, neither count I my life dear unto myself. (Acts 20:24)

7. Many *(is called, are called)*, but few *(is chosen, are chosen)*. (Matt. 22:14)

8. Be not afraid when one *(is made, are made)* rich, when the glory of his house is increased. (Ps. 49:16)

9. Blessed *(is, are)* every one that feareth the Lord; that walketh in his ways. (Ps. 128:1)

10. Many, O Lord my God, *(is, are)* thy wonderful works which thou hast done. (Ps. 40:5)

Teaching Help 10A: Spelling with ie and ei Words

To practice spelling *ie* and *ei* words unscramble the words described in the following sentences. Then use the circled letters from each word to form a sentence that fits the blanks at the end of the exercise.

◯ __ __ __ __   1. This word also means "to grab." *(zesie)*

◯ __ __ __ __   2. A person who is dedicated to God possesses this. *(pyite)*

__ ◯ __ __ __   3. If something is strange, it is described as this. *(reiwd)*

__ __ __ __ __ __ __ ◯ __   4. Something that is untrue is this. *(detcfulei)*

__ __ ◯ __ __ __   5. This is something that you hold to be true. *(lbefie)*

__ __ ◯ __ __ __   6. This is the blockade of an enemy city by an army. *(gseie)*

__ __ __ ◯ __   7. One controls a horse by these. *(seirn)*

__ __ __ ◯ __   8. This color is grayish yellow. *(bgiee)*

__ __ __ ◯ __   9. When you cut something, you do this to it. *(cepire)*

__ ◯ __ __ __ __ __ __   10. Tea and coffee contain this substance. *(cfaeifne)*

__ __ __ __ __ __ ◯   11. Milk is rich in this substance. *(tporien)*

__ __ ◯ __ __ __ __ __   12. When you pay back a person for money that you borrowed, you do this. *(ermburise)*

__ __ ◯ __ __ __   13. If you measure something for its heaviness, you do this to it. *(gwhei)*

__ ◯ __ __ __   14. This person is your brother's daughter. *(encie)*

__ __ __ __ __ ◯ __ __ __   15. If an idea is understandable, it is this. *(preaciveble)*

◯ __ __ __ __ __   16. In the wintertime we took a ride on one of these. *(ghesli)*

◯ __ __ __ __   17. If you give something up, you do this. *(ldiey)*

__ __ __ __ __ __ __ __   __ __ __   __ __   __ __ __ __.

© 2001 BJU Press. Limited license to copy granted on copyright page.

Name_____

Teaching Help 10B: Adding Suffixes

Combine a root from the first column and a suffix from the second column to create a word that best fits each description below. Then write the word in the blank.

debate	ment
happy	ly
assure	ing
duty	ed
boor	ful
loose	ance
bat	able
swim	ness
submit	ish
advance	er

_____ 1. Something that can be argued is this.

_____ 2. A person who is filled with joy has much of this.

_____ 3. If you are certain about something, you possess this.

_____ 4. A person who is careful to do what is expected of him is this.

_____ 5. A person who lacks culture is described as this.

_____ 6. If a rope is not tied tightly, it may hang in this manner.

_____ 7. In baseball this is the person who hits the ball.

_____ 8. When we go to the lake, we will spend our time doing this.

_____ 9. If you have given your will to someone else, you have done this to it.

_____ 10. If something has progressed, it has made this.

Teaching Help 11A: Capitalization

Congratulations! You have just been given a job at the local newspaper. For your first assignment you have been asked to edit the following article. Carefully read through the paragraph, paying special attention to the capitalization. Mark the errors and then rewrite the paragraph correctly in the space below.

       yesterday began as an ordinary Summer day for Eugene Saunders. But halfway through His walk home from the Grocery Store across the street from uncle ted's auto repair, Saunders saw what he described as "The Strangest Sight On Earth." When Saunders was a Colonel in the army, he spent time living in Jungles and Deserts around the World, places where he encountered many unusual sights and happenings. but this one topped them all. As he walked down darby lane, saunders heard someone running behind him. He turned, to see who was in such a hurry, just in time to jump out of the path of the largest Ostrich he had ever seen. on the broad back of the sprinting Bird sat a small Bear Cub wearing a White Sox baseball cap! Soon afterward, three men ran by. One stopped to explain to the bewildered Saunders that the circus had just arrived and that Olley The Ostrich and Buddy The Bear had decided to go sightseeing before their first Performance on Saturday night.

_____

_____

_____

_____

_____

_____

_____

_____

_____

_____

_____

_____

_____

Name _____

Teaching Help 11B: Capitalization

In the blank write the letter of the phrase that is capitalized correctly.

1. _____ A. an article from The *Wall Street Journal*
   B. an article from the *Wall Street Journal*
   C. an article from the *Wall Street journal*

2. _____ A. a picture of mount rushmore
   B. a picture of Mount rushmore
   C. a picture of Mount Rushmore

3. _____ A. leave at 11:00 A.M. to make your 1:15 P.M. flight
   B. leave at 11:00 A.M. to make your 1:15 p.m. flight
   C. leave at 11:00 a.m. to make your 1:15 P.M. flight

4. _____ A. my sister's Volleyball team
   B. my sister's volleyball team
   C. my sister's Volleyball Team

5. _____ A. His Puerto Rican Accent
   B. his Puerto Rican accent
   C. his puerto rican accent

6. _____ A. this poem by T. S. Eliot
   B. this poem by T. s. eliot
   C. this poem by t. s. Eliot

7. _____ A. take some Vitamin A
   B. take some vitamin a
   C. take some vitamin A

8. _____ A. your Junior year
   B. your junior year
   C. your Junior Year

9. _____ A. Dear Mr. and Mrs. Benson and Family,
   B. Dear Mr. and Mrs. Benson and family,
   C. dear Mr. and Mrs. Benson and family,

10. _____ A. birds fly South in the winter
    B. birds fly south in the Winter
    C. birds fly south in the winter

Teaching Help 12A: Punctuation

For this exercise imagine that you have a new pen pal in Germany. He is fourteen years old and his name is Kai. Write him a two-paragraph letter telling him about yourself, your classes, your family, your pets, your home, or your most embarrassing moment. Pay special attention to your punctuation.

Teaching Help 12B: Punctuation

Rewrite the following sentences, inserting any missing punctuation.

1. After reading Jules Vernes book Around the World in Eighty Days I wanted to take a trip in a hot-air balloon

_____

2. Alice do you know who invented the hot-air balloon

_____

3. Im not sure. Perhaps you should ask did you go to the library today?

_____

4. In September of 1973 the Montgolfier Brothers flew the first hot-air balloon loaded with precious cargo consisting of a duck a sheep and a cockerel

_____

_____

5. A few weeks later, Pilâtre de Rozier a science teacher and the marquis d'Arlandes an infantry officer became the first human passengers in a hot-air balloon

_____

_____

6. The two brave adventurous men flew five and a half miles over Paris

_____

7. Would you like to accompany me my wife and my dog, Rover, in a flight to St Louis asked my friend Col Adam Jennings who happens to be a hot-air balloon pilot

_____

_____

8. We take off at 630 AM tomorrow morning the pilot informed me

_____

9. I was so excited I could hardly sleep that night I woke up almost every hour, hoping it would be time for me to get up

_____

_____

10. My first hot-air balloon flight was an adventure Ill never forget

_____

Teaching Help 13A: Using a Library Catalog Entry

Answer the following questions by using the catalog entry below.

MATERIAL: Book

CALL NUMBER: J 551.5 G135

AUTHOR: Gallant, Roy A

TITLE: Exploring the weather. Illustrated by Lowell Hess.

EDITION: [1st ed.]

PUBLICATION: Garden City, N.Y., Garden City Books 1957

DESCRIPTION: 64 p. illus. 32 cm.

SUBJECT: Meteorology—Juvenile literature.

SUBJECT: Weather

1. What is the complete title of the book?_____

2. If you decided to search for this book by its author, under which letter of the alphabet would you search?_____

3. How many pages does the book contain?_____

4. Who is the illustrator of this book?_____

5. What company published the book?_____

6. What is the call number of the book?_____

7. In what specific section of the library would this book be found?_____

8. What year was the book published?_____

9. Under what subject headings would you find other books on the same topic?_____

10. Where was the book published?_____

Teaching Help 13B: Using the Readers' Guide

Use the following entry to answer each question.

FISHING

See also

Fishermen
Salt water fishing

Lake linnyn: a fisherman's paradise. Martin Jeeves. il *Tacklebox* v12 no5 p34-36+ Ag 2002

1. Who is the author of the article?_____

2. What is the volume number for the article?_____

3. When was the article published?_____

4. What is the title of the article?_____

5. What is the subject heading under which the article is listed?_____

6. Is this article illustrated?_____

7. On what page does the article begin?_____

8. What is the title of the magazine?_____

9. What is another subject heading one could search for related topics?_____

_____

10. Does the article end on page 36?_____

Teaching Help 13C: Special Reference Tools

In the blank write the letter of the reference tool best suited for finding the answer to each question.

A. almanac or yearbook
B. atlas or gazetteer
C. Bible concordance
D. book of quotations
E. biographical dictionary
F. desk dictionary
G. special-purpose dictionary
H. encyclopedia
I. index
J. thesaurus

_____ 1. What is the reference for the following verse: "Pray without ceasing"?

_____ 2. What is the Spanish word for *house?*

_____ 3. How many siblings did Jane Austen have?

_____ 4. Where is the Bay of Bengal located?

_____ 5. What is a synonym for the word *error?*

_____ 6. What does the word *frenzy* mean?

_____ 7. Where can you find a magazine article about piranhas?

_____ 8. Who won the Nobel Prize for Physics in 1990?

_____ 9. Which of Shakespeare's plays is the source of the following quotation: "To be, or not to be: that is the question"?

_____ 10. How can I learn more about zoological gardens?

Teaching Help 14A: Using the Parts of a Book

In each blank write the letter of the correct book section that would give you the information requested. Each answer will be used only once.

    A. title page
    B. table of contents
    C. list of illustrations
    D. introduction or preface
    E. acknowledgments
    F. text
    G. bibliography
    H. appendix
    I. glossary
    J. index

_____ 1. How many paragraphs are on the first page of Chapter 2?

_____ 2. How would you define the word *anther?*

_____ 3. Why was this book written?

_____ 4. On which pages are carnations discussed?

_____ 5. Who edited the book?

_____ 6. Where can you find a diagram that shows the parts of a flower?

_____ 7. Where does the author thank his colleagues for their advice and input?

_____ 8. Where can you find additional books on growing irises?

_____ 9. What three topics does Chapter 9 discuss?

_____ 10. On which page is there a photograph of an orchid?

Teaching Help 14B: Context Clues

In the blank write the letter of the choice that defines the italicized word in each sentence.

_____ 1. A cheetah has a long tail; however, a lynx is almost *anurous*.
   A. tailless
   B. hairy

_____ 2. Janessa will act as our *comprador*. She will tell Mr. Eliot our business plan, and then she will tell us Mr. Eliot's opinion.
   A. employer
   B. go-between

_____ 3. The shopkeeper called the police after he caught the young boy *pilfering* merchandise from his store.
   A. buying
   B. stealing

_____ 4. The *zephyr*, blowing against our faces, cooled us on the warm day.
   A. soft breeze
   B. still stream

_____ 5. I asked Randolph if he would like to go to a hockey game. His quick *rejoinder* was, "Sure, that sounds like fun."
   A. excuse
   B. reply

Teaching Help 15A: Outlining a Paper

Arrange the following list into the five main points of an outline. Be sure to order the items logically.

Laundry

Drying the clothes

Putting the clothes away

Organizing the supplies

Folding the clothes

Washing the clothes

Name_____

Teaching Help 15B: Composition Skills

Answer the following questions about the paragraph below. In the blank write the letter that corresponds to the correct answer.

On July 4, 1776, the Declaration of Independence was signed. Over a century later on July 10, 1890, Wyoming became the forty-fourth state. On July 16, 1945, the first atomic bomb was set off in New Mexico, and almost two and a half decades later, Neil Armstrong was the first man to walk on the moon. This event took place on July 20, 1969.

_____ 1. Which topic sentence best fits the paragraph?
    A. Many famous Americans were born in the month of July.
    B. Many important events have occurred in the month of July.

_____ 2. Which type of paragraph development does the author use in the paragraph?
    A. comparison/contrast
    B. fact

_____ 3. What type of paragraph organization does the author use in the paragraph?
    A. chronological
    B. order of importance

_____ 4. Which sentence best concludes the paragraph?
    A. All of these July incidents are national holidays.
    B. All of these July incidents have been significant in American history.

_____ 5. Which title best fits the paragraph?
    A. July: An Eventful Month
    B. The Month of July

In the blank write the letter that corresponds to the correct answer.

_____ 6. A topic sentence does *not*
    A. usually appear as the first sentence of the paragraph.
    B. introduce the topic.
    C. usually appear at the end of a paragraph.

_____ 7. In an essay a thesis statement is *not*
    A. similar to a topic sentence in a paragraph.
    B. a concluding sentence.
    C. a sentence which introduces the topic of the essay to the audience.

_____ 8. A good introduction does *not*
    A. catch the reader's interest.
    B. tell the reader, "I will talk about such-and-such in this paper."
    C. draw attention to the main idea of the topic.

_____ 9. A good conclusion does *not*
    A. repeat the topic sentence word for word.
    B. summarize the main idea of the paragraph.
    C. offer a solution to a problem.

_____ 10. Which of the following sentences is *not* true?
    A. Revision is not necessary for the experienced writer.
    B. Revision improves a person's writing.
    C. Revision helps a person to write better first drafts.

Teaching Help 15C: Revising

Underline the ten clichés in the following paragraphs. Rewrite each sentence that contains a cliché so that it will express the idea of the sentence more simply.

Pedro awoke at the crack of dawn. Today he was going to the county fair! Pedro ran into his brother's bedroom, but Carlos was still sleeping like a log. Pedro thought it was a crying shame, but he knew that Carlos wasn't as excited as he was. Why, it was just yesterday that Carlos said going to the fair bored him to tears. But Pedro knew that Carlos would have fun.

Pedro and Carlos visited the stables first. Pedro stroked one horse's head and fed the horse an apple. Carlos said he wouldn't touch the horse with a ten-foot pole. Pedro couldn't understand why Carlos was acting as though he were in the depths of despair. Pedro wasn't ready to throw in the towel, however, so he suggested they ride the Ferris wheel. Carlos seemed to brighten up at this idea. On the ride Carlos's spirits seemed to lift. He apologized for his bad behavior. After all was said and done, both boys had a good day.

1. _____
_____

2. _____
_____

3. _____
_____

4. _____
_____

5. _____
_____

6. _____
_____

7. _____
_____

8. _____
_____

9. _____
_____

10. _____
_____

Teaching Help 15D: Proofreading Checklist

Problems	Solutions
Grammar	
Do I have any fragments, fused sentences, or comma splices in my writing?	Locate what is missing in a fragment and complete the sentence. Divide the fused sentence and punctuate it correctly. Add an appropriate conjunction to the comma splice.
Usage	
Do my subjects and verbs agree? Do my pronouns and antecedents agree?	Put a singular subject with a singular verb and a plural subject with a plural verb. Check the rules for pronoun-antecedent agreement in Chapter 9.
Punctuation	
Have I omitted any internal punctuation marks or used any internal marks incorrectly? Have I used any incorrect end punctuation or omitted any end punctuation?	Read each sentence carefully. Check the rules for punctuation in Chapter 12.
Capitalization	
Does every sentence begin with a capital letter? Are all proper nouns capitalized?	Look for specific places, people, events, and objects. Check each sentence.
Spelling	
Have I misspelled any words?	Look deliberately at every word.
Other Checks	
Have I omitted or repeated any words?	Read your paper aloud.

Name________________________________

ESL Worksheet 3A: Using Some *Correctly*

When a sentence containing the word *some* is made negative using the word *not, some* is replaced with *any.* Replace the words in the left column with the words in the right column when making a sentence negative using the word *not.*

POSITIVE		NEGATIVE
some	⟶	any
somebody/someone	⟶	anybody/anyone
something	⟶	anything

Examples:

We looked at *some* kittens in the pet store.
We did *not* look at *any* kittens in the pet store.

The waitress was speaking with *somebody/someone.*
The waitress was*n't* speaking with *anybody/anyone.*

Something was falling from the shelf.
There was*n't anything* falling from the shelf.

To make the sentence negative without using the word *not,* add a word that already has a negative meaning.

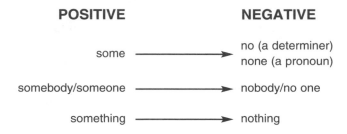

POSITIVE		NEGATIVE
some	⟶	no (a determiner) none (a pronoun)
somebody/someone	⟶	nobody/no one
something	⟶	nothing

Examples:

We looked at *some* kittens in the pet store.
We looked at *no* kittens in the pet store.

Some of the players forgot the rules of the game.
None of the players forgot the rules of the game.

The waitress was speaking with *somebody/someone.*
The waitress was speaking with *nobody/no one.*

Something was falling from the shelf.
Nothing was falling from the shelf.

ESL Worksheet 3B: Exercises in Using Some *Correctly*

Read the sentences containing *some.* **Then look at the choices for making the sentences negative. Circle the letter of each correct negative sentence. You may have more than one correct answer for some of the following items.**

1. McCarty bought his grandmother *some* pottery.
   A. McCarty didn't buy no pottery for his grandmother.
   B. McCarty bought no pottery for his grandmother.
   C. McCarty didn't buy any pottery for his grandmother.

2. *Someone* was cleaning the bowl he purchased.
   A. No one was cleaning the bowl he purchased.
   B. There wasn't anyone cleaning the bowl he purchased.
   C. There wasn't no one cleaning the bowl he purchased.

3. McCarty had dropped *something* in the pottery store.
   A. McCarty had not dropped anything in the pottery store.
   B. McCarty had not dropped nothing in the pottery store.
   C. McCarty had dropped nothing in the pottery store.

4. McCarty purchased *some* ceramic mugs.
   A. McCarty didn't purchase no ceramic mugs.
   B. McCarty didn't purchase any ceramic mugs.
   C. McCarty purchased no ceramic mugs.

5. He had *some* employees help him find a yellow teapot.
   A. He didn't have any employees help him find a yellow teapot.
   B. He had no employees help him find a yellow teapot.
   C. He didn't have no employees help him find a yellow teapot.

Read the sentences containing the word *some.* **Make each sentence negative.**

6. Addie wanted to bake something.

   _____

7. She baked some cookies.

   _____

8. Some of the cookies were burned.

   _____

9. Someone ate her cookies.

   _____

10. She gave some cookies to her neighbors.

   _____

ESL Worksheet 4A: Verb Tenses

When speaking or writing about events before or after your current situation, use different tenses based on which tense you are already using for general reference.

- If you are speaking or writing from a present-tense perspective, refer to previous events by using the present perfect and to events that happen later by using the future.

PRESENT	We *are going* to the beach this summer.
PRESENT PERFECT	We *have been going* there for the past five years.
FUTURE	We *will go* there next summer also.

- If you are speaking or writing from a past-tense perspective, refer to previous events by using the past perfect and to events that happen later by using the simple past again.

PAST	We *arrived* in plenty of time.
PAST PERFECT	We *had* not *been* there before.
PAST	Then we *went* for a walk on the beach.

- If you are speaking or writing from a future-tense perspective, refer to previous events by using the future perfect and to events that happen later by using the future again.

FUTURE	Our family *will* usually *rent* one big house during our vacation.
FUTURE PERFECT	After this summer, we *will have done* this for about fifteen years.
FUTURE	Next year we *will need* to rent a larger house.

ESL Worksheet 4B: Tense Check

Present Perfect

Use the present perfect tense when referring to something completed (finished) during the time period you are in or when referring to something that has continued until the present moment.

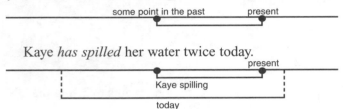

Kaye *has spilled* her water twice today.

Lewis *has visited* several European countries this summer.

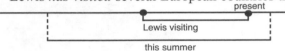

Past Perfect

Use the past perfect tense when referring to *X,* the first of two points in past time.

When we arrived at the party, the guests *had* (already) *eaten* dessert.

I *had written* four letters before lunch today.

Note: In informal usage the past tense sometimes substitutes for the past perfect when the time relationships are clear.

Future Perfect

Use the future perfect tense when referring to *X,* the first of two points in future time. In this case the perfect tense emphasizes that something happens *before* another future time or event.

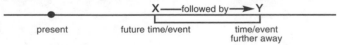

I *will have read* all of Romans by tomorrow morning.

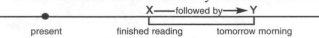

Grandpa and Grandma *will have returned* to Oregon by the end of October.

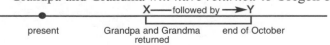

ESL Worksheet 4C: Using the Auxiliary Do *Correctly*

Do is generally used in three ways:

1. To help emphasize

    • Add the correct form of the auxiliary *do* only if the clause does not already have an auxiliary or a *be* verb.

    PRESENT TENSE   *does* (3rd-person singular subject)
                            do (all other subjects)

    PAST TENSE   *did* (all subjects)

    WRONG   I *do should go* to the grocery store.
    RIGHT   I *should go* to the grocery store.
    WRONG   We *do are going* to the zoo this afternoon.
    RIGHT   We *are going* to the zoo this afternoon.

    • Place *do* before the main verb. Notice that *do* takes the tense of the verb.

    He *walks* the dog on Mondays.   Jesslyn *broke* the glass vase.
    He *does walk* the dog on Mondays.   Jesslyn *did break* the glass vase.

    In a sentence that repeats information, the part that contains repeated information is often omitted.

    He might not walk the dog, but I hope he *does.* (walk the dog)
    Jesslyn did not mean to break the glass vase, but she *did.* (break the glass vase)

    • Place the stress, or loudness, on *do* for oral emphasis.

    We *did hike* this morning.
    I *do want* dessert.

2. To help make a sentence negative

    • Add the correct form of the auxiliary *do* only if the clause does not already have an auxiliary or a *be* verb.

    WRONG   Cameron *do* not *might ride* his bike to the park.
    RIGHT   Cameron *might* not *ride* his bike to the park.
    WRONG   I *do* not *am taking* German this year.
    RIGHT   I *am* not *taking* German this year.

    • Place *not* between *do* and the main verb. Notice that *do* takes the tense of the verb.

    Annelina *enjoys* running.   Annelina *ran* three miles on Tuesday.
    She *does* not *enjoy* ice skating.   She *did* not *run* on Wednesday.

3. To help ask a question

    Some questions require the use of *do.* Notice again that *do* takes the tense of the verb.

    Gerard *found* an old coin.   Gerard collects foreign coins.
    What *did* Gerard *find?*   *Does* Gerard *collect* foreign coins?

ESL Worksheet 4D: Forming Questions Correctly

English has two basic types of questions: *wh* questions and *yes/no* questions. Some questions use inverted order, and others do not. (*Inverted order* means that the order of the subject and the predicate is reversed.)

Wh questions

(questions that ask for information using *who/whom/whose, which, what, when, where, why,* or *how*)

- When questioning the subject or something in the subject, do not use inverted order. Replace the word in question with an interrogative pronoun.

    Jason will come tonight. ⟶ *Who* will come tonight? (Jason)

    Their house is on the corner. ⟶ *Whose* house is on the corner? (their house)

- When questioning something in the complete predicate, use these three steps:
    1. Replace the word in question with an interrogative pronoun.
    2. Move the interrogative pronoun before the subject.
    3. Follow one of the next three steps.

    - If there is an auxiliary, move the first auxiliary before the subject.

ORIGINAL	Jason will come tonight.
STEP 1	Jason will come *when?*
STEP 2	*When* Jason will come?
STEP 3	*When* will Jason come?

    - If there is no auxiliary but there is a form of *be (am, is, are, was,* or *were),* move the form of *be* before the subject.

ORIGINAL	Albany is New York's capital.
STEP 1	Albany is *what?*
STEP 2	*What* Albany is?
STEP 3	*What* is Albany?

    - If there is no auxiliary or no *be* verb form, insert the correct form of the auxiliary *do.* Then move the form of *do* before the subject.

ORIGINAL	Tobias played the piano softly.
STEP 1	Tobias played the piano *how?*
STEP 2	*How* Tobias played the piano?
STEP 3A	*How* Tobias did play the piano?
STEP 3B	*How* did Tobias play the piano?

    Notice the changes when *do* is added.

play	⟶ do play	How do you play it?
play*s*	⟶ do*es* play	How does he play it?
play*ed*	⟶ *did* play	How did he play it?

    The main verb *(play)* has no ending; the auxiliary *do* must show the correct present-tense or past-tense form.

Yes/no questions

(questions that require *yes* or *no* for an answer)

- If a sentence contains an auxiliary verb, move the first auxiliary before the subject.

    She *will write* a poem.
    Will she *write* a poem?

    He *has been pulling* weeds in the yard.
    Has he *been pulling* weeds in the yard?

- If a sentence contains no auxiliary but does have a *be* verb, move the *be* verb before the subject.

    The car *is* blue.
    Is the car blue?

    Alexis *was* a kindergarten teacher.
    Was Alexis a kindergarten teacher?

- If there is no auxiliary and no *be* verb, add some form of the verb *do* before the subject. Notice that *do* takes the tense of the verb.

    Lane *ate* three hot dogs.
    Did Lane *eat* three hot dogs?

    The yogurt *tastes* creamy.
    Does the yogurt *taste* creamy?

ESL Worksheet 4E: Exercises in Forming Questions Correctly

Change each sentence to a *yes/no* question. Remember to look at the verb tense for each sentence. Then use that same tense for the question.

1. Red is Max's favorite color.

   _____

2. Max would like a red truck.

   _____

3. Max will have enough money for the truck.

   _____

4. His car had broken down numerous times.

   _____

5. He has earned money for a new vehicle.

   _____

Change each sentence to a *wh* question. Use the word in parentheses to form the question. Write the question and the short answer in the blank.

6. Max's favorite color is red. *(whose)*

   _____

7. Max would like a red truck. *(what)*

   _____

8. Max will have enough money for the truck. *(who)*

   _____

9. His car had broken down numerous times because it had a bad engine. *(why)*

   _____

10. He has earned money for a new vehicle by working for a law firm. *(how)*

    _____

ESL Worksheet 5A: Article Usage

1. Proper Nouns

1.1   Always use *the* before a plural proper noun.
The Cermaks are both teachers.

1.2   Usually do not use an article before a singular proper noun.
Mr. Cermak is a teacher.

1.3   Do not use an article before most geographic names.*
Lisbon is in Portugal.

   *Exceptions include collective names and plurals *(the United Kingdom* or *the African nations),* land masses *(the Greek Isles),* bodies of water *(the Atlantic Ocean),* and geographic regions *(the West, the Arctic,* or *the Sahara).*

2. Specific Count and Noncount Nouns

2.1   Use *the* when both you and the hearer know what is referred to.
The scarf is Bridget's.
The rice is cooked.

2.2   Use *the* before a noun that has been mentioned before.
My uncle bought *a horse. The* horse is black.

2.3   Use *the* before a noun modified by a superlative or ordinal adjective.
The hottest day of the year was August 19.
The second Sunday in May is Mother's Day.

3. General Singular Count Nouns

3.1   Use *a* or *an* when representing one member of a class.
She rides *a unicycle.*

3.2   Use an article unless a possessive or a demonstrative is used with the noun.
She rides *this unicycle.*

3.3   Use *the* in general statements.
The unicycle is an unusual vehicle.

4. General Plural Count Nouns

4.1   Usually do not use an article with plural count nouns used in a general sense.
Balloons are on sale at the party store.

5. General Noncount Nouns

5.1   Usually do not use an article with noncount nouns used in a general sense (languages, school subjects, etc.).
Sara likes to study *history.*

5.2   Use *the* if a modifier follows the noun.
She especially enjoys studying *the* history of Africa.

ESL Worksheet 5B: Exercise in Article Usage

Choose the correct article *(a, an,* or *the)* to put in each blank. If no article is needed, put an *X* in the blank. Above each answer list the appropriate rule number from the Article Usage sheet.

_____ Joleen took _____ flight to Nebraska to visit her grandparents. Although _____ flight was short, she ate _____ two small bags of peanuts and drank one can of cola. _____ best part of her flight was that she had _____ window seat. She thought _____ this seat was great. She had fun watching _____ big, puffy clouds. Looking out her window, Joleen remembered some facts she learned about clouds in _____ science. Since her grandparents can't drive, _____ Kalmans, her grandparents' neighbors, picked her up at _____ airport. When she arrived at her grandparents' house, _____ first thing Joleen saw was _____ her grandma's big smile. Joleen knew that she was going to have fun with her relatives.

ESL Worksheet 5C: Adverb Placement

Adverbs of Manner

Examples: *slowly, well, somehow, carefully, shyly, quietly, sadly, quickly, joyfully*

Placement: Adverbs of manner usually come in one of three places:

1. Directly before the subject when the subject is not preceded by any introductory information (such as a prepositional phrase)

   WRONG   *Gracefully* above the fields the hawk soared.
               Above the fields, *gracefully* the hawk soared.
   RIGHT   *Gracefully* the hawk soared above the fields.

2. With the verb
   - If there are any auxiliaries, place the adverb after the first auxiliary.
     The hawk was *carefully* examining the ground for prey.

   - If there is no auxiliary but there is a *be* verb, place the adverb after the *be* verb.
     The hawk was *carefully* observant.

   - If there is no auxiliary and no *be* verb, place the adverb before the main verb.
     The hawk *carefully* examined the ground for prey.

3. After the direct object (especially if the direct object is the end of the clause)
   The hawk examined the ground *carefully*.

Note: Adverbs of manner should not be placed between the verb and its direct object.

       WRONG   The hawk examined *carefully* the ground.

Adverbs of Time and Frequency

Examples: *now, later, sometime, never, often, usually, seldom, sometimes*

Placement: Adverbs of time usually come in one of three places:

1. Before the subject (except for *never*)
   Sometimes Betty walks to school.

2. With the verb
   - After the first auxiliary
     LeeAnn had *often* thought about a visit to Saipan.

   - After a *be* verb
     Herbert is *always* polite.

   - Before any other verb
     Joseph *never* fails a test.

3. At the end of the sentence if not too far removed from the verb (except for *never*)

               RIGHT   Anna reads her Bible *daily*.
   TOO FAR REMOVED   John puts his books on the table in the corner *usually*.
             BETTER   John *usually* puts his books on the table in the corner.

Adverbs of Place

Examples: *here, below, outside, somewhere, everywhere, nowhere, down, northward*

Placement: Adverbs of place usually come after the verb or at the end of the clause.

> She looked *outside* for the dog.
> She looked for the dog *outside*.

Note: Although these rules will be helpful for placing adverbs correctly in a sentence, they are somewhat variable. Exceptions are possible, especially for emphasis.

Name _____

ESL Worksheet 5D: Exercises in Adverb Placement

Decide whether the italicized adverbs are placed correctly. If the placement is correct, write *C* in the blank to the left. If the placement is incorrect, write *I* in the blank and rewrite the sentence correctly.

_____ 1. Marta *usually* is a good student.

_____

_____ 2. The squirrel was climbing *quickly* the tree.

_____

_____ 3. David *shyly* told her his name.

_____

_____ 4. The book was *surprisingly* heavy.

_____

_____ 5. The bird abandoned its nest in the top of the tree *later.*

_____

_____ 6. *Slowly* the leaf floated to the ground.

_____

_____ 7. Kate told the story *joyfully.*

_____

_____ 8. John *seldom* writes letters.

_____

_____ 9. We *never* have sung in a choir.

_____

_____ 10. Kahlil *here* lives.

_____

© 2001 BJU Press. Limited license to copy granted on copyright page.

ESL Worksheets **77**

ESL Worksheet 5E: Making Sentences Negative Using Not

In English, sentences are usually made negative by adding *not*. English has three basic rules for correctly placing *not* in sentences.

- If there is an auxiliary (such as *will, have, may, do,* or *is*) in the sentence, place *not* after the first auxiliary.

    We will watch the sunset.
    We will *not* watch the sunset.

    I may be late to work.
    I may *not* be late to work.

- If there is no auxiliary but there is a *be* verb *(am, is, are, was, were),* place *not* after the *be* verb.

    Vanessa is athletic.
    Vanessa is *not* athletic.

    The tennis players are competitive.
    The tennis players are *not* competitive.

- If there is no auxiliary and no *be* verb, add some form of the auxiliary *do.* Place *not* between *do* and the other verb. Notice that *do* takes the tense of the verb. The part of the sentence in parentheses can be omitted if it is clearly understood by both the reader and the writer.

    Angelika practices her cello every day.
    Angelika *does not* (*practice* her cello every day).

    Jesse found a stray cat.
    Jesse *did not* (*find* a stray cat).

Name_____

ESL Worksheet 5F: Exercises in Making Sentences Negative Using Not

Rewrite the following sentences to make them negative. Add *not* **to each sentence. Change the form of the verb and add an auxiliary if necessary.**

Example: Gail often writes letters.
Gail does *not* often write letters.

1. The baby cries every night.

    _____

2. I can mail my letters this weekend.

    _____

3. I will buy new stamps.

    _____

4. Lana is a friendly person.

    _____

5. Jung is from Korea.

    _____

6. Isabel cleans her room every Saturday.

    _____

7. We will go to the concert next week.

    _____

8. There will be fireworks after the ball game.

    _____

9. Dad parks his car in the garage.

    _____

10. Forrest wears a suit to work.

    _____

ESL Worksheet 6A: Using Prepositions

General Rules

1. Do not leave necessary prepositions out of a sentence.

> **WRONG**   My aunt and uncle live an apartment.
>
> **RIGHT**   My aunt and uncle live *in* an apartment.

2. *During* is a preposition that forms a prepositional phrase (with no verb). *While* is a conjunction that usually introduces a dependent clause; it cannot be followed by a noun phrase. *During* and *while* cannot be used interchangeably.

> **PREPOSITION**   Louisa took notes *during the lecture.*
>
> **CONJUNCTION**   Louisa took notes *while the instructor lectured.*

3. Do not use a preposition when *home* is used with a verb of motion or direction. The same rule applies to *downtown* and *uptown*.

> **WRONG**   She was going *to* home.
>
> **RIGHT**   She was going home.

If the verb is not a verb of motion or direction, the preposition is usually necessary.

> I called her *at* home.
> Will she be *at* home this afternoon?

4. Do not use a preposition when *here* or *there* is used after the verb.

> **WRONG**   She walked *to* there. He ran *to* here.
>
> **RIGHT**   She walked there. He ran here.

5. Use *at* for the most specific time or location, *on* for more general time or location, and *in* for the most general time or location.

> Church starts *at* 10:45 A.M.
> We are having a special service *on* Thursday.
> Meet me *in* the morning.
>
> Diedre works *at* 526 Main Street.
> Diedre works *on* Main Street.
> Diedre works *in* Akron.

6. Many verbs and adjectives, and even some nouns, must be followed by particular prepositions. Sometimes changing the preposition changes the meaning.

> Hayden's knowledge of chemistry *resulted from* hours of study.
> (Hours of study caused his knowledge.)
>
> Hayden's preparation *resulted in* a good grade in the class.
> (His grade was the effect of his preparation.)
>
> His success was *a result of* his hard work.
> (His hard work caused his success.)

ESL Worksheet 6B: Exercises in Using Prepositions

Choose the correct word for each blank from the choices in parentheses. If none of the suggested words is correct, put an *X* in the blank.

1. Eli enjoys reading the newspaper _____ his lunch break. *(during, while)*

2. He reads the paper _____ he eats his lunch. *(during, while)*

3. To get home he must walk _____ downtown. *(at, to)*

4. When he is _____ home, he reads his mail. *(at, to)*

5. Today he received a letter from his aunt _____ Uruguay. *(in, on, at)*

6. She has been living _____ there for three years. *(in, at)*

7. When she left America, she had to part _____ many of her friends. *(with, from)*

8. She also had to part _____ many of her favorite household items. *(with, from)*

9. She will visit Eli _____ May 19. *(in, on, at)*

10. Her train will arrive _____ 6:00 P.M. *(in, on, at)*

ESL Worksheet 8A: How to Combine Sentences

Sentences can be combined in a variety of ways using a variety of connecting words. Sentences are composed of two kinds of clauses: dependent clauses and independent clauses. These clauses are connected mainly by three kinds of words: subordinating conjunctions, coordinating conjunctions, and conjunctive adverbs.

Clauses

DEPENDENT CLAUSE (DC) — A dependent clause has a subject and a predicate but contains an introductory word that makes it unable to express a complete thought and stand alone as a sentence.

INDEPENDENT CLAUSE (IC) — An independent clause contains a subject and a predicate, expresses a complete thought, and can stand alone as a sentence.

Connecting Words

SUBORDINATING CONJUNCTION (sc) — Subordinating conjunctions introduce dependent clauses.

COORDINATING CONJUNCTION (cc) — Coordinating conjunctions join two independent clauses.

CONJUNCTIVE ADVERB (ca) — Conjunctive adverbs are used with independent clauses and can usually be moved around within the clause. These joining words have a relationship of meaning rather than of grammar.

The following lists contain many commonly used connecting words.

MEANING	SUBORDINATING CONJUNCTIONS
Time	when, while, as, before, after, since, once, until, every time, whenever
Place	where, wherever
Cause	because, since, as, now that (meaning "because now")
Condition	if, unless
Manner	as if, as though
Purpose	so that
Concession	although, even though
Comparison	than

MEANING	COORDINATING CONJUNCTIONS	CONJUNCTIVE ADVERBS
Similarity and Association	and	besides, likewise, moreover, also
Choice	or	otherwise
Result or Consequence	so	accordingly, consequently, therefore, then, thus
Contrast	but, yet	however, nevertheless, still

ESL Worksheet 8A: How to Combine Sentences (continued)

There are seven common formulas for combining clauses. These formulas are listed in the right column, and they use the abbreviations given previously for clauses and connecting words. Pay close attention to the punctuation included in each formula. Notice that because the subordinating conjunction introduces the dependent clause, these two elements are enclosed in parentheses as a unit.

Example sentences: My friends went out for pizza. I baby-sat my little brother.

	Sample Combinations	Formulas
1.	IC , cc IC . My friends went out for pizza, but I baby-sat my little brother.	IC, cc IC.
2.	(sc DC), IC . While I baby-sat my little brother, my friends went out for pizza.	(sc DC), IC.
3.	IC (sc DC). My friends went out for pizza while I baby-sat my little brother.	IC (sc DC).
4.	IC . ca , IC . My friends went out for pizza. However, I baby-sat my little brother.	IC. ca, IC.
5.	IC ; ca , IC . My friends went out for pizza; however, I baby-sat my little brother.	IC; ca, IC.
6.	IC . IC, ca , IC continued . My friends went out for pizza. I, however, baby-sat my little brother.	IC. IC, ca, IC continued.
7.	IC . IC , ca . My friends went out for pizza. I baby-sat my little brother, however.	IC. IC, ca.

Notice the placement of commas in the correct sentences above:

- Place the comma after an adverbial clause that comes at the beginning of a sentence.
- Do not use a comma before an adverbial clause that comes at the end of a sentence.

ESL Worksheet 8B: Exercises in How to Combine Sentences

The following chart shows meaning similarities among the three main types of connecting words.

Coordinating Conjunctions	Conjunctive Adverbs	Subordinating Conjunctions
and	besides, likewise, moreover, also	—
or	otherwise	—
so	accordingly, consequently, then, therefore, thus	because, since
but, yet	however, nevertheless, still	while, whereas, although, even though

Combine the following sentences using the formulas indicated. Rewrite each sentence, adding the correct connecting word and the correct punctuation. You may leave the words in parentheses out of the sentence.

Example: Paige enjoys traveling. She visits countries in the Far East.

IC, cc IC. (Formula 1): ___Paige enjoys traveling, so she visits countries in the Far East.___

(sc DC), IC. (Formula 2): ___Since Paige enjoys traveling, she visits countries in the Far East.___

IC; ca, IC. (Formula 5): ___Paige enjoys traveling; therefore, she visits countries in the Far East.___

1. Paige plays golf. (On the other hand,) Reese plays hockey.

IC, cc IC. (Formula 1): _____

(sc DC), IC. (Formula 2): _____

IC. ca, IC. (Formula 4): _____

2. Paige may ride her bike to work. (If not,) she will drive to work.

IC, cc IC. (Formula 1): _____

IC. ca, IC. (Formula 4): _____

IC; ca, IC. (Formula 5): _____

ESL Worksheet 12: The Most Common Punctuation Marks in English

Mark	Name	Example
.	period	Baseball is his favorite sport.
!	exclamation point	The house is on fire!
?	question mark	Where do you live?
,	comma	I live in Salina, Kansas.
'	apostrophe	That isn't Julie's dog.
( )	parentheses	Elaine and Peggy (who are sisters) own a cat.
" "	quotation marks	Joe said, "Do you know Nicole?"
;	semicolon	George plays baseball; it is his favorite sport.
:	colon	He also enjoys these sports: soccer, tennis, and skiing.

Chapter 1: Sentence Patterns

Practice A

Label the sentence patterns in the following sentences. Above each word of the sentence pattern, write its label.

1. Some people design their own stationery.

2. The embossing process is simple.

3. Embossing gives paper a raised texture.

4. Embossed paper is often very elegant.

5. You can emboss with letters or patterns.

Practice B

Label the sentence patterns in the following sentences. Above each word of the sentence pattern, write its label.

6. Cherie is a collector of elegant writing paper and cards.

7. At least once a month, she writes her grandmother a letter about new events at home and at school.

8. Cherie is consistent with thank-you notes.

9. In appreciation for the kindness of others, she sends thank-you notes often.

10. Cherie's letters of kindness encourage her friends.

Practice C

Write a sentence for each of the following sentence patterns.

11. (S-InV) _____

12. (S-TrV-DO) _____

13. (S-TrV-IO-DO) _____

14. (S-LV-PN) _____

15. (S-LV-PA) _____

Chapter 1: Phrases and Clauses

Practice A

Identify each italicized group of words as either a phrase *(P)* or a clause *(C)*.

_____ 1. *An emu is a large Australian bird.*

_____ 2. *Underneath its thick feathers* lie two small wings.

_____ 3. The emu, *unable to fly,* runs very swiftly.

_____ 4. The emu weighs *about one hundred pounds.*

_____ 5. Emus can be troublesome *because they eat crops.*

Practice B

In each sentence underline any independent clauses once and any dependent clauses twice.

6. Cashmere goats are found mainly in India and Tibet.

7. Although they are found mainly in these areas, cashmere goats have been raised in some European countries.

8. When goats live higher in the mountains, they tend to have darker hair.

9. Cashmere goats are valuable because they have soft, silky wool.

10. Because it is so soft, cashmere wool is used to make fine sweaters and scarves.

Practice C

Identify each italicized group of words as a phrase *(P)*, an independent clause *(IC)*, or a dependent clause *(DC)*.

_____ 11. *Classified as an amphibian,* a newt is a type of salamander with thin skin and a long tail.

_____ 12. *Newts hatch from eggs* that are laid in the spring.

_____ 13. Newts generally live in the water, but because they have lungs, *some may live on land.*

_____ 14. *Having poisonous skin,* newts are not usually disturbed by predators.

_____ 15. *If a leg is lost,* a land newt is able to grow another one.

Name_____

Chapter 1: Sentence Problems

Practice A

Identify each group of words as a sentence *(S)* or a fragment *(F)*.

_____ 1. Nicholas II, the last czar of Russia, from 1894-1918.

_____ 2. Aspiring to strengthen Russia's power, he attempted greater military control in the Far East.

_____ 3. Losing the war, weakening his power and governmental control.

_____ 4. Reformers and revolutionists forced Nicholas to give up his power.

_____ 5. The Bolsheviks who shot and killed Nicholas, his wife, his son, and his four daughters.

Practice B

Identify each group of words as a sentence *(S)*, a fragment *(F)*, a fused sentence *(FS)*, or a comma splice *(CS)*.

_____ 6. Northern Ireland is one of the four divisions of the United Kingdom, the other three are England, Scotland, and Wales.

_____ 7. Northern Ireland separated from Ireland in 1920 now it is often called Ulster.

_____ 8. Most of the people in Northern Ireland who are largely Protestant.

_____ 9. Desiring to remain part of Great Britain, they have great contention with the remaining citizens who are mostly Roman Catholic.

_____ 10. Catholics desire Northern Ireland to join with the Republic of Ireland, violent disagreement persists between the two parties.

Practice C

Correct the sentence errors by rewriting the sentences correctly in the following blanks.

11. The Philippine Islands form one country in the Pacific Ocean, more than seven thousand islands make up the Philippines.

_____

_____

12. Originally, people came to the Philippines from Indonesia and Malaysia these people formed many different communities on different islands.

_____

_____

13. Spanish explorers colonized the islands in the 1500s, the islands were named for King Philip II.

_____

_____

14. In 1898 Spain gave the United States control of the islands on July 4, 1946, the Philippines were granted independence.

_____

_____

15. The Japanese temporarily took over the islands in 1941, General Douglas MacArthur regained control for the United States in 1944.

_____

_____

Chapter 2: Plural Forms of Nouns

Practice A

In the blank write the plural form of the italicized noun.

_____ 1. Almost every nation has an *army.*

_____ 2. The United States Army is the *branch* of the armed forces that is responsible for land operations.

_____ 3. The *chief* of staff of the United States Army supervises the members and organizations of the army.

_____ 4. The development of the *radio* aided military operations.

_____ 5. Many young people desire a *career* in the army.

Practice B

In the blank write the correct possessive form of the italicized phrase.

6. The army is the oldest branch of *the armed services of the nation.*

_____

7. *The beginning of the army* occurred in 1775 when the Continental Congress created the army to fight in the Revolutionary War.

_____

8. Army history records *the heroic acts of many soldiers.*

_____

9. *The first draft law of Congress* was passed in 1863.

_____

10. *The first military school of the United States* was opened at West Point in 1802.

_____

Practice C

Underline any errors with plurals or possessives. Rewrite the words correctly on the lines below.

The 1900's were a time of reorganization for the army. In 1903 Congress created the general staff system. Since that time, many chief of staffs have led the army. In 1907 the army's leaders set up an aeronautical division, which became the air force forty years later. The governments' end of the draft occurred in 1973. Afterward, the armed services' began recruiting volunteers. Several reorganizations in the late twentieth century were designed to increase the soldiers's efficiency as well as to cut costs.

_____

_____

Name_____

Chapter 2: Count and Noncount Nouns

Practice A
Label each italicized noun *C* (count) or *NC* (noncount).

_____ 1. The air force is responsible for military operations in the air and in *space*.

_____ 2. Satellites monitor the earth for any *sign* of enemy activity.

_____ 3. The air force gives *support* to other branches of the armed services.

_____ 4. The air force protects ground troops in *battle*.

_____ 5. A *plane* might deliver fresh troops or supplies.

Practice B
Underline each count noun once and each noncount noun twice.

6. Nuclear weapons have tremendous power for destruction.

7. Therefore, the air force uses advanced technology for many operations.

8. The air force does extensive research throughout the country.

9. Scientists and engineers at universities and in businesses provide great help to the air force.

10. The air force may also help track a hurricane or forecast the weather.

Practice C
Underline each count noun once and each noncount noun twice. (Consider only the common nouns.)

11. During the late 1980s, the Marine Corps had a strength of about 195,000 men and women.

12. Every great nation must have an effective defense.

13. The Marine Corps is trained for amphibious assault.

14. Marines throughout the world are prepared for trouble at any moment.

15. The Marine Corps guards embassies in other countries.

Chapter 2: Functions of Nouns in the Sentence

Practice A

Label each italicized noun *S* (subject), *DO* (direct object), *IO* (indirect object), *OP* (object of the preposition), *PN* (predicate noun), *App* (appositive), or *NA* (noun of direct address).

_____ 1. The Continental Congress established a marine *corps* on November 10, 1775.

_____ 2. The marines have been a vital *part* of many victories in many wars since that time.

_____ 3. During the War of 1812, Captain John Gamble became the only marine *officer* in command of a naval ship.

_____ 4. In the Civil War, marines fought in many land and naval *battles.*

_____ 5. Marines dealt their *enemies* many lethal blows in both world wars.

Practice B

Label each italicized noun *S* (subject), *DO* (direct object), *IO* (indirect object), *OP* (object of the preposition), *PN* (predicate noun), *App* (appositive), or *NA* (noun of direct address).

_____ 6. My father was in the navy, *Orville.*

_____ 7. The chief of naval operations, an *admiral*, is the highest ranking officer in the navy.

_____ 8. A nuclear-powered aircraft *carrier* joined the navy's fleet in 1989.

_____ 9. Some of the greatest weapons of the navy are undetectable *submarines*.

_____ 10. The navy maintains *command* of the sea.

Practice C

Write sentences using each noun in the function that is indicated.

11. navy *(predicate noun)* _____

12. battleship *(appositive)* _____

13. officer *(noun of direct address)* _____

14. ship *(object of the preposition)* _____

15. crew *(indirect object)* _____

Chapter 3: Personal Pronoun Usage

Practice A

Underline the correct pronoun from the choices in parentheses.

1. Has *(you, your)* family ever seen a yak?

2. My brother and *(I, me)* learned that the yak is the wild ox of Asia.

3. The cold, dry plateaus of Tibet suit *(they, them)* well.

4. My friend Hiroshi received two tickets to Tibet, so *(he, him)* and I made plans to go.

5. When we visited Tibet, I took some yak pictures of *(my, mine)* own.

Practice B

Underline the correct pronoun from the choices in parentheses.

6. *(Them, Those)* wild Tibetan yaks measure six feet tall at the shoulder.

7. Since this large animal weighs up to twelve hundred pounds, *(who, whom)* do you think could ride one?

8. Sarah told *(we, us)* that a yak carries its head low, with its nose almost touching the ground.

9. *(She, Her)* and Hiroshi recently completed a project about yaks for our biology class.

10. It's *(she, her)* who finds these creatures fascinating.

Practice C

Underline the correct pronoun from the choices in parentheses. In the blank, label the function of the pronoun *S* (subject), *DO* (direct object), *IO* (indirect object), *OP* (object of the preposition), or *PN* (predicate noun).

_____ 11. Sarah discovered many facts about yaks. It was *(she, her)* who told us that yaks charge furiously at their predators.

_____ 12. Although yaks look clumsy, *(they, them)* can slide down icy slopes, swim rivers, and climb up steep slopes.

_____ 13. Because of the noises domestic yaks make, people gave *(they, them)* the name "grunting ox."

_____ 14. Hiroshi also offered some valuable information about yaks. He surprised *(I, me)* with his knowledge of yaks.

_____ 15. After class I told him that I would like to learn more about yaks from *(he, him)*.

Chapter 3: Reflexive and Intensive Pronouns

Practice A

Label each italicized pronoun *reflexive* or *intensive*.

_____ 1. Hiroshi *himself* enjoys photographing the wild animals of foreign countries.

_____ 2. He has ventured out to many distant places by *himself.*

_____ 3. His brother Lee accompanied him on an adventure to Tibet, and they *themselves* took many incredible pictures.

_____ 4. Before the trip they researched the country for *themselves.*

_____ 5. Tibet *itself* is called the Roof of the World because it has the highest plateaus and mountains on earth.

Practice B

In each sentence underline the reflexive pronouns once and the intensive pronouns twice. If the pronoun is reflexive, write its function in the blank. If the pronoun is intensive, write the noun or pronoun it intensifies in the blank.

_____ 6. Mount Everest, itself one of the world's highest mountains, is located in southern Tibet.

_____ 7. Hiroshi and his brother themselves visited the city Ka-erh in western Tibet, a city which is possibly the highest in the world.

_____ 8. Tibet has been a part of China since 1950, but it once stood by *itself* for several years as an independent state.

_____ 9. Large parts of Tibet itself are wastelands.

_____ 10. Through his research Hiroshi taught himself the fact that Tibet has many wild animals besides yaks, animals such as tigers, monkeys, and wild horses.

Practice C

Rewrite each sentence, adding intensive pronouns to emphasize certain elements as suggested.

11. The entire region of Tibet receives less than ten inches of rain annually.
Emphasize that it is Tibet that receives this amount of rainfall.

_____

_____

12. The Himalayas block moisture-bearing winds that come sweeping up from India.
Emphasize that the mountains alone block the winds.

_____

_____

13. The climate is very windy, with sudden blizzards and violent winds being very common.
    Emphasize that the typical climate is very windy.

    _____

    _____

14. Tibet's population of two million lives mostly in the southern portion of the country.
    Emphasize that the people live in the country's southern region.

    _____

    _____

15. The official language of Tibet is Mandarin Chinese, but the traditional language is Tibetan.
    Emphasize that the traditional language is different from the official language.

    _____

    _____

Chapter 3: Indefinite Pronouns

Practice A

Underline each indefinite pronoun. In the blank, label the pronoun *singular* or *plural*.

_____ 1. Barley is one of Tibet's chief crops.

_____ 2. Most of the food the people eat contains barley flour.

_____ 3. Everyone understands the importance of the yak as a food source.

_____ 4. Several of the products made from yaks are milk, cheese, cloth, and shoe leather.

_____ 5. Many of the yaks are used for transportation.

Practice B

Underline each indefinite pronoun. In the blank, label the pronoun *singular* or *plural*.

_____ 6. Almost everybody in Tibet wears long robes with high collars and long sleeves.

_____ 7. While the robes are usually made of wool or sheepskin, some of the wealthy people wear robes made of silk.

_____ 8. Both of the visitors, Hiroshi and Lee, bought themselves traditional robes while visiting Tibet.

_____ 9. Each of the households weaves cloth and carpet.

_____ 10. Exporting wool generates much of their national income.

Practice C

In the blank write an appropriate indefinite pronoun to complete the sentence. Do not use the same pronoun more than once.

_____ 11. _?_ of Hiroshi's time was spent reading articles on Tibet.

_____ 12. Before traveling, _?_ should take the time to learn about the place he will be visiting.

_____ 13. Knowing _?_ about the country's culture and people will enrich your experience.

_____ 14. Learning a _?_ of the language would help a great deal.

_____ 15. Because Hiroshi diligently prepared, _?_ of his trips were fascinating and rewarding.

Chapter 3: Correcting Unclear Reference Problems

Practice A

Label each sentence *clear* or *unclear*.

_____ 1. When Hiroshi and his brother arrived back home, he became ill with the flu for a week and a half.

_____ 2. Even though he was not feeling well, Hiroshi was still excited about telling his friends about the trip to Tibet.

_____ 3. Asher told Hiroshi that he was happy he was home.

_____ 4. Once he felt better, Hiroshi cooked us a Tibetan meal and showed us his photos of the wild animals he saw. It was very good!

_____ 5. After seeing the excitement on Hiroshi's face when he was telling of his adventures, Asher has decided that he wants to visit Tibet for himself.

Practice B

Rewrite each sentence to make the pronoun-antecedent relationship clear.

6. Asher told Hiroshi that he wanted to go to Tibet next summer.

_____

_____

7. Hiroshi and Lee told Asher about their adventures in Tibet and showed him their pictures. He found them fascinating.

_____

_____

8. Hiroshi told us a story about his first ride on a yak. It was hilarious!

_____

_____

9. Yaks were transporting Hiroshi and a guide to a nearby village when they were both stung by huge wasps.

_____

_____

10. Hiroshi's yak reared up and then began to run as fast as it could. Finally, it halted abruptly. It frightened Hiroshi.

_____

_____

Practice C

Rewrite each sentence to make the pronoun-antecedent relationship clear.

11. Although it gave Hiroshi quite a scare, he was not afraid to get back on the rambunctious yak for the ride back into town.

   _____

   _____

12. Lee was seated calmly on another yak while he watched his brother's adventure. The expression on his face was priceless.

   _____

   _____

13. Lee quickly reached into his backpack and pulled out his camera to snap a picture of Hiroshi. The careening animal didn't seem to alarm him.

   _____

   _____

14. Asher told Lee he should have been more concerned for Hiroshi's safety.

   _____

   _____

15. We all laughed about the story and the picture. Even though Lee embellished the facts for greater dramatic effect, Hiroshi was able to laugh heartily at them.

   _____

   _____

Chapter 4: Principal Parts of Verbs

Practice A

Underline the correct verb from the choices in parentheses. Be sure to check for any auxiliary that may go with the verb you have chosen.

1. Samuel Pepys *(wrote, written)* a famous account of his life in the seventeenth century.

2. His *Diary,* which includes detailed events of his life, was *(gave, given)* to the general public in 1822.

3. Pepys was *(born, borned)* in London in 1633.

4. By 1673 Pepys had *(took, taken)* responsibility for the navy, which he significantly reformed.

5. Through his diaries we have *(got, gotten)* a rich description of England's culture and history.

Practice B

In the blank write the correct past or past participle form of the verb in parentheses.

_____ 6. The drug penicillin has *(keep)* dangerous bacteria from spreading.

_____ 7. Sir Alexander Fleming discovered penicillin when he noticed that some mold growing in a laboratory dish had *(kill)* the bacteria in the dish.

_____ 8. Bacteria cannot survive after the penicillin has *(break)* down their stiff cell walls.

_____ 9. Some types of penicillin have been *(know)* to cause allergic reactions, but most reactions are mild.

_____ 10. Types of penicillin are now commonly *(use)* for the treatment of throat and ear infections.

Practice C

In the blank write the correct past or past participle form of the verb in parentheses.

_____ 11. Yesterday my father *(hang)* a charming oil portrait over the piano.

_____ 12. The portrait has been on the table since we *(lay)* it there last week.

_____ 13. The kittens have *(drink)* the warm milk and gone to sleep.

_____ 14. By dinner time the kittens will have *(lie)* in the sun for two hours.

_____ 15. The dismantled raft has *(sink)* to the bottom of the lake.

Chapter 4: Perfect Tenses

Practice A

Label the tense of each italicized verb *present, present perfect, past, past perfect, future,* or *future perfect*.

_____ 1. Coral islands *have formed* from rocklike deposits that resist erosion.

_____ 2. Atolls, coral islands in the shape of rings, *may enclose* an entire lagoon.

_____ 3. By the time several ocean volcanoes became extinct, a group of coral islands *had formed* around their rims. These islands now make up part of the Tuamotu Archipelago in the South Pacific.

_____ 4. The islands of the Tuamotu Archipelago *were made* part of French Polynesia.

_____ 5. By next year the pearl-producing oysters of the lagoons *will have provided* one of the main sources of revenue for the islands.

Practice B

In the blank write the correct form of the verb in parentheses.

_____ 6. Numerous oyster farms *(cultivate, present perfect)* the famous black pearls of Tuamotu Archipelago.

_____ 7. A pearl *(begin, present)* to form after a foreign object enters the oyster's shell.

_____ 8. The oyster covers the object with coats of nacre. This process, after some time, *(begin, future perfect)* to form a pearl.

_____ 9. Most of the pearls in the South Pacific are black. However, oysters *(produce, present perfect)* pearls that are green and even white.

_____ 10. Natural pearls were once rare and expensive. Soon after farmers *(begin, past perfect)* to culture them, however, pearls became more available.

Practice C

In the blank write the correct form of the verb in parentheses.

_____ 11. At an oyster farm in French Polynesia, plastic garlands hanging in the water *(collect, future)* the floating larvae of oysters.

_____ 12. Before the tiny oysters are seven months old, workers *(place, future perfect)* them in hanging baskets for protection under the water.

_____ 13. Pearl cultivators found that pearls grew bigger and faster after they *(insert, past perfect)* a small bead inside the oyster to start the growth of the pearl.

_____ 14. After three years, the workers *(harvest, past)* the oysters and the black pearls.

_____ 15. Black pearls *(become, present perfect)* some of the most expensive pearls in the world.

Chapter 4: Progressive Tenses

Practice A

In the blank, label the tense of the italicized verb.

_____ 1. China is a type of ceramic that manufacturers *are using* mainly for fine dishes.

_____ 2. Makers of ceramic *were producing* this type of porcelain first in China; therefore, these products are often called china or chinaware.

_____ 3. After a fine piece of porcelain china is made, collectors *will be admiring* it for its strength and delicate appearance.

_____ 4. Since the very first appearance of porcelain, workers *have been making* it from two substances: kaolin and petuntze.

_____ 5. Before the appearance of porcelain, workers *had been creating* stoneware and earthenware from natural clay fired at high temperatures.

Practice B

In the blank write the progressive form of each italicized verb. Do not change the tense of the verb.

_____ 6. Manufacturers *produce* three main kinds of porcelain china.

_____ 7. Many collectors *have considered* hard-paste china the best porcelain.

_____ 8. When he makes the hard-paste china, the manufacturer *will fire* the materials at a much higher temperature because hard-paste china resists melting much better than other types of porcelain.

_____ 9. Several Europeans developed soft-paste china as they *attempted* to imitate hard-paste china.

_____ 10. Adding burned animal bones to kaolin and petuntze creates bone china. The English discovered and *have manufactured* most of the world's bone china.

Practice C

In the blank, label the tense of the italicized verb.

_____ 11. Rulers in China *desired* fine porcelain as far back as A.D. 960.

_____ 12. By the end of the 1700s, several European countries *had competed* with China in making porcelain.

_____ 13. The Germans *have decorated* beautiful fine china since the early 1700s.

_____ 14. This year English manufacturers *will have produced* famous bone china for almost two hundred fifty years.

_____ 15. Several American and Japanese manufacturers *will continue* to produce several lines of quality porcelain.

Chapter 5: Determiners

Practice A

Underline each adjective. Write *PA* over each predicate adjective. Draw an arrow from each other adjective to the noun it modifies.

1. Hibernation is an inactive state of some animals during winter.

2. These animals have a lower body temperature during hibernation.

3. An animal in this state needs little energy.

4. These animals' bodies adapt to harsh winter conditions.

5. The animals often appear dead.

Practice B

In the blank write an appropriate adjective from the category indicated in parentheses. Try to use a variety of adjectives.

_____ 6. _?_ scientists disagree on the hibernation of bears. *(indefinite)*

_____ 7. _?_ opinion is true? *(interrogative)*

_____ 8. Well, a _?_ body temperature does not fall as much as the temperature of other hibernators. *(possessive)*

_____ 9. _?_ scientists also state that a bear is easily awakened from sleep. *(demonstrative)*

_____ 10. _?_ scientists state, however, that a bear's heart rate drops; therefore, bears are true hibernators. *(indefinite)*

Practice C

Label the italicized adjectives *Art* (article), *P* (possessive), *D* (demonstrative), *Int* (interrogative), or *Ind* (indefinite).

_____ 11. *Many* hibernators eat large amounts of food in the fall.

_____ 12. *Which* animals are warm-blooded?

_____ 13. The food is stored in *their* bodies as fat.

_____ 14. *The* fat provides energy during hibernation.

_____ 15. *These* animals alternate periods of hibernation with periods of wakefulness.

Chapter 5: Using Modifiers Correctly

Practice A

Underline the correct adjective or adverb from the choices in parentheses.

1. Bats often scare people *(bad, badly)*.

2. Many times people are afraid because bats appear *(most, mostly)* at night.

3. Bats are valuable because they eat *(large, larger)* numbers of insects.

4. Bats often behave *(timid, timidly)*.

5. Although bats will not intentionally do *(any, no)* harm, they may have rabies.

Practice B

Underline the correct adjective or adverb from the choices in parentheses.

6. People seem *(different, differently)* in their opinions about bats.

7. People in western countries are *(more fearful, most fearful)* of bats than those in European countries are.

8. Most bats are *(real, really)* harmless to people.

9. Bats can probably see as *(good, well)* as human beings.

10. Of flying foxes and brown bats, flying foxes are *(larger, largest)*.

Practice C

Underline the correct adjective or adverb from the choices in parentheses.

11. Compared to those that inhabit exposed areas, bats that live in secluded areas tend to have *(duller, dullest)* markings.

12. Bats that have long, slender wings move the *(fastest, most fastest)* of all.

13. Other bats have *(shorter, more shorter)* wings.

14. Many bats look for a *(good, well)* place to hibernate in the fall or winter.

15. Do some North American bats not eat *(any, no)* food during their hibernation?

Name_____

Chapter 5: Misplaced Modifiers

Practice A
Label each sentence *C* (clear) or *U* (unclear).

_____ 1. Female bats feed their babies for only a few months.

_____ 2. Bats that perch securely attach themselves to rocks and twigs by their claws.

_____ 3. Not all bats have good night vision.

_____ 4. Bats with poor senses often rely on echoes to locate objects.

_____ 5. Echoes allow even the bat to know how its prey is moving.

Practice B
Rewrite the following sentences, correcting any problems with modifier positions.

6. Bats are mammals that can only fly.

7. All people do not know a lot of facts about bats.

8. People who fear bats incorrectly draw conclusions about bats.

9. All bats are not of the same species.

10. Some bats have only a wingspan of one foot.

Concept Reinforcements   **105**

Practice C

Rewrite the following sentences, correcting any problems with modifier positions.

11. The Kitti's hog-nosed bat nearly weighs two grams.

   _____

   _____

12. A bat's digesting its food quickly reduces its superfluous weight.

   _____

   _____

13. Only bats sleep during the day.

   _____

   _____

14. When I was in the woods, I just saw five bats.

   _____

   _____

15. I was so frightened that I fainted almost to the ground.

   _____

   _____

Name_____

Chapter 6: Functions of Prepositional Phrases

Practice A

Underline the word that each italicized prepositional phrase modifies. Label the phrase either *Adj* (adjectival) or *Adv* (adverbial).

_____ 1. *In Woodstock, Oxfordshire, England,* lies Blenheim Palace.

_____ 2. Queen Anne rewarded the Duke of Marlborough *with this home.*

_____ 3. The Duke's wife, Sarah, was a good friend *of the queen.*

_____ 4. An inscription *on the East Gate* tells when the palace was built.

_____ 5. Sir John Vanbrugh built the palace *between 1705 and 1722.*

Practice B

Place parentheses around each prepositional phrase. Label the phrase either *Adj* (adjectival) or *Adv* (adverbial).

_____ 6. Blenheim was designed in the English baroque style.

_____ 7. When I visited Blenheim, I toured the palace with my aunt.

_____ 8. The ceiling above the Great Hall is beautiful.

_____ 9. It was painted by Sir James Thornhill.

_____ 10. The painting is a picture of a triumphant Marlborough.

Practice C

Place parentheses around each prepositional phrase. Underline the word modified by the prepositional phrase. Label the prepositional phrase either *Adj* (adjectival) or *Adv* (adverbial).

_____ 11. My favorite room in the house was Sir Winston Churchill's birth room.

_____ 12. Blenheim was also the place where Sir Winston Churchill proposed to his wife.

_____ 13. As we walked among the rooms, we saw elegant dishes displayed.

_____ 14. I really liked the Meissen tureens with the lemon-slice handles.

_____ 15. Our guide told us an interesting story about these particular dishes.

Concept Reinforcements   107

Chapter 6: Coordinating and Correlative Conjunctions

Practice A
Underline the coordinating and correlative conjunctions in the following sentences.

1. We toured not only the Green Drawing Room but also the Red Drawing Room.

2. The Red Drawing Room houses a portrait of Lady Morton and Mrs. Killigrew.

3. I enjoyed looking at the paintings, but the tapestries on the walls really caught my attention.

4. Neither my aunt nor I could understand why the dog in the tapestry has horse's hooves.

5. Overall, I found the rooms to be elaborate yet delightful.

Practice B
Underline the coordinating and correlative conjunctions in each sentence once. Underline the words or phrases joined by the conjunctions twice.

6. When we toured the grounds of the palace, we visited the Italian Garden and the Great Avenue.

7. Both my aunt and I remarked that we had never seen such lovely sights.

8. I wanted to visit the Grand Bridge, but my aunt said that the walk was too far.

9. Instead, we chose to tour the Rose Garden, for walking among the flowers was less strenuous.

10. My aunt said that we could explore either the Butterfly House or the Marlborough Maze next.

Practice C
Combine a word or phrase from the first sentence with a word or phrase from the second sentence to make a compound sentence element joined by the type of conjunction indicated in parentheses. Use a variety of conjunctions. In the blank write the new sentence.

11. We saw butterflies in the Butterfly House. We also saw moths. *(correlative)*

_____

12. The Butterfly House accommodates Owl butterflies. The Butterfly House accommodates Heliconius butterflies. *(coordinating)*

_____

13. My aunt did not see any Monarch butterflies. I did not see any Monarch butterflies. *(correlative)*

_____

14. I ventured through the Marlborough Maze. My aunt did not. *(coordinating)*

_____

15. Surprisingly, I did not make any incorrect turns in the maze. I also did not get lost. *(coordinating)*

_____

Name_____

Chapter 6: Subordinating Conjunctions

Practice A
Underline the subordinating conjunctions in the following sentences.

1. After I made it through the maze, I rested with my aunt on a bench.
2. Although my aunt was tired, she still wanted to see more sights at the palace.
3. We decided to take a ride on the Blenheim's railway so that our feet could take a break.
4. Once we arrived back at the palace, we felt much better.
5. We visited the Grand Cascade since our strength was renewed.

Practice B
Place parentheses around the dependent clauses. Underline the subordinating conjunction that begins each clause.

6. When we finished admiring the falls, we walked along the lake.
7. My aunt told me then that she would like to walk across the Grand Bridge.
8. As we made our way across the bridge, we noticed many people taking photographs of the scenery.
9. While they took their photographs, my aunt and I looked at the view of the palace with our binoculars.
10. I wanted to learn more about the palace because it had intrigued me so much.

Practice C
Use a subordinating conjunction to combine the two sentences by making one a dependent clause. Try to represent the relationship between the two ideas. In the blank write the new sentence.

11. We toured the interior of the palace one more time. We returned home.

_____

12. We wanted to see the rooms again. There were a couple of rooms that we had missed.

_____

13. I didn't realize how much I had missed. We went on our second tour.

_____

14. Our second tour was better than our first. We learned more facts about the palace.

_____

15. I will visit Blenheim Palace again. I have the opportunity.

_____

Chapter 7: Participles

Practice A

Underline the present and past participles. Draw an arrow from each underlined participle to the noun it modifies.

1. Color enhances beauty, and varied colors often change moods and atmospheres.

2. Several shades of green can create a calm, relaxing atmosphere.

3. A subdued blue can be peaceful as well, or it can indicate a feeling of melancholy.

4. Red is associated with building excitement and even increased anger.

5. A vibrant yellow appears sunny and cheerful; decorating with yellow promotes a pleasant, inviting atmosphere.

Practice B

Underline the participial phrases. Draw an arrow from each underlined participial phrase to the noun it modifies. In the blank, label each underlined participial phrase *present* or *past*.

_____ 6. Color actually begins as light waves differing in length.

_____ 7. Our eyes perceive the various lengths as differently colored waves of light.

_____ 8. Red, having the longest wavelengths, appears at one end of the spectrum.

_____ 9. Appearing at the opposite end, the color violet has the shortest wavelengths.

_____ 10. The long yellow wavelengths combined with short blue wavelengths are reflected as medium wavelengths and appear green.

Practice C

A. Underline each participle and place parentheses around each participial phrase.
B. Draw an arrow from each participle to the word it modifies.
C. In the blank, label each participial phrase *present* or *past*.
D. Label the sentence patterns. Above each word of the sentence pattern write its label.

_____ 11. White waves of light bent by a prism display all the colors of the rainbow.

_____ 12. Light waves, not actually colored themselves, create the sense of color in the brain.

_____ 13. The eye contains three color-sensing cones.

_____ 14. Affecting more men than women, colorblindness is an inherited disorder.

_____ 15. People blinded to all color have achromatic vision.

Chapter 7: Gerunds

Practice A

Underline the gerunds. In the blank, label each underlined gerund _S_ (subject), _DO_ (direct object), _IO_ (indirect object), _OP_ (object of the preposition), or _PN_ (predicate noun).

_____ 1. Cooking prepares food and usually makes it taste better.

_____ 2. Creative meals result from obtaining new ideas and recipes.

_____ 3. If you give meal planning enough time, you can make meals much more efficiently.

_____ 4. One beneficial activity to ensure a healthful diet is planning the basics of nutrition.

_____ 5. If you include meeting basic nutrition requirements in your meals, your dinner time can be both healthful and delicious.

Practice B

Label each italicized word _G_ (gerund) or _P_ (participle).

_____ 6. _Baking_ requires the placement of food in an oven. Bread, cookies, and pastries are foods that are usually baked.

_____ 7. Many people enjoy the aroma of _baking_ bread.

_____ 8. When you are frying meat or vegetables, you will begin by _heating_ an amount of fat in a pan or skillet.

_____ 9. _Boiling_ requires that the food, usually vegetables, be kept in water at least 212°F.

_____ 10. Pasta also is often cooked in _boiling_ water.

Practice C

Place parentheses around the gerund or gerund phrase. In the blank, label the gerund or gerund phrase _S_ (subject), _DO_ (direct object), _IO_ (indirect object), _OP_ (object of the preposition), or _PN_ (predicate noun).

_____ 11. An appealing meal results from combining foods with variety in color, temperature, texture, and taste.

_____ 12. The coloring of food should be diverse. For example, a brightly colored fruit or vegetable adds variety to a meal.

_____ 13. Most cooks prefer including at least one hot food and one cold food in the menu.

_____ 14. Another creative idea is incorporating a theme into the menu.

_____ 15. Some favorite recipes and a little creativity give dining double pleasure and create an enjoyable atmosphere for friends, family, or guests.

Chapter 7: Infinitives

Practice A

Underline the infinitives. Not every sentence contains an infinitive.

1. The country of Congo happens to lie along the equator in west-central Africa.

2. Visitors from cooler, drier climates are likely to swelter in the heat and humidity.

3. Farming, hunting, and fishing have traditionally been the most common occupations of the people, but today many more have begun to acquire office and technical positions.

4. Trees and vegetation cover the northern region, and wild animals are known to inhabit the forests.

5. The Congo River, the world's fifth longest river, flows through Congo to the Atlantic Ocean.

Practice B

Underline the infinitives. Label the function of each infinitive *N* (noun), *Adj* (adjective), or *Adv* (adverb).

_____ 6. I decided to learn more about rural life in Africa.

_____ 7. To hunt is an activity that many people enjoy.

_____ 8. To kill their prey, hunters may use a bow and arrows.

_____ 9. Leaves and berries to supplement any game are often collected by some of the women.

_____ 10. The privilege to collect fruit and plants from farmers' fields is given to those who help farmers with their crops.

Practice C

Underline the infinitive phrases. Label the function of each infinitive phrase *N* (noun), *Adj* (adjective), or *Adv* (adverb).

_____ 11. Would you like to know the reason for the twenty-four-second shot clock in the National Basketball Association?

_____ 12. During the 1953–54 season, many NBA teams were in financial trouble. To go to a game was boring because the game moved very slowly.

_____ 13. At that time a team in the lead had no incentive to shoot the ball.

_____ 14. To save the game, Danny Biasone, owner of the Syracuse Nationals, proposed the twenty-four-second rule, which requires the shooting of a basket within twenty-four seconds after acquiring possession of the ball.

_____ 15. The rule went into effect at the beginning of the 1954–55 season. Scoring began to rise an average of fourteen points per game that year, and fans quickly responded to the increased excitement of the game.

Chapter 8: Independent and Dependent Clauses

Practice A

Label each italicized group of words *P* (phrase) or *C* (clause).

_____ 1. *Volcanoes are very interesting.*

_____ 2. There are three types *of volcanoes.*

_____ 3. Volcanoes are classified by the way *that they are formed.*

_____ 4. A person *who studies volcanoes* must be familiar with several terms.

_____ 5. Magma is melted rock found *under the earth's surface.*

Practice B

Label each italicized group of words *P* (phrase), *IC* (independent clause), or *DC* (dependent clause).

_____ 6. *Once magma has come to the earth's surface,* it is called lava.

_____ 7. Lava that is very fluid moves quickly, but *sticky lava does not move as fast.*

_____ 8. *Volcanoes also erupt rock fragments.*

_____ 9. These rock fragments range in size; they can be grains *of volcanic dust* or volcanic bombs.

_____ 10. *Since volcanic ash sometimes helps to create a mudflow,* it can be a harmful substance.

Practice C

Place parentheses around each dependent clause.

11. Whereas a shield volcano is formed by lava, cinder-cone volcanoes are formed by rock fragments.

12. Composite volcanoes received their name because they are formed by lava and rock fragments.

13. Although they may erupt sometime in the future, dormant volcanoes are considered inactive.

14. If a volcano erupts repeatedly, it is called an active volcano.

15. Once a volcano erupts on a regular basis, it is considered an intermittent volcano.

Chapter 8: Using Independent and Dependent Clauses

Practice A

Underline the coordinating conjunctions. Label each sentence *S* (simple) or *Cd* (compound). Not every sentence contains a coordinating conjunction.

_____ 1. There are four types of volcanic eruptions: Strombolian, Hawaiian, Peléean, and vulcanian.

_____ 2. Hawaiian volcanic eruptions are the least dangerous, but Peléean are the most destructive.

_____ 3. A volcano erupted on Mount Pelée in 1902, and it killed almost thirty-eight thousand people.

_____ 4. Mauna Loa is located in Hawaii; it is the world's largest active volcano.

_____ 5. Kilauea is also a Hawaiian volcano and is active.

Practice B

Label each sentence *S* (simple), *Cd* (compound), or *Cx* (complex).

_____ 6. Although many people think of volcanoes as devastating, volcanoes also have positive effects.

_____ 7. People use lava to make roads, and they use pumice as an abrasive.

_____ 8. In Iceland people use water from volcanic hot springs to heat their homes.

_____ 9. People from other countries are able to use geothermal energy since volcanoes produce underground steam.

_____ 10. Volcanoes are also helpful because they allow scientists to learn more about the earth.

Practice C

Label each sentence *S* (simple), *Cd* (compound), *Cx* (complex), or *Cd-Cx* (compound-complex).

_____ 11. Mexico City is the home of two volcanoes: Popocatépetl and Ixtacihuatl.

_____ 12. Popocatépetl is also called "Smoking Mountain," and it reaches 17,883 feet.

_____ 13. Did Popocatépetl receive its name because it is always emitting sulfur?

_____ 14. When my friends visited Mexico City last summer, they saw Popocatépetl; they were also able to see Ixtacihuatl.

_____ 15. After they returned home, I looked at their photographs, and I asked them whether they saw any other volcanoes.

Chapter 8: Kinds of Dependent Clauses

Practice A

In the blank write the word that the italicized clause modifies.

_____ 1. El Salvador is a country *that is well known for its volcanoes.*

_____ 2. Izalco, *which is one of El Salvador's volcanoes,* is called the Lighthouse of the Pacific.

_____ 3. I should visit El Salvador *when Izalco is not active.*

_____ 4. Iceland is an island *where there are two hundred volcanoes.*

_____ 5. Volcanoes fascinate me *because they are so powerful.*

Practice B

In the blank, label the italicized clause *Adj* (adjective) or *Adv* (adverb).

_____ 6. Mount St. Helens is a volcano *that is located in Washington.*

_____ 7. Many acres of forest were destroyed *when Mount St. Helens erupted.*

_____ 8. A volcanologist is a person *who studies why volcanoes erupt.*

_____ 9. *As a volcano threatens to erupt,* volcanologists try to study the volcanic activity.

_____ 10. Earthquakes, *which often occur before an eruption,* are good warnings that a volcano is going to erupt.

Practice C

Place parentheses around the dependent clauses. In the blank, label the clause *Adj* (adjective) or *Adv* (adverb).

_____ 11. Whenever a volcanologist wants to measure a volcano's expansion, he uses a tiltmeter.

_____ 12. A seismograph also aids a scientist because it is an earthquake identifier.

_____ 13. Mount Shasta is a volcano that has a smaller volcano located on its western slopes.

_____ 14. Mount Etna, which is located in Sicily, first erupted around 700 B.C.

_____ 15. Hawaii is the state where the largest volcano in the world is located.

Chapter 9: Simple and Compound Subjects

Practice A

Underline the verb in parentheses that agrees with the subject.

1. Birte *(visits, visit)* Denmark every year.

2. Her parents *(sails, sail)* to Denmark each spring.

3. Water *(surrounds, surround)* Denmark.

4. Many islands *(is located, are located)* near Denmark.

5. Denmark *(borders, border)* Germany.

Practice B

Questions 6-10: Proofread the following paragraph for errors in subject-verb agreement. Cross out each incorrect verb and write the correct verb above it.

This summer Thore and I plans to visit Denmark. Neither he nor I has ever been there before, so we are looking forward to our trip. While we are there, I hope to see the Royal Library or the National Museum. Thore's aunt and uncle says that they visited these sights a few years ago. Both his aunt and his uncle wishes that they could return to Denmark, but unfortunately they don't have the time or the money to go. Either my parents or my grandmother are giving me some spending money for the trip, so neither Thore nor I will have to worry about finances. I'm so thankful for their generosity!

Practice C

Combine the two sentences using a compound subject. Use the verb that agrees with the subject of your new sentence.

11. Norway is a Scandinavian country.
    Denmark is a Scandinavian country.

    _____

12. Norway lies closer to Denmark.
    Sweden lies closer to Denmark.

    _____

13. Poland does not border Denmark.
    Finland does not border Denmark.

    _____

14. Ålborg is a city in Denmark.
    Århus is a city in Denmark.

    _____

15. Afua does not speak Danish.
    Wilhelm does not speak Danish.

    _____

Chapter 9: Finding the Subject

Practice A

Underline the subject of each sentence. Then underline the verb in parentheses that agrees with the subject.

1. Copenhagen and Odense, not Helsinki, *(is, are)* cities in Denmark.

2. The people of Denmark *(is called, are called)* Danes.

3. There *(is, are)* over five million inhabitants who live in Denmark.

4. Who *(is, are)* a famous writer from Denmark?

5. Grundtvig, not Oehlenschläger, *(was, were)* a Danish hymn writer.

Practice B

Write in the blank the correct form of the verb in parentheses.

_____ 6. One of Denmark's most famous composers _?_ Carl A. Nielsen. *(be)*

_____ 7. My sister, not my brothers, _?_ to his symphonies. *(listen)*

_____ 8. There _?_ five areas of land in Denmark. *(be)*

_____ 9. The beaches of the Western Dune Coast _?_ along the upper western coast of Jutland. *(stretch)*

_____ 10. Bornholm, not the Northern Flat Plains, _?_ near the southern part of Sweden. *(lie)*

Practice C

Questions 11-15: Proofread the following paragraph for errors in subject-verb agreement. Cross out each incorrect verb and write the correct verb above it.

Hans Christian Andersen's greatest gift to Denmark were his fairy tales. His collection are stories for children and adults alike. Andersen also wrote plays and novels. However, his fairy tales, not his greatest novel, is still read outside of Scandinavia. In Andersen's collection there is fairy tales about both people and animals. His tales about human nature has entertained many generations.

Name_____

Chapter 9: Indefinite Pronouns and Problem Nouns as Subjects

Practice A

Underline the verb in parentheses that agrees with the subject.

1. Each of Tia's brothers *(owns, own)* a book of fairy tales by Hans Christian Andersen.

2. "The Emperor's New Clothes" *(is, are)* one of his famous stories.

3. Neither of the girls *(has read, have read)* "The Ugly Duckling."

4. *(Was, Were)* "Little Ida's Flowers" also authored by Andersen?

5. A group of children always *(crowds, crowd)* around the librarian whenever she starts to read one of Andersen's tales.

Practice B

Underline the verb in parentheses that agrees with the subject.

6. Today I read that seven dollars and sixty-eight cents *(is, are)* equal to one Danish krone.

7. None of Denmark *(is, are)* bordered by another Scandinavian country.

8. All of the country *(experiences, experience)* similar weather.

9. *(Does, Do)* some of the Danish people play board games?

10. I wonder if checkers *(is, are)* popular in Denmark.

Practice C

Underline the verb in parentheses that agrees with the subject.

11. My soccer team *(is, are)* taking a tour of Denmark next June.

12. Do you think athletics *(is, are)* important to the Danish people?

13. *(Does, Do)* any of you know about the educational system in Denmark?

14. I have read that most of the Danish people *(is, are)* literate.

15. Five years of high school education *(allows, allow)* a Danish student to be qualified for higher education.

Chapter 9: Pronoun-Antecedent Agreement

Practice A

Underline the pronoun in parentheses that agrees with the antecedent.

1. Neither Kirk nor his friend Thurston has taken *(his, their)* family to Tivoli Gardens.

2. Kristen and Ingrid took *(her, their)* American exchange student there last year.

3. Many like to take *(its, their)* friends to Tivoli Gardens at night.

4. Do all of the rides have *(its, their)* lights on at night?

5. One of the clowns gave me *(his, their)* blue balloon.

Practice B

In the blank write the pronoun that agrees with the antecedent.

_____ 6. I wish that my aunt would give me _?_ recipe for Danish kringle.

_____ 7. Most of my relatives enjoy coffee with _?_ Danish pastries.

_____ 8. Someone in the class remembered that _?_ mother used to make kringle at Christmastime.

_____ 9. Stanley hopes to visit _?_ great uncle who lives in Denmark.

_____ 10. Either Jayne or Krischa will buy a Danish flag when _?_ is in Denmark.

Practice C

Underline the antecedent of the pronoun in parentheses. Then underline the pronoun in the parentheses that agrees with the antecedent.

11. Denmark is a land with beaches, lakes, and farms. Many believe *(its, their)* countryside is beautiful.

12. Both of Kaysa's Danish grandfathers spent *(his, their)* lives on a farm.

13. One of her grandmothers lived *(her, their)* early life in the city.

14. As far as he knows, none of Kaleb's family members are Danish. *(It, They)* are Norwegian.

15. If anyone has an opportunity to visit Denmark, *(he, they)* should not let the opportunity pass him by.

Chapter 10: Spelling

Practice A

Label the italicized words *C* (correct) or *I* (incorrect).

_____ 1. Spelling words incorrectly has always caused me much *greif.*

_____ 2. Even my two *sister-in-laws* have tried to help me with my spelling.

_____ 3. Yesterday two unusual *events* occurred.

_____ 4. I spelled both *"nachos"* and "tomatoes" correctly.

_____ 5. A great *achievement* for me is spelling words correctly.

Practice B

Underline the correct word from the choices in parentheses.

6. I've tried to improve my spelling by *(keepping, keeping)* a list of words that I often misspell.

7. *(Recieve, Receive)* is one of the words that appears on my list.

8. I hope that this practice will be a good *(deterrent, deterent)* for some of my spelling problems.

9. Now I am *(beginning, begining)* to be a better speller.

10. I have also worked on *(memorizing, memorizeing)* specific spelling rules.

Practice C

Underline any misspelled words and write the corrections in the blanks.

_____ 11. Sometimes even a children's song like "Obedeince" can help a person with spelling.

_____ 12. Some words are decieving to the eye.

_____ 13. Often I believe that I have spelled a word inaccurately.

_____ 14. However, I remember that even though some words look wierd, they are still spelled correctly.

_____ 15. It's great to know that spelling is becoming easyer for me!

Chapter 10: Troublesome Verbs

Practice A

Underline the correct verb from the choices in parentheses.

1. I am determined that I *(shall, will)* learn to spell troublesome verbs correctly.

2. I have found that there are several ways that I *(may, can)* accomplish this task.

3. First, I can *(sit, set)* down to study the differences between the words.

4. I can also *(rise, raise)* my hand to ask my teacher a question about a word that I'm unsure of.

5. If I *(lie, lay)* a dictionary next to my desk, I will be able to double-check my spelling easily.

Practice B

Questions 6-10: Proofread the following paragraph for errors with troublesome verbs. Cross out each incorrect verb and write the correct verb above it.

Shall I tell you more tips about how you may remember to spell troublesome verbs correctly? One thing to remember is that some verbs shall have a direct object. Other verbs are used for preference or for permission. Some of these words seem tricky, but sit your mind at ease and lie your worries aside. These difficult words can be conquered. Are you ready to raise to the challenge?

Practice C

Write five sentences using the following italicized words correctly.

11. *rise*_____

12. past of *lay*_____

13. *will*_____

14. *may*_____

15. *sit*_____

Name_____

Chapter 10: Other Troublesome Words

Practice A

Label the italicized word *C* (correct) or *I* (incorrect).

_____ 1. The more spelling words I memorize, the *less* I have to look up in the dictionary.

_____ 2. My grandparents are *real* good spellers.

_____ 3. They think that *it's* fun to do crossword puzzles.

_____ 4. I think that they consider doing crossword puzzles to be *they're* hobby.

_____ 5. While they work on the puzzles, Grandpa always asks Grandma if she will *lend* him her reading glasses.

Practice B

Underline the correct word from the choices in parentheses.

6. On Saturday I bought some new *(stationary, stationery)*.

7. I plan to write to Grandpa and Grandma to ask for some wise *(council, counsel)*.

8. I respect my grandparents because they have had such a great *(affect, effect)* on my life.

9. Grandpa and Grandma wrote back and gave me several *(principals, principles)* to follow.

10. They also said that they would *(pray, prey)* for me.

Practice C

Questions 11-15: Proofread the following paragraph for errors with troublesome words. Cross out each error and write the correct word above it.

It was Grandpa's prophesy that I would receive an A on my next spelling test. I studied harder than I've ever studied before, so I was real pleased when my teacher passed back my test. I spelled every word correctly accept for one. I forgot how to spell the capitol of Florida. I'm still thankful that I was able to spell all of the other words correctly, though. As a reward for my hard work, Grandpa and Grandma are going to take me out for desert.

© 2001 BJU Press. Limited license to copy granted on copyright page.

Concept Reinforcements **123**

Chapter 11: Personal Names, Religions, Nationalities

Practice A

Underline each word that contains a capitalization error.

1. I asked pastor Dryer if he could tell me anything about buddhism.

2. He told me that it is an asian religion.

3. The Founder of this religion is known as the enlightened one.

4. Instead of following the Bible, many buddhists follow what is written in the tipitaka.

5. After hearing about this religion, I am thankful that my father in heaven has led me to the truth of his word.

Practice B

Underline each word that contains a capitalization error and write the correction in the blank. If the sentence is correct, write *C* in the blank.

_____ 6. My British literature teacher is Dr. Geoffrey A. Klein.

_____ 7. This week Dr. Klein is teaching us about spenserian stanza.

_____ 8. Robert Burns, who often wrote in scots, used this stanza form in some of his poems.

_____ 9. John Keats, a british poet, also used this poetic form in his poem "The Eve of St. Agnes."

_____ 10. "She dwells with Beauty—Beauty that must die" is a line from Keats's "Ode on Melancholy."

Practice C

Questions 11-15: Proofread the following paragraph for errors in capitalization. Cross out each error and write the correct letter above it.

Today my Dad told me about the swiss reformer Ulrich Zwingli. In the early 1500s, Zwingli read Erasmus's translation of the new testament, and he was greatly influenced by Erasmus. Zwingli preached against Roman catholicism. He believed that a person is saved by faith and not by works. In addition, Zwingli believed in the individual priesthood of the believer.

Name_____

Chapter 11: Place Names, Transportation, Astronomical Terms

Practice A

Label the italicized terms *C* (correctly capitalized) or *I* (incorrectly capitalized).

_____ 1. Neptune is the eighth planet from the *sun.*

_____ 2. Have you ever heard of the *Galaxy,* a large military jet?

_____ 3. Its steam exhaust system and its multitube boiler made the *rocket* a profitable steam loco-
motive in 1829.

_____ 4. The Jacobsens' address is 285 *starburst lane.*

_____ 5. The *state flag* of South Carolina has a crescent moon and a palmetto tree.

Practice B

In the blank write the letter of the choice that is capitalized correctly.

_____ 6. A. the southeast
B. the Far east
C. the Middle East

_____ 7. A. a Mountain Lake
B. Lake Oswego
C. a freshwater Lake

_____ 8. A. Auckland, new Zealand
B. Cape town, South Africa
C. Riyadh, Saudi Arabia

_____ 9. A. Mount Kilimanjaro
B. carlsbad caverns
C. a deep Valley

_____ 10. A. the capital of north Dakota
B. a river in New mexico
C. a bridge in West Virginia

Practice C

**Underline each word that contains a capitalization error and write the correction in the blank. If
the sentence is correct, write *C* in the blank.**

_____ 11. William Driver was originally from new England.

_____ 12. He was born in salem, Massachusetts, in 1803.

_____ 13. When he was twenty-one, he commanded his first ship, the *Charles doggett.*

_____ 14. Driver flew the American flag on his ship; he called the flag old Glory.

_____ 15. When Driver lived in tennessee in the mid-1860s, he hid his flag in a blanket.

Chapter 11: Businesses and Organizations, Cultural and Historical Terms, Titles and First Words

Practice A

In the blank write the letter of the choice that is capitalized correctly.

_____ 1. A. Levi's Blue jeans
B. Middle school
C. the Korean War

_____ 2. A. Father's day
B. Nobel Prize
C. Parent teacher Association

_____ 3. A. the school's Chess Club
B. Socialist
C. the colosseum in rome

_____ 4. A. Republican Party
B. the house of Representatives
C. Reform bill of 1832

_____ 5. A. the *San Francisco examiner*
B. a U-boat
C. a difficult Science quiz

Practice B

Underline each word that contains a capitalization error and write the correction in the blank. If the sentence is correct, write *C* in the blank.

_____ 6. Willis asked, "Would you like to go to a concert for your birthday?"

_____ 7. "I'd enjoy that," said Adrienne, "But what concert shall we attend?"

_____ 8. "There's a concert going on at Lake Erie college this weekend," answered Willis.

_____ 9. "I believe you're right," said Adrienne. "Aren't they playing Vivaldi's *The four Seasons?*"

_____ 10. "Yes, they are," replied Willis. "I think we can purchase tickets at Society bank."

Practice C

Questions 11-15: Rewrite the following letter on the blanks below, correcting any capitalization errors.

Dear Mr. and Mrs. Gamboe and family,

Thank you for inviting me to the singspiration at your home last night. I am so glad that we were able to sing my favorite hymn, "Be Thou my Vision." I think my favorite lines are "Heart of my own heart, whatever befall, / still be my Vision, o Ruler of all." These words encourage me to have God as my focus no matter what happens in my life. Overall, I thought the evening was very spiritually uplifting, and once again, I appreciate your hospitality.

sincerely,

Omari Gress

_____

_____

_____

_____

_____

_____

_____

_____

_____

_____

_____

_____

Chapter 12: Commas

Practice A

Label the following sentences *C* (correct) or *I* (incorrect).

_____ 1. A plant, that is a nuisance, is a weed.

_____ 2. Uncle Ralph, who enjoys gardening, is constantly ridding his garden of weeds.

_____ 3. The weed, with which he struggles the most, is the dandelion.

_____ 4. A weed, which grows in a garden, can often be a pretty flower.

_____ 5. This flower, which appears attractive, can actually be deadly.

Practice B

Identify the sentence that is punctuated correctly. In the blank write the letter of the choice that corresponds to the correct answer.

_____ 6. A. A dandelion is yellow, and grows in fields and yards.
B. A dandelion is yellow and grows in fields and yards.

_____ 7. A. The dandelion came from Europe, and it has a French name.
B. The dandelion came from Europe, and, it has a French name.

_____ 8. A. My little sister puts dandelions in a vase or a small glass pitcher.
B. My little sister puts dandelions in a vase, or a small glass pitcher.

_____ 9. A. The advertisement on the bag of weed killer is, "Destroy those dandelions!"
B. The advertisement on the bag of weed killer is "Destroy those dandelions!"

_____ 10. A. This weed killer should last us until August, 2006.
B. This weed killer should last us until August 2006.

Practice C

Insert any missing commas into the following sentences. If the sentence is correct, write *C* in the blank.

_____ 11. People who like dandelion leaves eat them cooked in some dishes or raw in a salad.

_____ 12. Dandelion leaves that are the tastiest are young leaves.

_____ 13. A dandelion's root which has hairlike branches grows to about three feet long.

_____ 14. Jacques who likes blowing on dandelions does not realize that he is actually spreading dandelion seeds.

_____ 15. Gardeners not only want to kill dandelions but also want to preserve the grass.

Chapter 12: Quotation Marks, Ellipses, and Underlining for Italics

Practice A

Label the following sentences *C* (correct) or *I* (incorrect).

_____ 1. "How are we going to get rid of all these weeds in our back yard? asked Yolanda."

_____ 2. "Well," answered Dee, "I don't know, but . . ."

_____ 3. "I was thinking, said Yolanda, that we should purchase a pesticide."

_____ 4. Dee thought that Yolanda had made a good suggestion.

_____ 5. The dictionary defines the word weed as "a plant considered undesirable . . . or troublesome."

Practice B

Insert any missing quotation marks into the following sentences.

6. The nursery rhyme says, A man of words and not of deeds / Is like a garden full of weeds.

7. According to St. Augustine, Anger is a weed; hate is the tree.

8. Isn't it interesting, said Philippe, how people associate weeds with vice?

9. I suppose, added Kassandra, that people dislike weeds just as much as they dislike evil deeds.

10. I think you're right, answered Philippe. Weeds damage plants just like sin damages people's lives.

Practice C

In the following sentences place quotation marks around the terms that require quotation marks and underline the terms that should be italicized.

11. The word gardening has two n's.

12. Thy Word Is like a Garden, Lord is a hymn I learned as a child.

13. Does Peg subscribe to Better Homes and Gardens?

14. Robert Louis Stevenson's A Child's Garden of Verses is a book of poetry for children.

15. Andrew Marvell wrote a poem entitled The Garden.

Chapter 12: Apostrophes

Practice A

Underline the word that is punctuated correctly from the choices in parentheses.

1. I hope *(its, it's)* going to rain.

2. The *(vegetables, vegetable's)* in our garden really need the rain.

3. *(Mom's, Moms')* carrots are growing fast.

4. *(Dads, Dad's)* allowing Emily and Erik to grow a tomato plant.

5. So far, *(Emily and Erik's, Emily's and Erik's)* plant does not have any tomatoes.

Practice B

Insert any missing apostrophes into the following sentences.

6. Wouldnt it be fun to grow watermelons?

7. Grandpa told me that he used to grow watermelons back in 44.

8. Aunt Francines string beans are ready to be picked.

9. I hope that my potatoes taste as good as Percys do.

10. The Lloyds garden is full of delicious vegetables.

Practice C

Questions 11-15: Insert any missing apostrophes into the following paragraph. Underline any words that have misplaced apostrophes.

Renee's and Larry's garden always produces beautiful squash. Larry says that there are two types of squash: summer squash and winter squash. Renee says that they've never grown winter squash, although the Williamses, their next-door neighbors, have grown winter squash since 95. Last year Larry and Renee grew zucchini. Its strange how people vary in their taste for vegetables. Larry likes his zucchini raw, but Renee likes her's fried. Summer is almost here, so theyll be enjoying more squash soon.

Chapter 12: Other Punctuation

Practice A

Identify the punctuation missing from each sentence. In the blank write the letter that corresponds to the correct answer.

A. semicolon
B. colon

_____ 1. Yellow crookneck is a summer squash banana squash is a winter squash.

_____ 2. You may start cooking the squash at 630 P.M.

_____ 3. Several states are important squash producers Texas, Florida, California, New Jersey, and New York.

_____ 4. There's only one way I like my squash prepared steamed

_____ 5. Squash is a healthy vegetable it is a low-calorie food.

Practice B

Identify the punctuation missing from each sentence. In the blank write the letter that corresponds to the correct answer.

A. hyphen
B. dash
C. parentheses

_____ 6. Corrina planted twenty four tomato plants.

_____ 7. She is growing three kinds of tomatoes: 1 cherry tomatoes, 2 Big Boy Hybrid tomatoes, and 3 Ponderosa tomatoes.

_____ 8. Solar Set another kind of tomato is grown in high temperatures at high levels of humidity.

_____ 9. The tomato although many consider it a vegetable is really a fruit.

_____ 10. People use tomatoes in ketchup, tomato sauce, and did you remember to pick up some tomato soup at the grocery store?

Practice C

Identify the punctuation missing from each sentence. In the blank write the letter that corresponds to the correct answer.

> A. semicolon
> B. colon
> C. hyphen
> D. dash
> E. parentheses

_____ 11. The tomato plant has hairy stems it also has yellow flowers.

_____ 12. Tomatoes they can grow in just about any type of soil are green before they ripen.

_____ 13. Tomatoes ripen into various colors red, orange, or yellow.

_____ 14. My sister in law likes to eat bacon, lettuce, and tomato sandwiches.

_____ 15. Ponderosa tomatoes a large variety are Dad's favorite.

Chapter 1: Taking Good Notes in Class

Date:

Class:

Topic:

Chapter and Page Numbers:

Main Ideas:

Chapter 2: Writing Good Paragraphs

Second Opinion
Use this form to make suggestions about the paragraph you are given.

1. Does the topic sentence define as well as introduce the subject of the paragraph?

    If not, how could the topic sentence be improved?

2. Is the paragraph developed by details or by examples?

    Are there enough details or examples to support the topic sentence sufficiently?

3. Are there any sentences in the paragraph that could be eliminated? Why do you say so?

4. What did you like best about this paragraph?

Name_____

Chapter 3: Writing Definitions

Critique the following definition of the word *dessert*.

The word *dessert* means anything that is eaten at the end of a meal. Most people think of it as the best part of the meal. Many kinds of desserts can be used as dessert. Desserts include apple pie, chocolate mousse, chocolate cake, ice cream, and fruit cobbler. Cookies are usually classified as snacks rather than as desserts. This also goes for candy bars, fruit, and milk shakes. Some people use *dessert* figuratively to mean an activity they cannot do until they get their chores done. Although *dessert* looks similar to the word *desert,* these words describe very different things.

- What is the fundamental problem with this definition?

- Does the definition contain any editorial statements?

- Are there any extraneous sentences in the definition?

- How universally true is this definition?

Chapter 4: Writing a Comparison and Contrast

Use the chart to help you organize your comparison and contrast.

Topic: _____ and _____	
Alike	**Different**

Topic Sentence:

Method of Organization:

Chapter 5: Writing About a Personal Experience

Self-Interview

- Why is this event significant to me?

- What would someone else find most interesting about this story?

- What details of the setting are essential for the story to be clear?

- What do I want the reader to feel?

- Where is the best place to begin the story?

Chapter 6A: Writing a Research Essay

Topic:

Purpose:

Thesis:

Outline:

Chapter 6B: Writing a Research Essay

Second Opinion
Use this form to make suggestions about the essay you are given.

1. Does each supporting paragraph begin with a good topic sentence?

2. Do all of the supporting paragraphs support the thesis statement?

3. Does the writer need to incorporate more transitions to make the paper flow more smoothly?

4. Does the writer correctly document each of his summaries, paraphrases, and quotations?

5. Examine the opening paragraph for the characteristics of a good introduction.

    Does it catch your interest?

    Does it introduce the topic of the essay?

    Does it draw attention to the main idea of the topic?

    Does the thesis statement appear as the last sentence?

6. Examine the concluding paragraph for the characteristics of a good conclusion.

    Is the first sentence a restatement of (not identical to) the thesis statement?

    Does the conclusion sum up the main ideas of the essay?

    Does the essay sound finished?

7. Does the essay contain problems with grammar, spelling, or punctuation?

8. Overall, is the essay clear?

9. Look at the bibliography.

    Is all the essential information present for each source? *(author, title, publication information)*

    Does the writer use hanging indentation?

    Are the titles of works correctly quoted or italicized?

10. Do you have any additional comments or suggestions?

Chapter 7: Writing Poetry

Quatrain

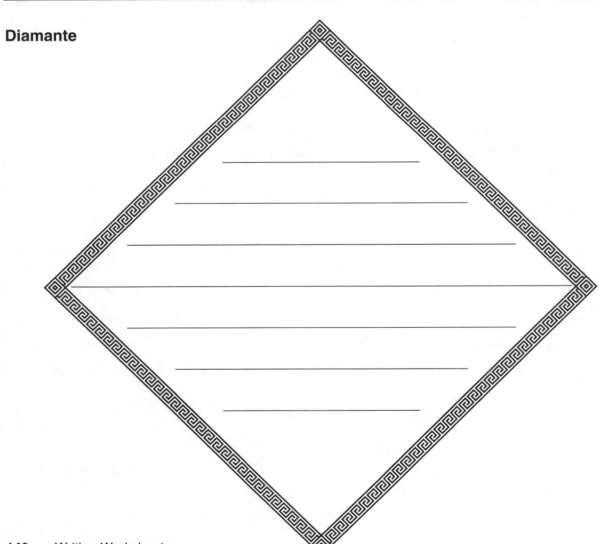

Diamante

Chapter 8: Writing a Devotional

Devotional Journal Page

Use this page to record and evaluate ideas for your devotional.

Date:

Observations/Reading/Conversations:

Devotional Ideas:

Possible Scripture References:

Chapter 9: Writing a Personal Response to Literature

In Someone Else's Shoes
Read someone else's personal response to literature and answer these questions.

1. Have you ever read this piece of literature?

2. Were you surprised that the person chose this piece of literature? Why or why not?

3. What was most effective about the person's response?

4. Was anything unclear?

5. If you have not read this piece of literature, do you think you would like to now?

Name_____

Chapter 10: Writing for the Media

Storyboard Template

Chapter 11: Recording an Oral History

Fill out this sheet before going to your interview with your subject.

Subject's Name:

Subject's Address:

Date and Time of Interview:

Have you . . .

- confirmed the date and time of the interview with the subject?

- asked the subject for permission to use a tape recorder?

- tested your tape recorder, gotten extra batteries, and inserted a blank tape?

- prepared to take notes by hand?

- written out your interview questions?

- determined which questions are most important and which questions could be left out?

- dressed appropriately?

Chapter 12: Letter Writing

E-valuate Your E-mail

If you received this e-mail message, what would you think?

Tone

- What is the sender's mood?

- Does the tone make you want to respond?

Format

- Which specific *do*s are demonstrated in the e-mail?

- Are there any *don't*s?

Clarity

- Do you follow the point from the beginning, or do you feel that you have joined the middle of a conversation?

- If you were the recipient, would you understand what was expected of you?

Mechanics

- Are the spelling and grammar correct?

- If there are abbreviations, are they easily recognized?

Chapter 1 Rubric
Writing an Essay Answer

MESSAGE

Organization
3 Essay contains a clear thesis, good supporting details, and an accurate restatement.
2 Essay contains a thesis, some supporting details, and a restatement.
1 Essay does not contain the necessary elements.

Development
3 Essay development shows a logical and effective progression of ideas.
2 Essay development shows good progression of ideas.
1 Essay development lacks good progression of ideas.

Support
3 Essay includes excellent examples and/or abundant, accurate support material.
2 Essay includes sufficient, valid support material.
1 Essay includes inadequate and/or inaccurate support material.

———— **MESSAGE SCORE**

MECHANICS

Grammar/Usage
3 Writer displays a command of agreement, pronoun reference, word usage, and complete sentences.
2 Writer demonstrates a basic understanding of agreement, pronoun reference, word usage, and complete sentences.
1 Writer makes errors in agreement, pronoun reference, word usage, or complete sentences.

Spelling
3 Writer uses and spells words above grade level.
2 Writer spells words on grade level.
1 Writer misspells grade-level words.

Capitalization/Punctuation
3 Writer demonstrates a command of grade-level capitalization and punctuation.
2 Writer demonstrates an understanding of grade-level capitalization and punctuation.
1 Writer misuses grade-level capitalization and/or punctuation.

———— **MECHANICS SCORE**
———— **TOTAL SCORE (Message plus Mechanics)**

| A 16-18 | B 14-15 | C 12-13 | D 10-11 | F 6-9 |

Overall, this writing . . .

Chapter 2 Rubric
Writing Good Paragraphs

	MESSAGE
	Originality 3 Paragraph shows originality of thought. 2 Paragraph includes some originality of thought. 1 Paragraph does not show originality of thought.
	Topic Sentence 3 Topic sentence is strongly stated and broad enough for a paragraph but sufficiently limited in focus; it effectively supports the thesis. 2 Topic sentence supports the thesis. 1 Topic sentence is too broad or too limited in its subject area and provides little or no support for the thesis.
	Details 3 Sentences include detailed support of the topic sentence. 2 Sentences include sufficient detail to support the topic sentence. 1 Sentences do not have enough detail to support the topic sentence.
_____	**MESSAGE SCORE**

	MECHANICS
	Grammar/Usage 3 Writer displays a command of agreement, pronoun reference, word usage, and complete sentences. 2 Writer demonstrates a basic understanding of agreement, pronoun reference, word usage, and complete sentences. 1 Writer makes errors in agreement, pronoun reference, word usage, or complete sentences.
	Spelling 3 Writer uses and spells words above grade level. 2 Writer spells words on grade level. 1 Writer misspells grade-level words.
	Capitalization/Punctuation 3 Writer demonstrates a command of grade-level capitalization and punctuation. 2 Writer demonstrates an understanding of grade-level capitalization and punctuation. 1 Writer misuses grade-level capitalization and/or punctuation.
_____	**MECHANICS SCORE**
_____	**TOTAL SCORE (Message plus Mechanics)**

A 16-18　　　B 14-15　　　C 12-13　　　D 10-11　　　F 6-9

Overall, this writing . . .

Chapter 3 Rubric
Writing Definitions

	MESSAGE
	Scope 3 Definition is both sufficiently limited and adequately encompassing. 2 Definition is slightly too limited or not sufficiently limited. 1 Definition is obviously too narrow or too broad.
	Objectivity 3 Definition remains free from the author's feelings or beliefs. 2 Definition incorporates the author's beliefs to a small degree. 1 Definition is obviously biased.
	Clarity 3 Definition uses concrete, accurate words. 2 Definition uses accurate but somewhat vague words. 1 Definition does not use concrete, accurate words.
_____	**MESSAGE SCORE**

	MECHANICS
	Grammar/Usage 3 Writer displays a command of agreement, pronoun reference, word usage, and complete sentences. 2 Writer demonstrates a basic understanding of agreement, pronoun reference, word usage, and complete sentences. 1 Writer makes errors in agreement, pronoun reference, word usage, or complete sentences.
	Spelling 3 Writer uses and spells words above grade level. 2 Writer spells words on grade level. 1 Writer misspells grade-level words.
	Capitalization/Punctuation 3 Writer demonstrates a command of grade-level capitalization and punctuation. 2 Writer demonstrates an understanding of grade-level capitalization and punctuation. 1 Writer misuses grade-level capitalization and/or punctuation.
_____ _____	**MECHANICS SCORE** **TOTAL SCORE (Message plus Mechanics)**

A 16-18   B 14-15   C 12-13   D 10-11   F 6-9

Overall, this writing . . .

Chapter 4 Rubric
Writing a Comparison and Contrast

	## MESSAGE
	Purpose
	3 The comparison/contrast paragraph clearly argues for/against a specific, workable topic.
	2 The comparison/contrast paragraph argues for/against a topic.
	1 The comparison/contrast paragraph does not argue for/against a workable topic.
	Research
	3 Paragraph evidences thorough research and study.
	2 Paragraph evidences moderate research and study.
	1 Paragraph evidences little or no research and study.
	Support
	3 The sentences thoroughly support the topic sentence.
	2 The sentences adequately support the topic sentence.
	1 The sentences do not support the topic sentence.
———	**MESSAGE SCORE**

	## MECHANICS
	Grammar/Usage
	3 Writer displays a command of agreement, pronoun reference, word usage, and complete sentences.
	2 Writer demonstrates a basic understanding of agreement, pronoun reference, word usage, and complete sentences.
	1 Writer makes errors in agreement, pronoun reference, word usage, or complete sentences.
	Spelling
	3 Writer uses and spells words above grade level.
	2 Writer spells words on grade level.
	1 Writer misspells grade-level words.
	Capitalization/Punctuation
	3 Writer demonstrates a command of grade-level capitalization and punctuation.
	2 Writer demonstrates an understanding of grade-level capitalization and punctuation.
	1 Writer misuses grade-level capitalization and/or punctuation.
———	**MECHANICS SCORE**
———	**TOTAL SCORE (Message plus Mechanics)**

A 16-18   B 14-15   C 12-13   D 10-11   F 6-9

Overall, this writing . . .

Chapter 5 Rubric
Writing About a Personal Experience

MESSAGE

Details
- 3 Details are well chosen and telling.
- 2 Details are sufficient.
- 1 More details are necessary for clarity.

Rough Draft
- 3 The rough draft is detailed and thorough.
- 2 The rough draft is sufficiently developed.
- 1 The rough draft is not well developed.

Word Choice
- 3 Word choice is precise and colorful.
- 2 Word choice is appropriate.
- 1 Word choice is careless and vague.

_____ **MESSAGE SCORE**

MECHANICS

Grammar/Usage
- 3 Writer displays a command of agreement, pronoun reference, word usage, and complete sentences.
- 2 Writer demonstrates a basic understanding of agreement, pronoun reference, word usage, and complete sentences.
- 1 Writer makes errors in agreement, pronoun reference, word usage, or complete sentences.

Spelling
- 3 Writer uses and spells words above grade level.
- 2 Writer spells words on grade level.
- 1 Writer misspells grade-level words.

Capitalization/Punctuation
- 3 Writer demonstrates a command of grade-level capitalization and punctuation.
- 2 Writer demonstrates an understanding of grade-level capitalization and punctuation.
- 1 Writer misuses grade-level capitalization and/or punctuation.

_____ **MECHANICS SCORE**

_____ **TOTAL SCORE (Message plus Mechanics)**

| A 16-18 | B 14-15 | C 12-13 | D 10-11 | F 6-9 |

Overall, this writing . . .

Chapter 6 Rubric
Writing a Research Essay

MESSAGE

Purpose
- 3 Student thoroughly explains topic and fully achieves his intended purpose for the intended audience.
- 2 Student explains topic and somewhat achieves his intended purpose for the intended audience.
- 1 Student does not explain topic well and does not achieve his intended purpose for the intended audience.

Outline
- 3 Outlining is detailed and thorough.
- 2 Outlining is sufficient.
- 1 Outlining does not have the necessary information or lacks clear organization.

Development
- 3 Essay development shows a logical and effective arrangement of ideas.
- 2 Essay development shows good arrangement of ideas.
- 1 Essay development lacks good arrangement of ideas.

Research
- 3 Essay contains abundant information from research with accurate citations of sources.
- 2 Essay contains some information from research with accurate citations of sources.
- 1 Essay contains little or no information from research, and/or citations are missing or inaccurate.

_____ **MESSAGE SCORE**

MECHANICS

Grammar/Usage
- 3 Writer displays a command of agreement, pronoun reference, word usage, and complete sentences.
- 2 Writer demonstrates a basic understanding of agreement, pronoun reference, word usage, and complete sentences.
- 1 Writer makes errors in agreement, pronoun reference, word usage, or complete sentences.

Spelling
- 3 Writer uses and spells words above grade level.
- 2 Writer spells words on grade level.
- 1 Writer misspells grade-level words.

Capitalization/Punctuation
- 3 Writer demonstrates a command of grade-level capitalization and punctuation.
- 2 Writer demonstrates an understanding of grade-level capitalization and punctuation.
- 1 Writer misuses grade-level capitalization and/or punctuation.

_____ **MECHANICS SCORE**

_____ **TOTAL SCORE (Message plus Mechanics)**

A 19-21   B 16-18   C 13-15   D 10-12   F 7-9

Overall, this writing . . .

Chapter 7A Rubric
Writing a Quatrain

	MESSAGE
	Rhyme 3 Quatrain has appropriate rhyme. 2 Quatrain maintains rhyme structure most of the time. 1 Quatrain does not rhyme.
	Form 3 Quatrain effectively maintains form. 2 Quatrain maintains form most of the time. 1 Quatrain does not maintain form.
	Sound 3 Poem sounds natural and unforced. 2 Poem has a few problems sounding natural and unforced. 1 Poem sounds unnatural and forced.
_____	**MESSAGE SCORE**

	MECHANICS
	Grammar/Usage 3 Writer displays a command of agreement, pronoun reference, word usage, and complete sentences. 2 Writer demonstrates a basic understanding of agreement, pronoun reference, word usage, and complete sentences. 1 Writer makes errors in agreement, pronoun reference, word usage, or complete sentences.
	Spelling 3 Writer uses and spells words above grade level. 2 Writer spells words on grade level. 1 Writer misspells grade-level words.
	Capitalization/Punctuation 3 Writer demonstrates a command of grade-level capitalization and punctuation. 2 Writer demonstrates an understanding of grade-level capitalization and punctuation. 1 Writer misuses grade-level capitalization and/or punctuation.
_____	**MECHANICS SCORE**
_____	**TOTAL SCORE (Message plus Mechanics)**

A 16-18   B 14-15   C 12-13   D 10-11   F 6-9

Overall, this writing . . .

Chapter 7B Rubric
Writing a Diamante

	MESSAGE
	Word Choice 3 Diamante uses original, striking words. 2 Diamante uses appropriate words. 1 Diamante uses dull, uninteresting words.
	Form 3 Diamante maintains diamond structure and parallelism throughout. 2 Diamante maintains an effective diamond structure. 1 Diamante does not maintain diamond structure and parallelism.
	Sound 3 Poem sounds natural and unforced. 2 Poem has a few problems sounding natural and unforced. 1 Poem sounds unnatural and forced.
_____	**MESSAGE SCORE**

	MECHANICS
	Grammar/Usage 3 Writer displays a command of agreement, pronoun reference, word usage, and complete sentences. 2 Writer demonstrates a basic understanding of agreement, pronoun reference, word usage, and complete sentences. 1 Writer makes errors in agreement, pronoun reference, word usage, or complete sentences.
	Spelling 3 Writer uses and spells words above grade level. 2 Writer spells words on grade level. 1 Writer misspells grade-level words.
	Capitalization/Punctuation 3 Writer demonstrates a command of grade-level capitalization and punctuation. 2 Writer demonstrates an understanding of grade-level capitalization and punctuation. 1 Writer misuses grade-level capitalization and/or punctuation.
_____ _____	**MECHANICS SCORE** **TOTAL SCORE (Message plus Mechanics)**

A 16-18   B 14-15   C 12-13   D 10-11   F 6-9

Overall, this writing . . .

Chapter 8 Rubric
Writing a Devotional

	MESSAGE
	Subject and Verse 3 The subject and appropriate choice of verse show obvious depth of thought. 2 The subject and choice of verse are appropriate. 1 The subject and choice of verse are not appropriate.
	Opening 3 The opening grabs the reader's attention. 2 The opening is appropriate. 1 The opening is dull and not sufficiently interesting.
	Application 3 The student draws an effective application. 2 The student draws an application. 1 The student does not draw an application.
	Audience 3 Style is effective for intended audience. 2 Style is appropriate for intended audience. 1 Style is inappropriate for intended audience.
_____	**MESSAGE SCORE**

	MECHANICS
	Grammar/Usage 3 Writer displays a command of agreement, pronoun reference, word usage, and complete sentences. 2 Writer demonstrates a basic understanding of agreement, pronoun reference, word usage, and complete sentences. 1 Writer makes errors in agreement, pronoun reference, word usage, or complete sentences.
	Spelling 3 Writer uses and spells words above grade level. 2 Writer spells words on grade level. 1 Writer misspells grade-level words.
	Capitalization/Punctuation 3 Writer demonstrates a command of grade-level capitalization and punctuation. 2 Writer demonstrates an understanding of grade-level capitalization and punctuation. 1 Writer misuses grade-level capitalization and/or punctuation.
_____ _____	**MECHANICS SCORE** **TOTAL SCORE (Message plus Mechanics)**

A 19-21   B 16-18   C 13-15   D 10-12   F 7-9

Overall, this writing . . .

Chapter 9 Rubric
Writing a Personal Response
to Literature

MESSAGE

Universality
3 Choice of experience demonstrates universality.
2 Choice of experience is appropriate.
1 Choice of experience does not demonstrate universality.

Explanation
3 Response gives ample explanation.
2 Response gives sufficient explanation.
1 Response gives insufficient explanation.

Relationship
3 Response shows clear and moving relationship between experience and literature.
2 Response shows sufficient relationship between experience and literature.
1 Response shows no relationship between experience and literature.

_____ **MESSAGE SCORE**

MECHANICS

Grammar/Usage
3 Writer displays a command of agreement, pronoun reference, word usage, and complete sentences.
2 Writer demonstrates a basic understanding of agreement, pronoun reference, word usage, and complete sentences.
1 Writer makes errors in agreement, pronoun reference, word usage, or complete sentences.

Spelling
3 Writer uses and spells words above grade level.
2 Writer spells words on grade level.
1 Writer misspells grade-level words.

Capitalization/Punctuation
3 Writer demonstrates a command of grade-level capitalization and punctuation.
2 Writer demonstrates an understanding of grade-level capitalization and punctuation.
1 Writer misuses grade-level capitalization and/or punctuation.

_____ **MECHANICS SCORE**
_____ **TOTAL SCORE (Message plus Mechanics)**

A 16-18   B 14-15   C 12-13   D 10-11   F 6-9

Overall, this writing . . .

Chapter 10 Rubric
Writing for the Media

<table>
<tr><td></td><td colspan="2"><h2>MESSAGE</h2></td></tr>
<tr><td></td><td colspan="2">

Approach
  3 Approach shows originality.
  2 Approach uses some originality.
  1 Approach does not show originality.
</td></tr>
<tr><td></td><td colspan="2">

Message
  3 Message is effective and powerful.
  2 Message is effective.
  1 Message is not effective.
</td></tr>
<tr><td></td><td colspan="2">

Storyboard
  3 Storyboard has clear, interesting panels and captures main thrust of announcement.
  2 Storyboard has sufficient panels.
  1 Storyboard does not have sufficient panels.
</td></tr>
<tr><td>_____</td><td colspan="2">**MESSAGE SCORE**</td></tr>
</table>

<table>
<tr><td></td><td colspan="2"><h2>MECHANICS</h2></td></tr>
<tr><td></td><td colspan="2">

Grammar/Usage
  3 Writer displays a command of agreement, pronoun reference, word usage, and complete sentences.
  2 Writer demonstrates a basic understanding of agreement, pronoun reference, word usage, and complete sentences.
  1 Writer makes errors in agreement, pronoun reference, word usage, or complete sentences.
</td></tr>
<tr><td></td><td colspan="2">

Spelling
  3 Writer uses and spells words above grade level.
  2 Writer spells words on grade level.
  1 Writer misspells grade-level words.
</td></tr>
<tr><td></td><td colspan="2">

Capitalization/Punctuation
  3 Writer demonstrates a command of grade-level capitalization and punctuation.
  2 Writer demonstrates an understanding of grade-level capitalization and punctuation.
  1 Writer misuses grade-level capitalization and/or punctuation.
</td></tr>
<tr><td>_____
_____</td><td colspan="2">**MECHANICS SCORE**
TOTAL SCORE (Message plus Mechanics)</td></tr>
</table>

A 16-18   B 14-15   C 12-13   D 10-11   F 6-9

Overall, this writing . . .

Chapter 11 Rubric
Recording an Oral History

MESSAGE

Organization
3 Organization shows forethought and planning.
2 Organization is adequate.
1 Organization shows lack of forethought and planning.

Details
3 Details and quotations are well chosen.
2 Details and quotations are effective.
1 Details and quotations are ineffective.

History
3 History includes ample variety to portray the subject thoroughly.
2 History includes enough variety to portray the subject accurately.
1 History does not include enough variety to portray the subject accurately.

Ending
3 Ending is memorable.
2 Ending is appropriate.
1 Ending is not memorable.

MESSAGE SCORE

MECHANICS

Grammar/Usage
3 Writer displays a command of agreement, pronoun reference, word usage, and complete sentences.
2 Writer demonstrates a basic understanding of agreement, pronoun reference, word usage, and complete sentences.
1 Writer makes errors in agreement, pronoun reference, word usage, or complete sentences.

Spelling
3 Writer uses and spells words above grade level.
2 Writer spells words on grade level.
1 Writer misspells grade-level words.

Capitalization/Punctuation
3 Writer demonstrates a command of grade-level capitalization and punctuation.
2 Writer demonstrates an understanding of grade-level capitalization and punctuation.
1 Writer misuses grade-level capitalization and/or punctuation.

MECHANICS SCORE
TOTAL SCORE (Message plus Mechanics)

A 19-21   B 16-18   C 13-15   D 10-12   F 7-9

Overall, this writing . . .

Chapter 12 Rubric
Letter Writing

	MESSAGE
	Tone 3 Tone is sincere and personal. 2 Tone is acceptable. 1 Tone is not appropriate.
	Details 3 Letter includes abundant, specific detail. 2 Letter includes sufficient detail. 1 Letter does not include enough detail.
	Length 3 Letter has an appropriate length. 2 Letter is too long. 1 Letter is short and abrupt.
_____	**MESSAGE SCORE**

	MECHANICS
	Grammar/Usage 3 Writer displays a command of agreement, pronoun reference, word usage, and complete sentences. 2 Writer demonstrates a basic understanding of agreement, pronoun reference, word usage, and complete sentences. 1 Writer makes errors in agreement, pronoun reference, word usage, or complete sentences.
	Spelling 3 Writer uses and spells words above grade level. 2 Writer spells words on grade level. 1 Writer misspells grade-level words.
	Capitalization/Punctuation 3 Writer demonstrates a command of grade-level capitalization and punctuation. 2 Writer demonstrates an understanding of grade-level capitalization and punctuation. 1 Writer misuses grade-level capitalization and/or punctuation.
_____	**MECHANICS SCORE**
_____	**TOTAL SCORE (Message plus Mechanics)**

A 16-18	B 14-15	C 12-13	D 10-11	F 6-9

Overall, this writing . . .

Chapter 1 Pretest: Sentences

I. Four Kinds of Sentences

Identify each sentence as *declarative, exclamatory, imperative,* or *interrogative.* Place the appropriate punctuation mark at the end of each sentence.

_____*declarative*_____   1. Many interesting salvation stories are found in the Book of Acts.

_____*exclamatory*_____   2. Wow! God works in such miraculous ways !

_____*interrogative*_____   3. Have you accepted Christ as Savior ?

_____*declarative*_____   4. Christ tells us to give the salvation message to all people.

_____*imperative*_____   5. Obey His commandment to witness throughout the whole world.

II. Subjects and Predicates

Draw a vertical line between the complete subject and the complete predicate of each sentence.

6. Paul and his companions | looked for a place of worship in Philippi.

7. They | found a group of women by a river outside the city.

8. One woman, Lydia, | knew about God but did not know Him personally.

9. The salvation message | was given by Paul and his companions that morning by the river.

10. Lydia | believed and was saved.

III. Inverted Order and Imperative Sentences

In each sentence underline the simple subject once and the simple predicate twice. If the subject is understood, write the understood *You* to the left of the number.

11. Have <u>you</u> <u>heard</u> about the salvation story of Saul?

12. There <u>are</u> so many interesting <u>circumstances</u> in that story.

13. <u>Did</u> <u>Saul</u> <u>murder</u> many Christians?

14. Present at the trial of Stephen <u>was</u> <u>Saul</u>.

You   15. <u>Read</u> in the Book of Acts about the rest of the story.

IV. Sentence Patterns

Label the sentence pattern in each sentence _S-InV, S-TrV-DO, S-TrV-IO-DO, S-LV-PN,_ or _S-LV-PA._ Above each word of the sentence pattern write its label.

            S   LV   PN
16. Cornelius was a centurion of the Italian band.

      S   LV   PA
17. He was devout.

              S   TrV   IO   DO
18. One day God sent him a vision.

        S   TrV   DO
19. God had answered his prayers.

                S   InV
20. Cornelius's men went to Joppa.

V. Phrases and Clauses

Label each italicized group of words _P_ (phrase), _IC_ (independent clause), or _DC_ (dependent clause).

___P___ 21. Peter was staying in Joppa _with a tanner named Simon._

___P___ 22. _In the middle of the day,_ Peter went onto the housetop to pray.

___DC___ 23. _When he was on the housetop,_ he fell into a trance.

___DC___ 24. A great sheet _that was filled with animals_ was lowered before him.

___IC___ 25. _God told Peter to eat the meat._

VI. Sentence Problems

Label each word group _S_ (sentence), _F_ (fragment), _FS_ (fused sentence), or _CS_ (comma splice).

___F___ 26. Peter, thinking about the vision's meaning.

___CS___ 27. Peter heard the message from Cornelius's men, he went with them to Cornelius's house.

___FS___ 28. Cornelius had called his relatives together he called his close friends too.

___CS___ 29. Peter preached Christ, the Holy Ghost came upon those who were present.

___S___ 30. God is no respecter of persons.

Chapter 2 Pretest: Nouns

I. Plural Nouns
In the blank write the plural form of the noun.

toll bridges	1. toll bridge
tomatoes	2. tomato
m's	3. *m*
halves	4. half
flagpoles	5. flagpole
businesses	6. business
children	7. child
sisters-in-law	8. sister-in-law
countries	9. country
car washes	10. car wash

II. Possessive Nouns
In the blank write the correct possessive form of the noun in parentheses.

Duane's   11. _?_ geography teacher told him that France is the biggest country in Europe. *(Duane)*

cousin's   12. My _?_ pen pal lives in Nice, the fifth largest city in France. *(cousin)*

parents'   13. Aimee took her _?_ camera with her when she visited France. *(parents)*

Louis XIV's   14. She saw _?_ home, the Palace of Versailles. *(Louis XIV)*

friend's   15. To climb to the top of Mont Blanc has been my _?_ lifelong dream. *(friend)*

III. Common and Proper Nouns
Underline each noun. Above each noun, label it *C* (common) or *P* (proper).

16. The <u>Edict of Nantes</u>(P) gave religious <u>freedom</u>(C) to French <u>Huguenots</u>(P).

17. <u>Joan of Arc</u>(P) was a <u>heroine</u>(C) of the <u>Hundred Years' War</u>(P).

18. The first <u>king</u>(C) of <u>France</u>(P) was <u>Hugh Capet</u>(P).

19. Those who supported the <u>monarchy</u>(C) during the <u>French Revolution</u>(P) were sent to the <u>guillotine</u>(C).

20. The <u>Arc de Triomphe</u>(P) commemorates a <u>conquest</u>(C) of <u>Napoleon</u>(P).

IV. Count and Noncount Nouns

In the blank write *count* or *noncount* for each italicized word.

__count__ 21. France possesses eight island *territories*.

__noncount__ 22. France produces more *barley* than the United States does.

__noncount__ 23. The *scenery* in France is beautiful.

__count__ 24 The Loire River is France's longest *river*.

__count__ 25. The French Riviera is a favorite *place* to vacation in Europe.

V. Collective and Compound Nouns

Underline the compound nouns once and the collective nouns twice.

26. The Normans were a Viking group that invaded the region known today as Normandy.

27. Charles Martel led the French army at the Battle of Tours in 732.

28. Alsace is a region of France that is rich in farmland.

29. The Bourbon family reigned in France from 1589 to 1792 and from 1814 to 1830.

30. France is the world's second largest producer of sugar beets.

VI. Noun Functions

Label the function of each italicized noun *S* (subject), *DO* (direct object), *IO* (indirect object), *OP* (object of the preposition), *PN* (predicate noun), *App* (appositive), or *NA* (noun of direct address).

__OP__ 31. The Tuileries Palace is located next to the Louvre in *Paris*.

__App__ 32. Louis XVI, the *"Sun King,"* reigned from 1661 to 1715.

__PN__ 33. Pierre-Auguste Renoir was a famous French impressionistic *painter*.

__IO__ 34. The British gave *Napoleon* the epithet "Corsican Ogre."

__OP__ 35. The Pyrenees Mountains separate France from *Spain*.

__App__ 36. Claude Debussy, a French *composer*, demonstrated his musical talent at a young age.

__S__ 37. *Guy de Maupassant* was a writer who was a contemporary of Debussy.

__DO__ 38. The ancient Greeks established *Marseilles,* France's oldest and largest city.

__PN__ 39. Mont-Saint-Michel is a *fortress* that was constructed by Philip II.

__NA__ 40. *Marcia,* what is the name of the river that flows through Paris?

Chapter 3 Pretest: Pronouns

I. Pronouns and Antecedents

Underline each pronoun and write its antecedent in the blank.

_____*people*_____   1. Many people are very conscious of the style of clothes <u>they</u> wear.

_____*person*_____   2. The clothes a person wears can often give <u>him</u> authority.

_____*businessman*_____   3. A businessman often wears a suit so that <u>he</u> can look professional.

_____*teacher*_____   4. A teacher dresses in such a way that <u>she</u> will not appear intimidating to students.

_____*Claudia*_____   5. Claudia, do <u>you</u> prefer to wear comfortable clothing?

II. Pronoun Case and Function

Underline the correct pronoun from the choices in parentheses. In the blank, label the function of the pronoun _S_ (subject), _DO_ (direct object), _OP_ (object of the preposition), _IO_ (indirect object), _PN_ (predicate noun), or _App_ (appositive).

__*DO*__   6. The clothing styles of people from foreign lands fascinate my cousin and *(I, <u>me</u>)*.

__*S*__   7. *(<u>We</u>, Us)* two have purchased many items of clothing from different countries.

__*IO*__   8. When I was in Japan, I bought *(she, <u>her</u>)* a beautiful green kimono.

__*S*__   9. Last summer *(<u>she</u>, her)* and her husband visited Mexico and brought me back a sombrero.

__*OP*__   10. My father said that he will buy a dirndl dress for *(I, <u>me</u>)* when he goes to Germany this April.

__*DO*__   11. My brother already owns some lederhosen. He bought *(they, <u>them</u>)* in Bavaria.

__*PN*__   12. Grateful recipients of two lovely silk sarongs were *(<u>my mother and I</u>, me and my mother)*.

__*App*__   13. When Deborah went to Russia, she purchased fur caps for her uncles, Richard and *(he, <u>him</u>)*.

__*OP*__   14. The sari that my cousin bought in India looks very attractive on *(she, <u>her</u>)*.

__*IO*__   15. Jack gave *(we, <u>us</u>)* girls berets that he found at a boutique in Paris.

III. Case, Person, and Gender of Personal Pronouns

Identify the correct case, person, or gender of each italicized personal pronoun. In the blank write the letter that corresponds to the correct answer.

__*C*__   16. A waitress sometimes wears a hairnet to keep *her* hair pulled back.
     A. subjective
     B. objective
     C. possessive

_C_ 17. Do construction workers always wear hardhats when *they* are at work?
  A. first person
  B. second person
  C. third person

_A_ 18. Whenever *he* rides his motorcycle, Brad always wears a helmet.
  A. masculine
  B. feminine
  C. neuter

_A_ 19. Did Kirsten wear a veil when *she* got married?
  A. subjective
  B. objective
  C. possessive

_B_ 20. Did *you* know that a milliner is a person who styles hats?
  A. first person
  B. second person
  C. third person

IV. Demonstrative and Interrogative Pronouns

Underline the demonstrative and interrogative pronouns. Label each underlined pronoun
D (demonstrative) or *I* (interrogative).

_I_ 21. <u>What</u> is the traditional dress of Scotland?

_D_ 22. The customary clothing is <u>this</u>: the kilt and the plaid.

_D_ 23. Are <u>these</u> always worn together?

_I_ 24. <u>When</u> did the Scots first start wearing kilts?

_I_ 25. To <u>whom</u> should I address other questions concerning traditional dress?

V. Reflexive and Intensive Pronouns

Underline the reflexive and intensive pronouns. Label each underlined pronoun *R* (reflexive) or
I (intensive).

_I_ 26. I <u>myself</u> did not know that the first sweaters were worn before and after sporting events to keep athletes warm.

_I_ 27. Since wool sweaters can be itchy, Ryan <u>himself</u> prefers to wear cotton sweaters.

_R_ 28. My mother crocheted <u>herself</u> an angora sweater.

_I_ 29. The pattern on the sweater <u>itself</u> is very interesting.

_R_ 30. Joy and Ellen purchased new cardigans for <u>themselves</u>.

VI. Indefinite and Relative Pronouns

Underline the indefinite pronouns once and the relative pronouns twice.

31. Anne-Marie's ski vest, <u><u>which</u></u> is filled with down, is <u>one</u> of her warmest items of clothing.

32. My aunt, <u><u>who</u></u> is always prepared for inclement weather, carries a plastic poncho in her purse.

33. Moths have eaten through <u>some</u> of the jackets <u><u>that</u></u> are in the closet.

34. Dad has worn the same wool overcoat for years. It's hard to believe <u>all</u> of its buttons are still intact.

35. <u>Several</u> have told Alec to buy a jacket <u><u>that</u></u> has a hood.

VII. Correcting Unclear Reference

Rewrite each sentence to make the pronoun reference clear. *(Answers may vary.)*

36. As soon as Kim tied Margaret's scarf, she was ready to go to the opera.

     As soon as Kim tied Margaret's scarf, Margaret was ready to go to the opera.

37. Ruffs were pleated collars worn in the sixteenth and seventeenth centuries that were popular.

     Ruffs were pleated collars that were popular in the sixteenth and seventeenth centuries.

38. The two storeowners had filled their small shop with all sorts of neckwear. Scarfs were displayed on racks, and ties were arranged on round tables. In addition, a number of colorful cravats graced the shelves on the wall. Overall, they had given it a pleasant atmosphere.

     The two storeowners had filled their small shop with all sorts of neckwear. Scarfs were displayed on

     racks, and ties were arranged on round tables. In addition, a number of colorful cravats graced the

     shelves on the wall. Overall, the storeowners had given the shop a pleasant atmosphere.

39. Mr. Cline told Stephen that his tie was very colorful.

     Mr. Cline told Stephen, "Your tie is very colorful."

40. They say that styles have changed drastically throughout the years.

     Clothing designers say that styles have changed drastically throughout the years.

Name_____

Chapter 4 Pretest: Verbs

I. Recognizing the Complete Verb

Underline the complete verb in each sentence. Underline each auxiliary twice. Do not underline interrupting adverbs.

1. Insects <u>are</u> a part of God's marvelous creation.

2. My brother <u>is</u> <u>keeping</u> an insect collection.

3. All of his insects <u>are</u> <u>displayed</u> in a glass case.

4. I <u>like</u> the butterflies the best.

5. <u>Do</u> you <u>own</u> a butterfly net?

II. Sentence Patterns

Label the sentence pattern in each sentence *S-InV, S-TrV-DO, S-TrV-IO-DO, S-LV-PN,* or *S-LV-PA.* Above each word of the sentence pattern write its label.

6.   **S**   **InV**
   A butterfly begins as an egg.

7.   **S**   **LV**   **PN**
   Then it becomes a caterpillar.

8.   **S**   **LV**   **PN**
   The third stage of a butterfly's life cycle is the pupating stage.

9.   **S**   **TrV**   **DO**
   The caterpillar forms a chrysalis.

10.   **S**   **InV**
    The adult butterfly emerges from its chrysalis.

11.   **S**   **LV**   **PA**
    Many moths look similar to butterflies.

12.   **S** **LV**   **PN**
    Their life cycle is the same as the butterfly's.

13.   **S**   **TrV** **IO**   **DO**
    The moth spins itself a cocoon.

14.   **S**   **TrV** **DO**
    Many moths produce silk.

15.   **S**   **LV**   **PN**
    Butterfly watching can be an enjoyable pastime.

III. Verb Tenses

In the blank, label the tense of the italicized verb *present, past, future, present perfect, past perfect,* or *future perfect.* Not all answers will be used.

_____**present**_____ 16. Butterflies and moths *feed* themselves through their proboscises.

_____**past perfect**_____ 17. A monarch butterfly *had trapped* itself between the window and the screen.

_____**past**_____ 18. Quincy *bought* a mesh-screened cage to house his butterfly caterpillars.

_____**future perfect**_____ 19. If Felicia catches one more butterfly, she *will have caught* twenty-three specimens.

_____**future**_____ 20. I hope that she *will remember* to show her collection to me.

In the blank, label the tense of the italicized verb *present progressive, past progressive, future progressive, present perfect progressive, past perfect progressive,* or *future perfect progressive.* Not all answers will be used.

___present progressive___ 21. I *am planning* an insect collection for my biology class.

___future progressive___ 22. I *will be working* on it all semester long.

___present perfect progressive___ 23. I *have been catching* every insect that I see.

___past progressive___ 24. Yesterday I *was sitting* on the porch, and I noticed a Japanese beetle.

___past perfect progressive___ 25. I *had been reading* a book about insects, so I was able to identify the beetle.

IV. Other Uses for Auxiliaries

Underline the complete verb. If the sentence contains *do* or *will* as an auxiliary, label the auxiliary according to its use: *E* (emphasis), *Q* (question), or *N* (negative).

___N___ 26. Some people <u>do</u> not <u>know</u> the difference between an insect and an arachnid.

___Q___ 27. <u>Did</u> the book <u>discuss</u> their differences?

___N___ 28. Yes, arachnids <u>do</u> not <u>have</u> only six legs; instead, they have eight legs.

___E___ 29. Many insects <u>do have</u> two sets of wings.

___Q___ 30. <u>Will</u> some insects <u>open</u> and <u>close</u> their wings several times before flight?

V. Active and Passive Voice

Underline the complete verb and label it *A* (active) or *P* (passive).

___P___ 31. Cockroaches <u>are considered</u> household pests.

___A___ 32. Dogs and cats <u>are</u> common flea hosts.

___P___ 33. The Asian carpenter bee <u>is known</u> as the world's largest bee.

___A___ 34. Wasps often <u>kill</u> grubs.

___A___ 35. Some mosquitoes <u>have spread</u> diseases among humans.

VI. Mood

In the blank, label the mood of the italicized verb *indicative* or *imperative.*

___imperative___ 36. *Mount* the insects in your collection with a straight pin.

___indicative___ 37. The bee *stung* me on my right hand.

___imperative___ 38. Please *get* me the fly swatter.

___indicative___ 39. Mr. Eckard *says* that ladybugs are helpful insects.

___imperative___ 40. Linda, *help* me catch this lacewing.

Chapter 5 Pretest: Adjectives and Adverbs

I. Adjectives

Underline the adjectives. Write *PA* over each predicate adjective. Draw an arrow from each other adjective to the noun or pronoun it modifies.

1. It is hard to believe that people lived without many of the household items that we enjoy today.

2. A refrigerator, an electric stove, and a dishwasher are several items that a person may use daily.

3. All of my kitchen appliances are Kenmore appliances.

4. Which brand do you prefer?

5. Ours are General Electric appliances.

6. That mixer is efficient because it has six different speeds.

7. I like to use the blender to make ice-cream shakes.

8. The toaster, handy and compact, toasts bagels and bread.

9. Microwaves are especially popular.

10. We still own the same microwave that we purchased in 1994.

II. Adverbs

Underline the adverbs. Draw an arrow from each adverb to the word it modifies.

11. The vacuum cleaner quickly removed the dirt on the floor.

12. A vacuum cleaner that has a rather long hose is much simpler to use.

13. Change the bag on your vacuum regularly.

14. I can easily reach difficult places with the attachments on my vacuum.

15. I often use the vacuum to clean my car.

III. Comparisons

Underline the correct adjective or adverb from the choices in parentheses.

16. Of all of the stoves we have owned, I think our electric stove is the *(better, best)*.

17. Compared with our old refrigerator, our new one is *(wide, wider)*.

18. The microwave heats food *(quickly, more quickly)* than the oven does.

19. The electric can opener is a *(more efficient, most efficient)* alternative to the hand-held variety.

20. The coffeemaker should be placed *(closer, closest)* to the sink than where it is now.

IV. Using Modifiers Correctly

Underline the correct word from the choices in parentheses.

21. I think it would be *(difficult, difficultly)* to wash all of one's clothes by hand.

22. Clothing that is stained *(bad, badly)* can easily be washed in a washing machine.

23. If you overload the washing machine, it will not work *(good, well)*.

24. When the washing machine is overloaded, it often sounds very *(strange, strangely)*.

25. Our washing machine may be old, but it still does a *(good, well)* job.

26. The dryer is a machine that dries clothing *(quick, quickly)*.

27. One should not put *(anything, nothing)* in the dryer that is likely to shrink.

28. When I took my clothes out of the dryer, they felt *(warm, warmly)*.

29. After you unload the dryer, look *(careful, carefully)* to make sure that you have not left any items inside.

30. Those who have had a *(bad, badly)* experience at a Laundromat are thankful if they own their own machines at home.

V. Problems with Modifier Positions

Rewrite the following sentences, correcting any problems with modifier positions. *(Answers may vary.)*

31. Our dishwasher only has two racks.

    Our dishwasher has only two racks.

32. All dishwasher racks are not arranged the same way.

    Not all dishwasher racks are arranged the same way.

33. People who wash their dishes thoroughly rinse them before placing them in the dishwasher.

    People who thoroughly wash their dishes rinse them before placing them in the dishwasher.

34. Adrienne even washes her fine china in the dishwasher.

    Adrienne washes even her fine china in the dishwasher.

35. A person who has washed dishes frequently realizes how helpful a dishwasher can be.

    A person who frequently washes dishes realizes how helpful a dishwasher can be.

Chapter 6 Pretest: Prepositions, Conjunctions, and Interjections

I. Prepositional Phrases

Place parentheses around each prepositional phrase. Underline the object of the preposition.

1. Geneva says she wants a new watch(for her <u>birthday</u>.)

2. The watch(with the iridescent <u>face</u>) has no numbers(on <u>it</u>.)

3. (Before this <u>week</u>,) I had never worn a watch.

4. Now I am never late(to <u>school</u>.)

5. (Instead of a <u>wristwatch</u>,) Zane carries a pocket watch.

II. Functions of Prepositional Phrases

Place parentheses around each prepositional phrase. Label the prepositional phrase *Adj* (adjectival) or *Adv* (adverbial). Draw an arrow from each phrase to the word it modifies.

Adv   6. Jared's signal watch beeps(on the hour.)

Adv   7. Last week it beeped(during the church service.)

Adj   8. The jewelry store(around the corner)sells both costly and inexpensive watches.

Adj   9. The watches(in the glass case)are very expensive.

Adv   10. Mr. Hobi times our sprints(with his stopwatch.)

III. Using Prepositions Correctly

Underline the correct preposition from the choices in parentheses.

11. *(<u>Among</u>, Between)* all the clocks in the Schneiders' house, the clock in the hall chimes the loudest.

12. The movers carried the grandfather clock *(in, <u>into</u>)* the living room.

13. They placed it *(<u>beside</u>, besides)* the grandmother clock.

14. *(Beside, <u>Besides</u>)* long-case clocks, there are also table clocks.

15. Monique placed her new mantle clock *(<u>between</u>, among)* the two candlesticks.

Label each italicized word *Prep* (preposition) or *Adv* (adverb).

Adv   16. When the alarm clock went *off,* I accidentally pressed the snooze button.

Adv   17. I then woke *up* an hour late.

Prep   18. When I walked *into* the office, my supervisor gave me a stern look.

Prep   19. I explained *to* him what had happened, and then he started to laugh.

Adv   20. He said that my being late was all right as long as I did not get *behind* in my work.

Correct each misplaced prepositional phrase by rewriting the sentence correctly in the blank. If the sentence is correct, write *C* in the blank.

21. The cuckoo pops out every half-hour in the cuckoo clock.

   The cuckoo in the cuckoo clock pops out every half-hour.

22. From the Black Forest, Sven bought a cuckoo clock made of wood.

   Sven bought a cuckoo clock made of wood from the Black Forest.

23. Many colleges and universities have a clock tower on their campuses.

   _C_

24. In her rose garden, Great-grandmother told us that she wanted a sundial.

   Great-grandmother told us that she wanted a sundial in her rose garden.

25. Weight-driven clocks have a weight from the drum of the clock that hangs.

   Weight-driven clocks have a weight that hangs from the drum of the clock.

IV. Conjunctions

Underline the conjunctions in the following sentences. In the blank, label the conjunctions *coordinating, correlative,* or *subordinating.*

correlative   26. <u>Both</u> "How Soon Hath Time" <u>and</u> "On Time" are poems by John Milton.

coordinating   27. Mallory has two watches, <u>but</u> only one tells the correct time.

coordinating   28. In early days, people used water clocks <u>and</u> hourglasses to keep track of time.

correlative   29. Water clocks were used <u>not only</u> for tracking the time during the day <u>but also</u> for timing the duration of speeches in Roman courts of law.

correlative   30. The early hourglasses held <u>either</u> sand <u>or</u> mercury.

coordinating   31. Today some people use hourglasses for kitchen timers <u>or</u> game timers.

subordinating   32. <u>Before</u> these devices were created, people kept time by relying on the length of their shadows.

correlative   33. The first mechanical clocks had <u>neither</u> pendulums <u>nor</u> hands.

subordinating   34. <u>Although</u> these clocks lacked certain mechanisms, they did have a bell to announce the hour.

subordinating   35. Many improvements had to be made to the early clocks <u>because</u> they were often inaccurate.

V. Interjections

Underline each interjection in the following sentences.

36. Could you wind the clock downstairs, <u>please</u>?

37. <u>Wow</u>! I can't believe how old your antique clock is.

38. <u>Hey</u>, do you know of a good jeweler who could fix my watch?

39. As a matter of fact, <u>yes</u>, Mr. Kuntz just repaired my watch last week.

40. <u>Well</u>, could you tell me where his store is located?

Chapter 7 Pretest: Verbals

I. Participles
Underline the participles. Draw an arrow from each underlined participle to the noun it modifies.

1. Many biblical characters are <u>developing</u> characters.

2. Jacob and Esau are two brothers who had a <u>maturing</u> relationship with each other.

3. Jacob and Esau were both <u>favored</u> sons.

4. Esau was a <u>cunning</u> hunter.

5. Esau became a <u>deceived</u> brother.

II. Participial Phrases
Underline the participial phrases. Draw an arrow from each underlined phrase to the noun it modifies. In the blank, label each underlined participial phrase *present* or *past*.

_____*past*_____ 6. <u>Tired from work in the field</u>, Esau asked Jacob for some food.

_____*present*_____ 7. <u>Taking advantage of his brother's ravenous state</u>, Jacob gave Esau pottage.

_____*present*_____ 8. Esau, <u>swearing that he would keep his promise</u>, sold his birthright to Jacob.

_____*past*_____ 9. <u>Blinded by old age</u>, Isaac was also deceived by Jacob.

_____*present*_____ 10. <u>Dressing Jacob in Esau's clothing</u>, Rebekah helped Jacob to trick his father.

III. Gerunds and Gerund Phrases
Underline the gerunds. Place parentheses around the gerund phrases. In the blank, label the gerund or gerund phrase *S* (subject), *DO* (direct object), *IO* (indirect object), *OP* (object of the preposition), or *PN* (predicate noun).

_OP_ 11. Jacob was also able to fool his father by (<u>offering</u> him savory meat.)

_DO_ 12. As a result of his deceitfulness, Jacob received (the <u>blessing</u> from his father.)

_S_ 13. Esau wanted the birthright, but (his <u>weeping</u>) could not change what had already transpired.

_S_ 14. (<u>Serving</u> Jacob in the future) became Esau's lot in life.

_OP_ 15. Since Jacob received what Esau wanted, Esau entertained the thought of (<u>killing</u> his brother.)

_PN_ 16. Rebekah knew that Esau's plan was (<u>murdering</u> Jacob.)

_PN_ 17. She said that Jacob's best escape would be (<u>running</u> away.)

_S_ 18. (Jacob's <u>fleeing</u>) led him to his mother's brother, Laban.

_IO_ 19. Jacob gave (<u>working</u> for Laban) his utmost attention because he loved Rachel so much.

_DO_ 20. After these years, Jacob received (a <u>calling</u> from the Lord.)

IV. Infinitives and Infinitive Phrases

Underline the infinitives. Place parentheses around the infinitive phrases. In the blank, label the function of each infinitive *N* (noun), *Adj* (adjective), or *Adv* (adverb).

N   21. (To return home)was God's command to Jacob.

N   22. Jacob obeyed God and decided(to leave Laban's house.)

Adv   23. (To get to his homeland,)Jacob traveled through Esau's territory.

Adv   24. Jacob sent messengers(to speak with Esau.)

Adj   25. Although God had promised him prosperity, Jacob felt that overwhelming Esau with gifts was the thing(to do now.)

N   26. (To give Esau a gift of cattle)was Jacob's plan of appeasing Esau.

Adj   27. Jacob's efforts(to satisfy his brother)worked better than he had expected.

Adv   28. Esau ran(to greet Jacob.)

N   29. Then he wanted(to know about Jacob's family.)

Adv   30. Jacob's family came before Esau(to bow before him.)

V. Participles, Gerunds, and Infinitives

Underline the verbals (not the entire phrases). In the blank, label each verbal *P* (participle), *G* (gerund), or *I* (infinitive). If the verbal is a modifier, draw an arrow from the verbal to the word it modifies.

I   31. Jacob decided to obey God no matter what the cost.

P   32. Although Jacob was God's chosen man, he demonstrated humility before his brother.

G   33. One way that Jacob showed his humility was his bowing before Esau.

I   34. Jacob no longer sought to scheme for Esau's ill.

G   35. Jacob's offering Esau a gift showed that he had changed in his relationship with Esau.

G   36. Esau's tears were no longer for sorrowing .

I   37. On the contrary, he cried to express his joy.

I   38. Esau was not greedy to take Jacob's gifts.

P   39. Esau's surprising response shows that God can change a bitter heart.

P   40. The reconciliation of these estranged brothers demonstrates that all things are possible with God.

Chapter 8 Pretest: Clauses

I. Phrases and Clauses

Label each italicized group of words *P* (phrase), *IC* (independent clause), or *DC* (dependent clause).

__DC__ 1. *Although numerous trees fill the world,* they are very different from one another.

__P__ 2. The majority of trees fall into one *of two categories.*

__IC__ 3. *These two categories are broadleaf trees and needleleaf trees.*

__DC__ 4. Other trees *that do not fit* into these classifications are palms, ginkgoes, and cycads.

__IC__ 5. *Broadleaf trees produce vibrantly colored leaves* in the fall.

II. Using Independent and Dependent Clauses

Label each sentence *S* (simple), *Cd* (compound), *Cx* (complex), or *Cd-Cx* (compound-complex).

__S__ 6. In the winter, broadleaf trees are characterized by their bare branches.

__Cx__ 7. In the spring, broadleaf trees produce flowers that grow into fruit.

__S__ 8. The birch and the beech are two broadleaf trees.

__Cd__ 9. The birch has papery bark, and the beech has papery leaves.

__Cx__ 10. Actually, there is a particular type of birch that is called the paper birch.

__S__ 11. The paper birch is also known as the canoe birch or the white birch.

__Cd-Cx__ 12. The paper birch got its name because its bark has the consistency of paper, and the canoe birch received its name because the Indians made canoes out of its bark.

__Cx__ 13. The white birch grows in North America, whereas the European white birch grows in the northern part of Europe.

__Cd__ 14. People use the wood of yellow birches and sweet birches to make furniture, and they use the wood of gray birches to manufacture spools.

__Cd-Cx__ 15. The river birch grows in a moist climate, and it has a bark that can turn from salmon pink to almost black.

III. Adjective Clauses

In the blank write the word(s) modified by the italicized adjective clause.

__yellow birch__ 16. The yellow birch, *which is also called the silver birch,* can reach a height of fifty to seventy-five feet.

__Robert Frost__ 17. Robert Frost, *who was a New England poet,* wrote a poem entitled "Birches."

__trees__ 18. Frost describes the birches as trees *that have been bent.*

<u>   reasons   </u> 19. Frost offers two reasons *that the trees are curved.*

<u>   boy   </u> 20. Either the ice storm has bowed them, or they have been bent by a boy *whose hobby is birch swinging.*

IV. Adverb Clauses

In the blank write the word(s) modified by the italicized adverb clause.

<u>   grow   </u> 21. *Although many trees are classified differently,* they often grow beside one another.

<u>   exist   </u> 22. Palm trees exist *where the environment is warm.*

<u>   possess   </u> 23. *Even though the majority of palms have one trunk,* some possess several trunks growing from the same roots.

<u>   collects   </u> 24. Reina always collects coconuts *whenever she visits her aunt in Hawaii.*

<u>   carries   </u> 25. *After she obtains several coconuts,* she carries them back to her aunt's house.

Place parentheses around the dependent clauses. In the blank, label each clause *Adj* (adjective) or *Adv* (adverb).

<u> *Adj* </u> 26. Palms are trees(that provide many benefits.)

<u> *Adj* </u> 27. Chairs and baskets(that are woven)are often made of palm leaves.

<u> *Adj* </u> 28. Raffia,(which is commonly used in decorating,)comes from the Madagascar palm.

<u> *Adv* </u> 29. I often use raffia(when I need to tie a package.)

<u> *Adj* </u> 30. Palm Springs is a city in California(where palm trees line the streets.)

<u> *Adv* </u> 31. Palm Sunday occurred(before Christ was crucified.)

<u> *Adj* </u> 32. Palm Sunday commemorates the day(when people placed palm branches on the ground before Jesus' entry into Jerusalem.)

<u> *Adv* </u> 33. (When they placed the palm branches on the ground,)they cried, "Hosanna!"

<u> *Adv* </u> 34. (Although some palms produce poisonous seeds,)most produce nontoxic seeds.

<u> *Adv* </u> 35. (After we had bored holes into the coconuts,)we drank the milk inside.

Chapter 9 Pretest: Agreement

I. Subjects and Predicates
Underline the simple subject in each sentence. Underline the verb that agrees with the subject.

1. Scientific <u>studies</u> *(has taught, <u>have taught</u>)* us many fascinating things.

2. How does a <u>person</u> *(<u>solve</u>, solves)* a scientific problem?

3. <u>Scientists</u> *(<u>follow</u>, follows)* the scientific method.

4. First, a <u>scientist</u> *(establish, <u>establishes</u>)* a problem.

5. Preliminary <u>research</u> *(<u>is</u>, are)* profitable for the scientist who is trying to establish a problem.

II. Compound Subjects
Underline the verb that agrees with the subject.

6. Latasha or Kami *(<u>knows</u>, know)* where to get the best information for the science project.

7. Neither Tyler nor Jerome *(<u>has started</u>, have started)* his scientific research.

8. Both Helen and Melita *(is, <u>are</u>)* responsible for observing and recording the data.

9. Our biology teacher and our chemistry teacher *(is conducting, <u>are conducting</u>)* experiments in the lab.

10. Either Mr. McCarnan or Mrs. Holmes *(<u>works</u>, work)* at the Center of Science and Industry.

III. Finding the Subject
Underline the simple subject in each sentence. Underline the correct verb from the choices in parentheses.

11. Here *(<u>is</u>, are)* a <u>section</u> of our book that talks about heredity.

12. <u>Cells</u> *(is, <u>are</u>)* one thing that we will study in this chapter.

13. One <u>function</u> of cells *(<u>is</u>, are)* respiration.

14. There *(is, <u>are</u>)* also other important <u>roles</u> for cells in the body.

15. The <u>genes</u>, not the nucleus, *(is, <u>are</u>)* the "blueprints" of the cell.

16. Cell <u>division</u> *(<u>is</u>, are)* the formation of two cells from one cell.

17. The <u>process</u> of mitosis *(<u>is</u>, are)* the replication of genes from the parent cell to the two new daughter cells.

18. What *(is, <u>are</u>)* the four <u>phases</u> of mitosis?

19. The <u>first</u> of these phases *(<u>is</u>, are)* prophase.

20. <u>Prophase</u>, <u>metaphase</u>, and <u>anaphase</u>, but not telophase, *(is, <u>are</u>)* stages of mitosis in which the cell has a spindle.

IV. Indefinite Pronouns and Problem Nouns as Subjects
Underline the verb that agrees with the subject.

21. Genetics *(is, are)* the study of heredity.

22. "Where did you get your curly hair and gray eyes?" *(is, are)* a question that people often ask Tiffany.

23. "Gregor Mendel's Findings" *(is, are)* the title of one of the sections in the genetics chapter in our book.

24. Most of the students in the class *(enjoys, enjoy)* Punnett squares.

25. Each *(works, work)* out the combinations on his own.

26. Then the class *(divides, divide)* into groups to compare results.

27. Charles's group *(is, are)* discussing their results with each other.

28. Today the news *(is, are)* featuring an article about modern genetics.

29. Many of us students *(plans, plan)* to read the article.

30. "Be sure to take good notes and study hard for your test" *(is, are)* the advice that Mrs. Klinger gave us before we left biology class.

V. Number and Gender with Noun Antecedents
In the blank write an appropriate personal pronoun to complete the sentence.

_____*it*_____ 31. Hemophilia is often called "the disease of royalty," and _?_ is also called "the bleeder's disease."

_____*her*_____ 32. Although Queen Victoria did not have this disease, she passed it along to _?_ offspring.

_____*they*_____ 33. Alice and Beatrice, Victoria's daughters, carried the hemophilic gene; consequently, _?_ had children and grandchildren who were hemophiliacs.

_____*he, she*_____ 34. A *carrier* is a person who carries a gene for a trait; however, _?_ does not show the trait.

_____*He*_____ 35. Alexis, a great-grandson of Victoria, was also a hemophiliac. _?_ was heir to the Russian throne.

VI. Compound Antecedents
Underline the correct pronoun from the choices in parentheses.

36. Both dominant and recessive traits reveal *(itself, themselves)* in a person's biological makeup.

37. Neither Shelley nor Marienne can roll *(her, their)* tongue.

38. Valerie or her two sisters will carry *(her, their)* father's gene for colorblindness.

39. Hank and Patrick have arched feet like both of *(his, their)* parents.

40. Neither Jessica's uncles nor her father has a cleft in *(his, their)* chin.

182 Key to Pretests

© 2001 BJU Press. Reproduction prohibited.

VII. Indefinite Pronouns as Antecedents

If the italicized pronoun does not agree with its antecedent, write the correct pronoun in the blank. If the sentence does not contain an agreement error, write *C* in the blank.

_____*their*_____ 41. Both of my aunts have dimples in *her* right cheeks.

_____*his*_____ 42. Each of Emil's brothers has *their* father's nose.

_____*her*_____ 43. Neither of my nieces has *their* mother's straight hair.

_____*C*_____ 44. All the members of the Merrill family have *their* grandfather's hazel eyes.

_____*her*_____ 45. One of the girls in my youth group has a widow's peak in *their* hairline.

_____*C*_____ 46. Some of the other girls wish that *they* had one as well.

_____*him*_____ 47. Not everyone appreciates the traits God has given *them*.

_____*them*_____ 48. Quite often only a few are thankful to God for the traits He has given *him*.

_____*C*_____ 49. However, no one should be disappointed with the way God has made *him*.

_____*he*_____ 50. God always designs someone so that *they* can glorify Him.

Chapter 10 Pretest: Spelling and Troublesome Words

I. Spelling

Underline any misspelled words and write the corrections in the blank. If the sentence is correct, write *C* in the blank.

1. I would never think of <u>skiping</u> breakfast on a Sunday morning.

   skipping

2. Mother always prepares our family a <u>bountyful</u> breakfast.

   bountiful

3. This morning she cooked pancakes, bacon, eggs, and fried potatoes.

   C

4. Mom's hearty breakfasts are a favorite part of my <u>deit</u>.

   diet

5. After breakfast Dad, the leader of our home, directs us in our family devotions.

   C

6. I forgot to bring my Bible to the table, so I had to <u>retreive</u> it from my bedroom.

   retrieve

7. Today we discussed practicing <u>holyness</u> in our <u>dayly</u> <u>lifes</u>.

   holiness, daily, lives

8. Some think that only those who have committed heinous crimes need to be deterred from sin.

   C

9. However, in God's eyes sins such as <u>conciet</u> and laziness are just as wicked as <u>theivery</u> or lying.

   conceit, thievery

10. Nevertheless, Christ's death on the cross made <u>atonment</u> for all sin.

    atonement

II. Troublesome Verbs

Underline the correct verb from the choices in parentheses.

11. My family always *(<u>sits</u>, sets)* on the fourth row at church.

12. Whenever I see a hymnal *(<u>lying</u>, laying)* on the floor, I place it in the hymn rack.

13. The music director always has us *(<u>rise</u>, raise)* to our feet for the third hymn.

14. I asked Father if I *(<u>may</u>, can)* hold my own hymnal.

15. I think I *(shall, <u>will</u>)* never lose my love for singing hymns in church.

III. Other Troublesome Words

Underline the correct word from the choices in parentheses.

16. For the past several months, our pastor has been preaching about prophets and their *(prophecies, prophesies)*.

17. He has preached on Jonah, Amos, Obadiah, *(etc., and others)*.

18. Last week his message was entitled, "*(Prophecy, Prophesy)* the Truth!"

19. This message contained *(fewer, less)* points *(than, then)* his previous sermons, so I have been able to remember his points quite easily throughout the week.

20. What he said has *(affected, effected)* my thinking, and I have been looking for opportunities to witness to my unsaved neighbors.

21. I am *(real, really)* glad that I was able to talk to my unsaved friend Stacey yesterday.

22. She doesn't have a Bible, so I *(lent, loaned)* her one of mine.

23. I told her that she may *(borrow, loan)* it for as long as she likes.

24. I was able to share with her that Christ *(Hisself, Himself)* gave His life for her.

25. I was able to tell her that she needs to *(accept, except)* Christ as her personal Savior.

IV. Homonyms

Underline the correct word from the choices in parentheses.

26. After I shared the gospel with Stacey, I told her that I would *(pray, prey)* for her.

27. It is sobering to think of all the people that Satan *(prays, preys)* upon.

28. However, it is comforting to know that God will never *(desert, dessert)* His children.

29. Christians can always go to God's Word for *(council, counsel)*.

30. I am going to use my new *(stationary, stationery)* to write some letters to my unsaved relatives.

31. My unsaved uncle lives in St. Paul, the *(capital, capitol)* of Minnesota.

32. He is a man of good *(principals, principles)*; however, he still needs Christ to save him.

33. Christians should remember to pray for the many unsaved legislators at the *(capitol, Capitol)*.

34. We should also keep in mind the unsaved persons who serve on our local city *(council, counsel)*.

35. Hard-hearted people often seem to be *(stationary, stationery)* in their beliefs, but we Christians need to remember that God is in control of people's hearts.

V. Possessive Pronouns v. Contractions
Underline the correct word from the choices in parentheses.

36. *(Its, It's)* a humbling experience to witness to someone *(whose, who's)* making fun of you.

37. However, *(they're, there)* not really scorning you.

38. *(Their, They're)* scorn is actually mocking *(your, you're)* God.

39. *(Your, You're)* not going to allow another person's behavior to keep you from witnessing, are you?

40. Remember that *(theirs, there's)* always the chance that a seed will be planted in that unsaved person's life.

Chapter 11 Pretest: Capitalization

I. Proper Nouns: Personal Names, Religions, Nationalities

Underline any word that is an example of a capitalization error and write the correction in the blank. If the sentence is correct, write *C* in the blank.

1. Last semester my brother Jeff took a poetry class with <u>dr.</u> Joachim <u>r.</u> Langenscheidt.

   Dr., R.

2. Although he was <u>austrian</u>, Dr. Langenscheidt spoke impeccable English.

   Austrian

3. On the first day of class, he shared how he had come to know the <u>redeemer</u>.

   Redeemer

4. He grew up in a <u>catholic</u> home, but he came to Christ after reading a <u>german</u> <u>new testament</u> that his aunt Ingrid had given him.

   Catholic, German, New Testament

5. Dr. Langenscheidt told Jeff's class that he has always had a love for poetry.

   C

6. As he read more of the <u>bible</u>, he realized that God had filled <u>his</u> Word with books of poetry.

   Bible, His

7. Dr. Langenscheidt always begins his poetry class by teaching from the <u>proverbs</u>.

   Proverbs

8. Although he does put an emphasis on <u>old testament</u> poetry, he also teaches other types of poetry.

   Old Testament

9. Jeff really enjoyed learning about the differences between <u>elizabethan</u> and <u>petrarchan</u> sonnets.

   Elizabethan, Petrarchan

10. Jeff told me that his favorite poem was one in which John Milton addresses Time.

   C

II. Proper Nouns: Place Names, Transportation, Astronomical Terms

Underline any word that is an example of a capitalization error and write the correction in the blank. If the sentence is correct, write *C* in the blank.

11. Although I really wanted to go to Australia, I plan to spend my summer vacation in the <u>midwest</u>.

 Midwest

12. Justine promised to take me sailing on <u>lake</u> Michigan.

 Lake

13. She also said that we need to visit <u>chicago</u> and <u>green bay</u>.

 Chicago, Green Bay

14. When we are in Ohio, she said that we could take a boat ride on the <u>*goodtime II*</u>.

 Goodtime II

15. If we take the ride at night, perhaps we'll be able to spot <u>ursa major</u>.

 Ursa Major

16. I've always wanted to see <u>saturn's</u> rings, but I don't think that we'll be able to see them without a telescope.

 Saturn's

17. Justine's dad said that he would take us to a train museum that displays models of old trains.

 C

18. The <u>Museum</u> is located downtown on 1400 <u>main street</u>.

 museum, Main Street

19. Her dad's favorite train is named <u>*royal blue*</u>.

 Royal Blue

20. Before I return to the South, I want to visit the <u>great plains</u> and the <u>ozark plateau</u>.

 Great Plains, Ozark Plateau

III. Proper Nouns: Businesses and Organizations, Cultural and Historical Terms

In the blank write the letter of the choice that is capitalized correctly.

___*A*___ 21. A. Oxford University
 B. a Grocery store
 C. february

___C___ 22. A. the Cia
　　　　　 B. the American cancer society
　　　　　 C. Pepsi

___C___ 23. A. The Language Club
　　　　　 B. Senior class field trip
　　　　　 C. Bull Moose Party

___A___ 24. A. Tower of London
　　　　　 B. winter Festival
　　　　　 C. Castle drawbridge

___B___ 25. A. Presidents' day
　　　　　 B. Valentine's Day
　　　　　 C. fourth of July

___A___ 26. A. Pulitzer Prize
　　　　　 B. statue of liberty
　　　　　 C. Industrial revolution

___C___ 27. A. world war I
　　　　　 B. april showers
　　　　　 C. Empire State Building

___B___ 28. A. Trade school
　　　　　 B. Saturday at the zoo
　　　　　 C. declaration of independence

___C___ 29. A. Phi beta kappa
　　　　　 B. Football team
　　　　　 C. Boston Red Sox

___B___ 30. A. Program for Better literacy
　　　　　 B. Federal Deposit Insurance Corporation
　　　　　 C. national guard

IV. Titles and First Words

In the blank write the letter of the choice that is capitalized correctly.

___A___ 31. A. My dad delivers our local newspaper, the *Plain Dealer*.
　　　　　 B. Edmund Waller wrote the poem "Of the last verses of the Book."
　　　　　 C. Miss Green subscribes to *Good housekeeping* magazine.

___B___ 32. A. chapter 21
　　　　　 B. Act III
　　　　　 C. "The Sands of time are Sinking"

___A___ 33. A. Monet's painting *The Road Bridge at Argenteuil*
　　　　　 B. Literature
　　　　　 C. *Good morning America*

_B___ 34. A. "Are you going to lunch?" Asked Sheila. "I don't think so," replied Brooke.
        B. "Let's go to supper," suggested Sheila, "and then we can talk."
        C. Brooke replied, "well, I believe I'll have time to do that."

_B___ 35. A. My heart is like a singing bird whose nest is in a watered shoot;
           my heart is like an apple tree whose boughs are bent with thickest fruit;
        B. My heart is like a singing bird whose nest is in a watered shoot;
           My heart is like an apple tree whose boughs are bent with thickest fruit;
        C. my heart is like a singing bird whose nest is in a watered shoot;
           my heart is like an apple tree whose boughs are bent with thickest fruit;
           (from "A Birthday" by Christina Rossetti)

_C___ 36. A. The geese fly in a v-formation.
        B. Did Blythe make a b+ in Science 101?
        C. The first note I learned to identify on the piano was middle C.

_B___ 37. A. Dear Pastor Ashbrook and church family,
        B. Sincerely yours,
        C. your loving son,

_A___ 38. A.
              I. Gathering the materials
              II. Wrapping the gift
              III. Decorating the wrapped box
        B.
              I. Gathering the Materials
              II. Wrapping the Gift
              III. Decorating the Wrapped Box
        C.
              I. Gathering the Materials
              II. Wrapping the Gift
              III. Decorating the wrapped Box

_B___ 39. A. Did Beethoven write the "moonlight sonata"?
        B. Have you read *Pride and Prejudice?*
        C. I love to study Fine Arts.

_C___ 40. A. Grandma always reminds me, "call me when you get home."
        B. Who will defend us, o prince?
        C. Do you think that I will be invited to the Spanish party?

Chapter 12 Pretest: Punctuation

I. End Marks and Special Uses of Periods

Identify the sentence or address that is punctuated correctly. In the blank write the letter that corresponds to the correct answer.

___A___ 1. A. I met with the pastor on Tuesday at 11:00 A.M.
           B. I met with the pastor on Tuesday at 11:00 AM.

___B___ 2. A. He asked me whether I had ever memorized any verses from the Epistle to the Philippians?
           B. He asked me whether I had ever memorized any verses from the Epistle to the Philippians.

___A___ 3. During our interview he gave me three things to remember:
           A. 1. Be a servant.
              2. Be content.
              3. Rejoice in the Lord.
           B. 1 Be a servant.
              2 Be content.
              3 Rejoice in the Lord.

___A___ 4. A. He said I may send any further questions to him at the following address:
              Rev. James Smythe, P.O. Box 11, Willoughby, OH 44094.
           B. He said I may send any further questions to him at the following address:
              Rev James Smythe, PO Box 11, Willoughby, OH 44094.

___A___ 5. A. Did you know that the apostle Paul wrote Philippians around A.D. 60?
           B. Did you know that the apostle Paul wrote Philippians around AD 60.

II. Commas in a Series and After Introductory Elements

Identify the sentence that is punctuated correctly. In the blank write the letter that corresponds to the correct answer.

___B___ 6. A. Paul addresses the Epistle to the Philippians to the saints, bishops and deacons at Philippi.
           B. Paul addresses the Epistle to the Philippians to the saints, bishops, and deacons at Philippi.

___A___ 7. A. In the opening verses he expresses his earnest, joyful prayer for them.
           B. In the opening verses he expresses his earnest joyful prayer for them.

___A___ 8. A. Paul says that he longs after the Philippians, and he prays that their love would abound.
           B. Paul says that he longs after the Philippians and he prays that their love would abound.

___B___ 9. A. In verse 12, Paul explains why God has allowed him to be in prison.
           B. In verse 12 Paul explains why God has allowed him to be in prison.

___B___ 10. A. First he says that all those in the palace know about his bonds for Christ.
             Second he says that others outside the palace also know about his bonds for Christ.
             Finally he says that other Christians are bolder to speak for Christ.
           B. First, he says that all those in the palace know about his bonds for Christ.
             Second, he says that others outside the palace also know about his bonds for Christ.
             Finally, he says that other Christians are bolder to speak for Christ.

III. Commas to Set Off Certain Sentence Elements and Incorrect Commas

Identify the sentence that is punctuated correctly. In the blank write the letter that corresponds to the correct answer.

___A___ 11. A. Paul says that some people preached Christ with contention, not with sincerity.
            B. Paul says that some people preached Christ with contention not with sincerity.

___A___ 12. A. Yes, there were others who did preach Christ out of love.
            B. Yes there were others who did preach Christ out of love.

___B___ 13. A. Chapter 2 which tells of Christ's humility is one of my favorite chapters.
            B. Chapter 2, which tells of Christ's humility, is one of my favorite chapters.

___A___ 14. A. A person who humbles himself acts in a Christlike manner.
            B. A person, who humbles himself, acts in a Christlike manner.

___B___ 15. A. Paul hopes that Timothy will be able to visit the Philippians, and, he also says that he himself would like to see them.
            B. Paul hopes that Timothy will be able to visit the Philippians, and he also says that he himself would like to see them.

IV. Commas with Quotations, Dates, and Addresses and Commas in Letters

Insert any missing commas in the following sentences. If the sentence is correct, write *C* in the blank.

_____ 16. "In the second chapter of Philippians‚" said Merle‚"Paul talks about Epaphroditus."

___C___ 17. "Does Paul mention why Epaphroditus was sick?" asked Nadine.

_____ 18. I hope to have all of Philippians memorized by my next birthday, May 7‚2002.

_____ 19. Please send the commentary on Philippians to my new address: 872 Bank Street‚ Painesville‚Ohio 44077.

_____ 20. Pastor West always closes his letters in the following manner: "In Christ‚Rev. Scott West."

V. Semicolons and Colons

Insert any missing semicolons or colons in the following sentences.

21. The first part of Philippians 2 discusses Christ's humility and exaltation‚the first part of Philippians 3 discusses Paul's credentials.

22. Paul warns the Philippians to beware of the following‚dogs, evil workers, and the concision.

23. Paul was of the people of Israel‚Paul was of the tribe of Benjamin.

24. Philippians 3:14 has been my life verse since I was ten.

25. One theme that appears to be repeated throughout Philippians is this‚likemindedness.

VI. Quotation Marks, Italics, and Ellipses

Identify the punctuation mark missing from each sentence. In the blank write the letter that corresponds to the correct answer. (If necessary, you may use your Bible to answer these questions.)

A. quotation marks
B. italics
C. ellipses

__B__ 26. The word joy is repeated throughout the Epistle to the Philippians.

__A__ 27. How many times does Paul use this word throughout the book? asked A. J.

__C__ 28. Peg said, "I believe it appears um, actually, I'm not certain how many times, but"

__A__ 29. "I'd like to hear what songs you'd like to sing, said Ryan. Perhaps we could sing a hymn."

__A__ 30. Irene suggested, "Why don't we sing Joyful, Joyful, We Adore Thee?"

__B__ 31. Have you ever read the book Be Joyful?

__C__ 32. Philippians 4:7 says, "And the peace of God shall keep your hearts and minds through Christ Jesus."

__B__ 33. In its last issue, New Testament News carried a ten-page article on the Epistle to the Philippians.

__A__ 34. The article was entitled Philippians: A Prison Epistle.

__B__ 35. Cole's painting, The Rejoicing Christian, is a magnificent piece of art.

VII. Apostrophes, Hyphens, Dashes, and Parentheses

Identify the punctuation mark missing from each sentence. In the blank write the letter that corresponds to the correct answer.

A. apostrophe
B. hyphen
C. dash
D. parentheses

__B__ 36. This morning I read Philippians 4:113.

__D__ 37. At the beginning of Philippians 4, Paul requests that two women Euodias and Syntyche be likeminded.

__C__ 38. The next verse talks about Clement do you think that Euodias and Syntyche heeded Paul's exhortation?

__A__ 39. Paul rejoices in the Lord for the Philippians generosity.

__A__ 40. Im so glad that Ive been able to read this book of the Bible.

Teaching Help 1: Sentences

Join the clauses from the right column to the clauses in the left column by using an appropriate conjunction from the middle column. Some combinations may be written as two separate sentences, and the same conjunction may be used more than once. Remember to use the proper punctuation when combining the clauses. *(Answers may vary.)*

Early fans were made of palm leaves		the lorgnette fan even had an eyeglass
	but	
People used fans to cool themselves		in China both men and women carried fans
Some painters included fans in their paintings		by the Victorian period fans had radii of more than twenty inches
	yet	
A "broken" fan resembles a leaf		people often carried them as part of their attire
The Japanese invented the folding fan in A.D. 700	so	the Portuguese brought the folding fan to Europe
Many people associate fans with women		a banner fan looks like a flag
	however	
In the early 1800s fans had about an eight-inch radius		Anthony Van Dyck painted ostrich-feather fans in some of his paintings
Fans were an important accessory	or	they used fans to chase away flies
Fan handles were often fashioned from ivory or tortoise shell	and	later fans were made of ostrich or peacock feathers
Some fans incorporated very interesting features		some were crafted from bone or sandalwood

1. *Early fans were made of palm leaves, but later fans were made of ostrich or peacock feathers.*

2. *People used fans to cool themselves, or they used fans to chase away flies.*

3. *Some painters included fans in their paintings. Anthony Van Dyck painted ostrich-feather fans in some of his paintings.*

4. *A "broken" fan resembles a leaf; however, a banner fan looks like a flag.*

5. *The Japanese invented the folding fan in A.D. 700, but the Portuguese brought the folding fan to Europe.*

6. *Many people associate fans with women, yet in China both men and women carried fans.*

7. *In the early 1800s fans had about an eight-inch radius, yet by the Victorian period fans had radii of more than twenty inches.*

8. *Fans were an important accessory, so people often carried them as part of their attire.*

9. *Fan handles were often fashioned from ivory or tortoise shell, but some were crafted from bone or sandalwood.*

10. *Some fans incorporated very interesting features. The lorgnette fan even had an eyeglass.*

Teaching Help 2A: Forms and Kinds of Nouns

Fill in the blanks with the correct answer to each question. Then find each answer in the scrambled letters below.

___proper___	1.	What kind of noun names a specific person, place, thing, or idea?
___collective___	2.	What kind of noun names a group?
___compound___	3.	What kind of noun combines two or more words?
___pastries___	4.	What is the plural form of *pastry?*
___echoes___	5.	What is the plural form of *echo?*
___autos___	6.	What is the plural form of *auto?*
___knives___	7.	What is the plural form of *knife?*
___criteria___	8.	What is the plural form of *criterion?*
___species___	9.	What is the plural form of *species?*
___beaches___	10.	What is the plural form of *beach?*

```
T B M I C W S A S H R T D E E T S S
E E T E S H C T O G S C G N O E E C
A A D R P I S B S A P N S I O N I C
S C O N O E M A D L A O A T D N E E
H H O H F L E H E S M U N E E I M
E S P C O U N T V S T A E R O T E O
O C A A T A R I B S R E C H O E S O
C E N S A O T N N T I E C E C C M A
B U E H I C W O T M E T S I O H N H
O I E T E M I D B A S O E E M S X S
L P W L N R A K C C T O F I M E L P
E S L A E A T N N U R B Y D O C O E
L O T T E R D R A I W I S A N H A C
C T I E E C F G R K V S T H F O R I
X R A P A S T R Y S R E D E E S A E
C A O H E A D L E L H S S T R H T S
O R A B K N I F E S I H E E S I D S
P C O M P O U N D S H O E X F W A E
```

Teaching Help 2B: Nouns

Answer the following questions about the paragraph below.

_____**names**_____ 1. What noun is a subject in sentence 5?

_____**creature**_____ 2. What noun is a predicate noun in sentence 2?

_____**creatures**_____ 3. What noun is a direct object in sentence 10?

_____**starfish**_____ 4. What noun is an indirect object in sentence 9?

_____**ocean**_____ 5. What noun is the object of the preposition in sentence 1?

_____**Benjamin**_____ 6. What noun is a noun of direct address in sentence 1?

_____**brother**_____ 7. What noun is an appositive in sentence 4?

_____**Justin's**_____ 8. What possessive noun appears in sentence 7?

_____**starfish**_____ 9. What compound noun appears in sentence 3?

_____**Justin**_____ 10. What proper noun appears in sentence 6?

¹ Benjamin, did you see the starfish my brother found at the ocean? ² I think it's a fascinating creature. ³ As he was walking along the shore, he found the starfish between some rocks. ⁴ Justin, my brother, told me that starfish are sometimes called sea stars.
⁵ Both names are appropriate, I think. ⁶ I asked Justin if all starfish have five appendages, and Justin said that some starfish have more than forty! ⁷ I noticed that Justin's starfish was missing an arm, but Justin said that the starfish would grow another arm to replace it.
⁸ Isn't that amazing! ⁹ I wanted to give the starfish a name, but Justin said that we should return the starfish to the ocean. ¹⁰ Perhaps we'll find some more sea creatures tomorrow.

Teaching Help 3: Pronouns

In the blank write the pronoun that completes each sentence correctly. Choose the pronoun from the list below. *(Answers may vary.)*

I	she
me	her
we	they
us	them
who	himself
whom	themselves
he	
him	

__We__ 1. _?_ girls were admiring the artwork around your house.

__Who__ 2. _?_ painted that portrait in your hallway?

__me__ 3. It has captured the attention of Katarina and _?_ .

__he__ 4. Charles Willson Peale painted that picture. His family and _?_ were well-known American painters.

__whom__ 5. From _?_ did his family learn to draw?

__himself__ 6. Many of them learned from Charles Willson Peale _?_ .

__them__ 7. Raphaelle and Rembrandt Peale were two of his sons. Do you think he named _?_ after the famous artists?

__themselves__ 8. Raphaelle and Rembrandt Peale _?_ became prominent artists.

__they__ 9. Still life and portrait painters were _?_ .

__her__ 10. Sarah Miriam Peale was Charles Willson Peale's niece. Some have named _?_ as the first female American portrait painter.

Teaching Help 4: Verbs

Answer the following questions. Then use your answers to complete the crossword puzzle.

Across

auxiliary 6. An _?_ helps the main verb.

Intransitive 9. _?_ verbs do not have a complement.

future 11. The verb *will read* is in what tense?

indicative 12. A declarative sentence is written in the _?_ mood.

passive 13. In _?_ voice the subject receives the action of the verb.

Down

active 1. In _?_ voice the subject is the doer of the action.

emphasis 2. The auxiliary *do* creates _?_, makes a sentence negative, or forms a question.

has 3. To form the present perfect tense, use *have* or _?_.

linking 4. A state-of-being verb is a _?_ verb.

Transitive 5. _?_ verbs have direct objects.

Progressive 7. _?_ verbs show continuous action.

Perfect 8. _?_ tense verbs express completion of an action.

imperative 10. The _?_ mood is used for commands and requests.

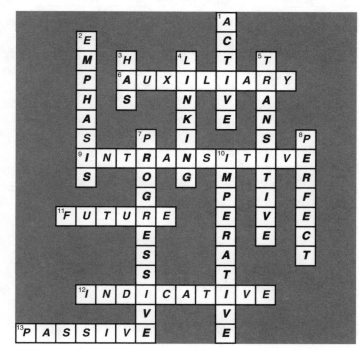

Teaching Help 5A: Adjectives and Adverbs

Fill in appropriate modifiers to complete the paragraph. *(Answers will vary.)*

As Colin and I approached the _____**old**_____, _____**gray**_____ house, we heard
    (adjective)   *(adjective)*

a _____**loud**_____ noise behind us. At first we were _____**very**_____ frightened, but we
    (adjective)   *(adverb)*

_____**soon**_____ discovered that the sound we heard was only a _____**stray**_____ cat. We
    (adverb)   *(adjective)*

continued to walk _____**slowly**_____ towards the _____**front**_____ door and then
                          (adverb)   *(adjective)*

_____**carefully**_____ stepped onto the _____**rickety**_____ steps. Trying the door handle, we
    (adverb)   *(adjective)*

discovered that the knob was _____**rusty**_____, but we were still able to open the door
                                      (adjective)

_____**quite**_____ easily. As we entered the house, we _____**immediately**_____ noticed that there were
    (adverb)   *(adverb)*

cobwebs everywhere. It was obvious that this house had been deserted for _____**many**_____ years.
                                                                                  (adjective)

Colin found a broom in a _____**nearby**_____ closet, and he started brushing away the cobwebs.
                              (adjective)

Although the house was _____**dirty**_____ and _____**dusty**_____, we figured that it wouldn't
                            (adjective)   *(adjective)*

take long to clean it up. After we explored the rest of the house, we _____**quickly**_____ decided that
                                                                          (adverb)

this place would be the _____**perfect**_____ spot for our _____**new**_____ club.
                              (adjective)   *(adjective)*

Teaching Help 5B: Adjectives and Adverbs

Choose the correct modifier from the choices in parentheses.

1. The sky looks *(ominous, ominously)*.

2. Dark clouds appear *(quick, quickly)*.

3. We look *(expectant, expectantly)* at the sky.

4. The distant thunder sounds *(loud, loudly)*.

5. We remain *(safe, safely)* in our house.

6. We needed the rain *(bad, badly)*.

7. It has watered our lawn *(good, well)*.

8. Now the air smells *(fresh, freshly)*.

9. The sunshine feels *(good, well)*.

10. We hope that the weather will stay *(warm, warmly)*.

Teaching Help 6A: Prepositions

Rewrite the scrambled sentences. In each rewritten sentence place parentheses around each prepositional phrase and underline each object of the preposition. *(Answers may vary.)*

1. botanical garden visited on a I Saturday. ___*I visited a botanical garden (on Saturday).*___

2. I stayed The weather the shade in was very warm whenever so I could. ___*The weather was very warm,*___ ___*so I stayed (in the shade) whenever I could.*___

3. the tall trees was cool under It the shade of. ___*It was cool (under the shade) (of the tall trees).*___

4. a stone bridge I walked hanging from it ivy over that had. ___*I walked (over a stone bridge) that had ivy*___ ___*hanging (from it).*___

5. winding stream a Beneath was the bridge. ___*(Beneath the bridge) was a winding stream.*___

6. everyone of Melinda took by standing a photograph the fountains. ___*Melinda took a photograph*___ ___*(of everyone) standing (by the fountains).*___

7. walking exotic plants among enjoyed I the. ___*I enjoyed walking (among the exotic plants).*___

8. gardens explored until We the 4:00 P.M. ___*We explored the gardens (until 4:00 P.M.)*___

9. learned I greenhouse inside that some were edible of the plants the. ___*I learned that some (of the plants)*___ ___*(inside the greenhouse) were edible.*___

10. worn out Melinda our tour after I and were. ___*Melinda and I were worn out (after our tour).*___

Name

Teaching Help 6B: Conjunctions

Rewrite the following paragraph by adding appropriate coordinating and correlative conjunctions. Use a variety of conjunctions. *(Answers may vary.)*

Peacocks belong to the pheasant family. The male is called a peacock. The female is called a peahen. The peacock is a peafowl. The peahen is a peafowl. The Indian peacock is a species of peafowl. The Javanese peacock is a species of peafowl. Indian peafowl live in India. Indian peafowl live in Sri Lanka. A Congo peacock feather was found in 1913. The Congo peacock was not discovered until 1936. A male peafowl possesses a train. He also possesses a head ornament. The female does not have a train. She does not have a head ornament. Some peacocks are wild. Some peacocks are tame. Wild peacocks inhabit open forests during the day. They roost in trees at night. Peacocks are mentioned in an ancient Greek play. They are also mentioned in the Bible.

Peacocks belong to the pheasant family. The male is called a peacock, but the female is called a peahen.

Both the peacock and the peahen are peafowl. The Indian peacock and the Javanese peacock are species of

peafowl. Indian peafowl live in India or Sri Lanka. A Congo peacock feather was found in 1913, yet the Congo

peacock was not discovered until 1936. A male peafowl possesses not only a train but also a head ornament.

The female has neither a train nor a head ornament. Peacocks are either wild or tame. Wild peacocks inhabit

open forests during the day, but they roost in trees at night. Peacocks are mentioned not only in an ancient

Greek play but also in the Bible.

Teaching Help 7A: Participles and Gerunds

Use the following phrases to form a sentence with a gerund and a sentence with a participle.
(Answers will vary.)

1. growing sunflowers

   A. participle:_ *The growing sunflowers turned their faces toward the sun.*_

   B. gerund:_ *One of my uncle's hobbies is growing sunflowers.*_

2. running water

   A. participle:_ *The running water was cool to the touch.*_

   B. gerund:_ *Running water through your hair will cool you off on a hot day.*_

3. cooking vegetables

   A. participle:_ *The cooking vegetables sent a delicious aroma throughout the kitchen.*_

   B. gerund:_ *Cooking vegetables with a roast enhances the flavor of the meat.*_

4. dripping ice cream

   A. participle:_ *I watched the dripping ice cream run down Vera's waffle cone.*_

   B. gerund:_ *I can never eat an ice-cream cone without dripping ice cream on myself.*_

5. training employees

   A. participle:_ *The training employees attended a seminar on safety in the workplace.*_

   B. gerund:_ *Roger's occupation is training employees.*_

Teaching Help 7B: Infinitives

Place parentheses around each infinitive in Philip P. Bliss's hymn "Dare to Be a Daniel."

Standing by a purpose true,

Heeding God's command,

Honor them, the faithful few!

All hail to Daniel's Band!

Chorus:

Dare (to be) a Daniel,

Dare (to stand) alone!

Dare (to have) a purpose firm!

Dare (to make) it known!

Many mighty men are lost,

Daring not (to stand,)

Who for God had been a host,

By joining Daniel's Band!

Many giants, great and tall,

Stalking thro' the land,

Headlong to the earth would fall,

If met by Daniel's Band!

Hold the gospel banner high!

On to vict'ry grand!

Satan and his host defy,

And shout for Daniel's Band!

Teaching Help 8: Clauses

Identify the sentence type. In the blank write the letter that corresponds to the correct answer.

___*B*___ 1. Lord Baden-Powell was a British soldier who started the Boy Scouts in 1908.
A. simple
B. complex

___*A*___ 2. He wrote *Aids to Scouting,* and he also wrote *Scouting for Boys.*
A. compound
B. complex

___*A*___ 3. The Wolf Cubs, which are also known as the Cub Scouts, were also founded by Lord Baden-Powell.
A. complex
B. compound-complex

___*B*___ 4. Boys who belong to the Cub Scouts are under the age of eleven, and boys who belong to the Boy Scouts are eleven years old or older.
A. compound
B. compound-complex

___*A*___ 5. The left-hand handshake and the fleur-de-lis badge are symbols associated with the Boy Scouts.
A. simple
B. compound

___*B*___ 6. The Girl Guides, which were begun by Baden-Powell and his sister Agnes, were founded in 1910; in America they became known as the Girl Scouts in 1912.
A. compound
B. compound-complex

___*B*___ 7. Juliette Low is the one who started the first Girl Scout troop in America.
A. simple
B. complex

___*A*___ 8. She had already organized troops in England and Scotland.
A. simple
B. compound

___*A*___ 9. Daisies, Brownies, and Juniors are troops for younger girls, and Cadettes and Seniors are troops designed for older girls.
A. compound
B. compound-complex

___*A*___ 10. Boy Scouts and Girl Scouts learn about good citizenship and good conduct.
A. simple
B. compound

For each *A* or *B* you chose above choose the corresponding letter below. For example, if you chose *A* for question 1, write *W* in the blank. If you chose *B*, write *B* in the blank. If your answers are correct, you will form the motto of the Boy Scouts.

1. A=W, B=B
2. A=E, B=Y
3. A=P, B=A
4. A=T, B=R

5. A=E, B=G
6. A=S, B=P
7. A=H, B=A

8. A=R, B=O
9. A=E, B=W
10. A=D, B=I

___*B*___ ___*E*___   ___*P*___ ___*R*___ ___*E*___ ___*P*___ ___*A*___ ___*R*___ ___*E*___ ___*D*___

Name_____

Teaching Help 9: Indefinite Pronouns and Subject-Verb Agreement

To complete the Bible verse underline the correct verb from the choices in parentheses.

1. All the words of my mouth *(is, are)* in righteousness; there *(is, are)* nothing froward or perverse in them. (Prov. 8:8)

2. *(Is, Are)* any thing too hard for the Lord? (Gen. 18:14)

3. There *(is, are)* none that doeth good, no, not one. (Rom. 3:12)

4. Some *(trusts, trust)* in chariots, and some in horses: but we will remember the name of the Lord our God. (Ps. 20:7)

5. Divers weights, and divers measures, both of them *(is, are)* alike abomination to the Lord. (Prov. 20:10)

6. None of these things *(moves, move)* me, neither count I my life dear unto myself. (Acts 20:24)

7. Many *(is called, are called)*, but few *(is chosen, are chosen)*. (Matt. 22:14)

8. Be not afraid when one *(is made, are made)* rich, when the glory of his house is increased. (Ps. 49:16)

9. Blessed *(is, are)* every one that feareth the Lord; that walketh in his ways. (Ps. 128:1)

10. Many, O Lord my God, *(is, are)* thy wonderful works which thou hast done. (Ps. 40:5)

Teaching Help 10A: Spelling with ie and ei Words

To practice spelling *ie* and *ei* words unscramble the words described in the following sentences. Then use the circled letters from each word to form a sentence that fits the blanks at the end of the exercise.

(s) e i z e   1. This word also means "to grab." *(zesie)*

(p) i e t y   2. A person who is dedicated to God possesses this. *(pyite)*

w (e) i r d   3. If something is strange, it is described as this. *(reiwd)*

d e c e i t f u (l)   4. Something that is untrue is this. *(detcfulei)*

b e (l) i e f   5. This is something that you hold to be true. *(lbefie)*

s (i) e g e   6. This is the blockade of an enemy city by an army. *(gseie)*

r e i (n) s   7. One controls a horse by these. *(seirn)*

b e i (g) e   8. This color is grayish yellow. *(bgiee)*

p i e r (c) e   9. When you cut something, you do this to it. *(cepire)*

c (a) f f e i n e   10. Tea and coffee contain this substance. *(cfaeifne)*

p r o t e i (n) 11. Milk is rich in this substance. *(tporien)*

r e i m (b) u r s e   12. When you pay back a person for money that you borrowed, you do this. *(ermburise)*

w (e) i g h   13. If you measure something for its heaviness, you do this to it. *(gwhei)*

n i (e) c e   14. This person is your brother's daughter. *(encie)*

p e r c e i v (a) b l e   15. If an idea is understandable, it is this. *(preaciveble)*

(s) l e i g h   16. In the wintertime we took a ride on one of these. *(ghesli)*

(y) i e l d   17. If you give something up, you do this. *(ldiey)*

S p e l l i n g   c a n   b e   e a s y .

Teaching Help 10B: Adding Suffixes

Combine a root from the first column and a suffix from the second column to create a word that best fits each description below. Then write the word in the blank.

debate	ment
happy	ly
assure	ing
duty	ed
boor	ful
loose	ance
bat	able
swim	ness
submit	ish
advance	er

_____debatable_____ 1. Something that can be argued is this.

_____happiness_____ 2. A person who is filled with joy has much of this.

_____assurance_____ 3. If you are certain about something, you possess this.

_____dutiful_____ 4. A person who is careful to do what is expected of him is this.

_____boorish_____ 5. A person who lacks culture is described as this.

_____loosely_____ 6. If a rope is not tied tightly, it may hang in this manner.

_____batter_____ 7. In baseball this is the person who hits the ball.

_____swimming_____ 8. When we go to the lake, we will spend our time doing this.

_____submitted_____ 9. If you have given your will to someone else, you have done this to it.

_____advancement_____ 10. If something has progressed, it has made this.

Teaching Help 11A: Capitalization

Congratulations! You have just been given a job at the local newspaper. For your first assignment you have been asked to edit the following article. Carefully read through the paragraph, paying special attention to the capitalization. Mark the errors and then rewrite the paragraph correctly in the space below.

yesterday began as an ordinary Summer day for Eugene Saunders. But halfway through His walk home from the Grocery Store across the street from uncle ted's auto repair, Saunders saw what he described as "The Strangest Sight On Earth." When Saunders was a Colonel in the army, he spent time living in Jungles and Deserts around the World, places where he encountered many unusual sights and happenings. but this one topped them all. As he walked down darby lane, saunders heard someone running behind him. He turned, to see who was in such a hurry, just in time to jump out of the path of the largest Ostrich he had ever seen. on the broad back of the sprinting Bird sat a small Bear Cub wearing a White Sox baseball cap! Soon afterward, three men ran by. One stopped to explain to the bewildered Saunders that the circus had just arrived and that Olley The Ostrich and Buddy The Bear had decided to go sightseeing before their first Performance on Saturday night.

Yesterday began as an ordinary summer day for Eugene Saunders. But halfway through his walk home

from the grocery store across the street from Uncle Ted's Auto Repair, Saunders saw what he described as

"the strangest sight on earth." When Saunders was a colonel in the army, he spent time living in jungles and

deserts around the world, places where he encountered many unusual sights and happenings. But this one

topped them all. As he walked down Darby Lane, Saunders heard someone running behind him. He turned,

to see who was in such a hurry, just in time to jump out of the path of the largest ostrich he had ever seen.

On the broad back of the sprinting bird sat a small bear cub wearing a White Sox baseball cap! Soon

afterward, three men ran by. One stopped to explain to the bewildered Saunders that the circus had just

arrived and that Olley the Ostrich and Buddy the Bear had decided to go sightseeing before their first

performance on Saturday night.

Name_____

Teaching Help 11B: Capitalization

In the blank write the letter of the phrase that is capitalized correctly.

1. __B__   A. an article from The *Wall Street Journal*
           B. an article from the *Wall Street Journal*
           C. an article from the *Wall Street journal*

2. __C__   A. a picture of mount rushmore
           B. a picture of Mount rushmore
           C. a picture of Mount Rushmore

3. __A__   A. leave at 11:00 A.M. to make your 1:15 P.M. flight
           B. leave at 11:00 A.M. to make your 1:15 p.m. flight
           C. leave at 11:00 a.m. to make your 1:15 P.M. flight

4. __B__   A. my sister's Volleyball team
           B. my sister's volleyball team
           C. my sister's Volleyball Team

5. __B__   A. His Puerto Rican Accent
           B. his Puerto Rican accent
           C. his puerto rican accent

6. __A__   A. this poem by T. S. Eliot
           B. this poem by T. s. eliot
           C. this poem by t. s. Eliot

7. __C__   A. take some Vitamin A
           B. take some vitamin a
           C. take some vitamin A

8. __B__   A. your Junior year
           B. your junior year
           C. your Junior Year

9. __A__   A. Dear Mr. and Mrs. Benson and Family,
           B. Dear Mr. and Mrs. Benson and family,
           C. dear Mr. and Mrs. Benson and family,

10. __C__ A. birds fly South in the winter
           B. birds fly south in the Winter
           C. birds fly south in the winter

Teaching Help 12B: Punctuation

Rewrite the following sentences, inserting any missing punctuation.

1. After reading Jules Vernes book Around the World in Eighty Days I wanted to take a trip in a hot-air balloon

   After reading Jules Verne's book Around the World in Eighty Days, I wanted to take a trip in a hot-air balloon.

2. Alice do you know who invented the hot-air balloon

   Alice, do you know who invented the hot-air balloon?

3. Im not sure. Perhaps you should ask did you go to the library today?

   I'm not sure. Perhaps you should ask—did you go to the library today?

4. In September of 1973 the Montgolfier Brothers flew the first hot-air balloon loaded with precious cargo consisting of a duck a sheep and a cockerel

   In September of 1973, the Montgolfier Brothers flew the first hot-air balloon, loaded with precious cargo

   consisting of a duck, a sheep, and a cockerel.

5. A few weeks later, Pilâtre de Rozier a science teacher and the marquis d'Arlandes an infantry officer became the first human passengers in a hot-air balloon

   A few weeks later, Pilâtre de Rozier, a science teacher, and the marquis d'Arlandes, an infantry officer,

   became the first human passengers in a hot-air balloon.

6. The two brave adventurous men flew five and a half miles over Paris

   The two brave, adventurous men flew five and a half miles over Paris. or !

7. Would you like to accompany me my wife and my dog, Rover, in a flight to St Louis asked my friend Col Adam Jennings who happens to be a hot-air balloon pilot

   "Would you like to accompany me, my wife, and my dog, Rover, in a flight to St. Louis?" asked my friend

   Col. Adam Jennings, who happens to be a hot-air balloon pilot.

8. We take off at 630 AM tomorrow morning the pilot informed me

   "We take off at 6:30 A.M. tomorrow morning," the pilot informed me.

9. I was so excited I could hardly sleep that night I woke up almost every hour, hoping it would be time for me to get up

   I was so excited I could hardly sleep that night; I woke up almost every hour, hoping it would be time for

   me to get up.

10. My first hot-air balloon flight was an adventure Ill never forget

    My first hot-air balloon flight was an adventure I'll never forget. or !

Teaching Help 13A: Using a Library Catalog Entry

Answer the following questions by using the catalog entry below.

MATERIAL: Book

CALL NUMBER: J 551.5 G135

AUTHOR: Gallant, Roy A

TITLE: Exploring the weather. Illustrated by Lowell Hess.

EDITION: [1st ed.]

PUBLICATION: Garden City, N.Y., Garden City Books 1957

DESCRIPTION: 64 p. illus. 32 cm.

SUBJECT: Meteorology—Juvenile literature.

SUBJECT: Weather

1. What is the complete title of the book? **Exploring the Weather**

2. If you decided to search for this book by its author, under which letter of the alphabet would you search? **G**

3. How many pages does the book contain? **64**

4. Who is the illustrator of this book? **Lowell Hess**

5. What company published the book? **Garden City Books**

6. What is the call number of the book? **J 551.5 G135**

7. In what specific section of the library would this book be found? **the juvenile section**

8. What year was the book published? **1957**

9. Under what subject headings would you find other books on the same topic? **meteorology or weather**

10. Where was the book published? **Garden City, New York**

Teaching Help 13B: Using the Readers' Guide

Use the following entry to answer each question.

FISHING

See also

Fishermen
Salt water fishing

Lake linnyn: a fisherman's paradise. Martin Jeeves. il *Tacklebox* v12 no5 p34-36+ Ag 2002

1. Who is the author of the article? __Martin Jeeves__

2. What is the volume number for the article? __12__

3. When was the article published? __August 2002__

4. What is the title of the article? __"Lake Linnyn: A Fisherman's Paradise"__

5. What is the subject heading under which the article is listed? __Fishing__

6. Is this article illustrated? __yes__

7. On what page does the article begin? __34__

8. What is the title of the magazine? __Tacklebox__

9. What is another subject heading one could search for related topics? __Fishermen or Salt water fishing__

10. Does the article end on page 36? __no__

Name_____

Teaching Help 13C: Special Reference Tools

In the blank write the letter of the reference tool best suited for finding the answer to each question.

A. almanac or yearbook
B. atlas or gazetteer
C. Bible concordance
D. book of quotations
E. biographical dictionary
F. desk dictionary
G. special-purpose dictionary
H. encyclopedia
I. index
J. thesaurus

C 1. What is the reference for the following verse: "Pray without ceasing"?

G 2. What is the Spanish word for *house?*

E 3. How many siblings did Jane Austen have?

B 4. Where is the Bay of Bengal located?

J 5. What is a synonym for the word *error?*

F 6. What does the word *frenzy* mean?

I 7. Where can you find a magazine article about piranhas?

A 8. Who won the Nobel Prize for Physics in 1990?

D 9. Which of Shakespeare's plays is the source of the following quotation: "To be, or not to be: that is the question"?

H 10. How can I learn more about zoological gardens?

Teaching Help 14A: *Using the Parts of a Book*

In each blank write the letter of the correct book section that would give you the information requested. Each answer will be used only once.

    A. title page
    B. table of contents
    C. list of illustrations
    D. introduction or preface
    E. acknowledgments
    F. text
    G. bibliography
    H. appendix
    I. glossary
    J. index

F 1. How many paragraphs are on the first page of Chapter 2?

I 2. How would you define the word *anther?*

D 3. Why was this book written?

J 4. On which pages are carnations discussed?

A 5. Who edited the book?

H 6. Where can you find a diagram that shows the parts of a flower?

E 7. Where does the author thank his colleagues for their advice and input?

G 8. Where can you find additional books on growing irises?

B 9. What three topics does Chapter 9 discuss?

C 10. On which page is there a photograph of an orchid?

Teaching Help 14B: Context Clues

In the blank write the letter of the choice that defines the italicized word in each sentence.

___A___ 1. A cheetah has a long tail; however, a lynx is almost *anurous.*
   A. tailless
   B. hairy

___B___ 2. Janessa will act as our *comprador.* She will tell Mr. Eliot our business plan, and then she will tell us Mr. Eliot's opinion.
   A. employer
   B. go-between

___B___ 3. The shopkeeper called the police after he caught the young boy *pilfering* merchandise from his store.
   A. buying
   B. stealing

___A___ 4. The *zephyr,* blowing against our faces, cooled us on the warm day.
   A. soft breeze
   B. still stream

___B___ 5. I asked Randolph if he would like to go to a hockey game. His quick *rejoinder* was, "Sure, that sounds like fun."
   A. excuse
   B. reply

Teaching Help 15A: Outlining a Paper

Arrange the following list into the five main points of an outline. Be sure to order the items logically.

Laundry

Drying the clothes

Putting the clothes away

Organizing the supplies

Folding the clothes

Washing the clothes

Laundry
I. Organizing the supplies
II. Washing the clothes
III. Drying the clothes
IV. Folding the clothes
V. Putting the clothes away

Name_____

Teaching Help 15B: Composition Skills

Answer the following questions about the paragraph below. In the blank write the letter that corresponds to the correct answer.

   On July 4, 1776, the Declaration of Independence was signed. Over a century later on July 10, 1890, Wyoming became the forty-fourth state. On July 16, 1945, the first atomic bomb was set off in New Mexico, and almost two and a half decades later, Neil Armstrong was the first man to walk on the moon. This event took place on July 20, 1969.

___*B*___ 1. Which topic sentence best fits the paragraph?
    A. Many famous Americans were born in the month of July.
    B. Many important events have occurred in the month of July.

___*B*___ 2. Which type of paragraph development does the author use in the paragraph?
    A. comparison/contrast
    B. fact

___*A*___ 3. What type of paragraph organization does the author use in the paragraph?
    A. chronological
    B. order of importance

___*B*___ 4. Which sentence best concludes the paragraph?
    A. All of these July incidents are national holidays.
    B. All of these July incidents have been significant in American history.

___*A*___ 5. Which title best fits the paragraph?
    A. July: An Eventful Month
    B. The Month of July

In the blank write the letter that corresponds to the correct answer.

___*C*___ 6. A topic sentence does *not*
    A. usually appear as the first sentence of the paragraph.
    B. introduce the topic.
    C. usually appear at the end of a paragraph.

___*B*___ 7. In an essay a thesis statement is *not*
    A. similar to a topic sentence in a paragraph.
    B. a concluding sentence.
    C. a sentence which introduces the topic of the essay to the audience.

___*B*___ 8. A good introduction does *not*
    A. catch the reader's interest.
    B. tell the reader, "I will talk about such-and-such in this paper."
    C. draw attention to the main idea of the topic.

___*A*___ 9. A good conclusion does *not*
    A. repeat the topic sentence word for word.
    B. summarize the main idea of the paragraph.
    C. offer a solution to a problem.

___*A*___ 10. Which of the following sentences is *not* true?
    A. Revision is not necessary for the experienced writer.
    B. Revision improves a person's writing.
    C. Revision helps a person to write better first drafts.

Teaching Help 15C: Revising

Underline the ten clichés in the following paragraphs. Rewrite each sentence that contains a cliché so that it will express the idea of the sentence more simply. *(Answers will vary.)*

Pedro awoke <u>at the crack of dawn</u>. Today he was going to the county fair! Pedro ran into his brother's bedroom, but Carlos was still <u>sleeping like a log</u>. Pedro thought it was <u>a crying shame</u>, but he knew that Carlos wasn't as excited as he was. Why, it was just yesterday that Carlos said going to the fair <u>bored him to tears</u>. But Pedro knew that Carlos would have fun.

Pedro and Carlos visited the stables first. Pedro stroked one horse's head and fed the horse an apple. Carlos said he wouldn't touch the horse <u>with a ten-foot pole</u>. Pedro couldn't understand why Carlos was acting as though he were in the <u>depths of despair</u>. Pedro wasn't ready to <u>throw in the towel</u>, however, so he suggested they ride the Ferris wheel. Carlos seemed to <u>brighten up</u> at this idea. On the ride Carlos's <u>spirits seemed to lift</u>. He apologized for his bad behavior. <u>After all was said and done</u>, both boys had a good day.

1.   *Pedro awoke early.*

2.   *Pedro ran into his brother's bedroom, but Carlos was still sleeping soundly.*

3.   *Pedro thought it was a shame, but he knew that Carlos wasn't as excited as he was.*

4.   *Why, it was just yesterday that Carlos said going to the fair was boring.*

5.   *Carlos said he wouldn't touch the horse at all.*

6.   *Pedro couldn't understand why Carlos was acting so unhappy.*

7.   *Pedro wasn't ready to give up, however, so he suggested they ride the Ferris wheel.*

8.   *Carlos seemed interested in this idea.*

9.   *On the ride Carlos's attitude improved.*

10.   *In the end, both boys had a good day.*

Name_____

ESL Worksheet 3B: Exercises in Using Some *Correctly*

Read the sentences containing *some*. Then look at the choices for making the sentences negative. Circle the letter of each correct negative sentence. You may have more than one correct answer for some of the following items.

1. McCarty bought his grandmother *some* pottery.
   A. McCarty didn't buy no pottery for his grandmother.
   (B) McCarty bought no pottery for his grandmother.
   (C) McCarty didn't buy any pottery for his grandmother.

2. *Someone* was cleaning the bowl he purchased.
   (A) No one was cleaning the bowl he purchased.
   (B) There wasn't anyone cleaning the bowl he purchased.
   C. There wasn't no one cleaning the bowl he purchased.

3. McCarty had dropped *something* in the pottery store.
   (A) McCarty had not dropped anything in the pottery store.
   B. McCarty had not dropped nothing in the pottery store.
   (C) McCarty had dropped nothing in the pottery store.

4. McCarty purchased *some* ceramic mugs.
   A. McCarty didn't purchase no ceramic mugs.
   (B) McCarty didn't purchase any ceramic mugs.
   (C) McCarty purchased no ceramic mugs.

5. He had *some* employees help him find a yellow teapot.
   (A) He didn't have any employees help him find a yellow teapot.
   (B) He had no employees help him find a yellow teapot.
   C. He didn't have no employees help him find a yellow teapot.

Read the sentences containing the word *some*. Make each sentence negative. *(Answers will vary.)*

6. Addie wanted to bake something.

   Addie did not want to bake anything.

7. She baked some cookies.

   She baked no cookies.

8. Some of the cookies were burned.

   None of the cookies were burned.

9. Someone ate her cookies.

   No one ate her cookies.

10. She gave some cookies to her neighbors.

    She didn't give any cookies to her neighbors.

ESL Worksheet 4E: Exercises in Forming Questions Correctly

Change each sentence to a *yes/no* question. Remember to look at the verb tense for each sentence. Then use that same tense for the question.

1. Red is Max's favorite color.

   Is red Max's favorite color?

2. Max would like a red truck.

   Would Max like a red truck?

3. Max will have enough money for the truck.

   Will Max have enough money for the truck?

4. His car had broken down numerous times.

   Had his car broken down numerous times?

5. He has earned money for a new vehicle.

   Has he earned money for a new vehicle?

Change each sentence to a *wh* question. Use the word in parentheses to form the question. Write the question and the short answer in the blank.

6. Max's favorite color is red. *(whose)*

   Whose favorite color is red? Max's

7. Max would like a red truck. *(what)*

   What would Max like? a red truck

8. Max will have enough money for the truck. *(who)*

   Who will have enough money for the truck? Max

9. His car had broken down numerous times because it had a bad engine. *(why)*

   Why had his car broken down numerous times? because it had a bad engine

10. He has earned money for a new vehicle by working for a law firm. *(how)*

    How has he earned money for a new vehicle? by working for a law firm

Name_____

ESL Worksheet 5B: Exercise in Article Usage

Choose the correct article *(a, an,* or *the)* to put in each blank. If no article is needed, put an *X* in the blank. Above each answer list the appropriate rule number from the Article Usage sheet.

1.2
___X___ Joleen took ___**a**___ flight to Nebraska to visit her grandparents. Although
3.1

2.2
___**the**___ flight was short, she ate ___**X**___ two small bags of peanuts and drank one can
4.1

of cola. ___**The**___ best part of her flight was that she had ___**a**___ window seat. She
2.3   **3.1**

thought ___**X**___ this seat was great. She had fun watching ___**the**___ big, puffy clouds.
3.2   **2.1**

Looking out her window, Joleen remembered some facts she learned about clouds in

___X___ science. Since her grandparents can't drive, ___**the**___ Kalmans, her grandparents'
5.1   **1.1**

neighbors, picked her up at ___**the**___ airport. When she arrived at her grandparents'
2.1

house, ___**the**___ first thing Joleen saw was ___**X**___ her grandma's big smile. Joleen knew
2.3   **3.2**

that she was going to have fun with her relatives.

ESL Worksheet 5D: Exercises in Adverb Placement

Decide whether the italicized adverbs are placed correctly. If the placement is correct, write _C_ in the blank to the left. If the placement is incorrect, write _I_ in the blank and rewrite the sentence correctly.

_____**I**_____ 1. Marta *usually* is a good student.

        (Usually) Marta is (usually) a good student.

_____**I**_____ 2. The squirrel was climbing *quickly* the tree.

        The squirrel was (quickly) climbing the tree (quickly).

_____**C**_____ 3. David *shyly* told her his name.

_____**C**_____ 4. The book was *surprisingly* heavy.

_____**I**_____ 5. The bird abandoned its nest in the top of the tree *later*.

        (Later) The bird (later) abandoned its nest in the top of the tree.

_____**C**_____ 6. *Slowly* the leaf floated to the ground.

_____**C**_____ 7. Kate told the story *joyfully*.

_____**C**_____ 8. John *seldom* writes letters.

_____**I**_____ 9. We *never* have sung in a choir.

        We have never sung in a choir.

_____**I**_____ 10. Kahlil *here* lives.

        Kahlil lives here.

Name_____

ESL Worksheet 5F: Exercises in Making Sentences Negative Using Not

Rewrite the following sentences to make them negative. Add *not* **to each sentence. Change the form of the verb and add an auxiliary if necessary.**

> **Example:** Gail often writes letters.
> Gail does *not* often write letters.

1. The baby cries every night.

   The baby does not cry every night.

2. I can mail my letters this weekend.

   I cannot mail my letters this weekend.

3. I will buy new stamps.

   I will not buy new stamps.

4. Lana is a friendly person.

   Lana is not a friendly person.

5. Jung is from Korea.

   Jung is not from Korea.

6. Isabel cleans her room every Saturday.

   Isabel does not clean her room every Saturday.

7. We will go to the concert next week.

   We will not go to the concert next week.

8. There will be fireworks after the ball game.

   There will not be fireworks after the ball game.

9. Dad parks his car in the garage.

   Dad does not park his car in the garage.

10. Forrest wears a suit to work.

    Forrest does not wear a suit to work.

ESL Worksheet 6B: Exercises in Using Prepositions

Choose the correct word for each blank from the choices in parentheses. If none of the suggested words is correct, put an *X* in the blank.

1. Eli enjoys reading the newspaper _____*during*_____ his lunch break. *(during, while)*

2. He reads the paper _____*while*_____ he eats his lunch. *(during, while)*

3. To get home he must walk _____*X*_____ downtown. *(at, to)*

4. When he is ___*at*___ home, he reads his mail. *(at, to)*

5. Today he received a letter from his aunt ___*in*___ Uruguay. *(in, on, at)*

6. She has been living ___*X*___ there for three years. *(in, at)*

7. When she left America, she had to part ___*from*___ many of her friends. *(with, from)*

8. She also had to part ___*with*___ many of her favorite household items. *(with, from)*

9. She will visit Eli _____*on*_____ May 19. *(in, on, at)*

10. Her train will arrive _____*at*_____ 6:00 P.M. *(in, on, at)*

Name_____

ESL Worksheet 8B: Exercises in How to Combine Sentences

The following chart shows meaning similarities among the three main types of connecting words.

Coordinating Conjunctions	Conjunctive Adverbs	Subordinating Conjunctions
and	besides, likewise, moreover, also	—
or	otherwise	—
so	accordingly, consequently, then, therefore, thus	because, since
but, yet	however, nevertheless, still	while, whereas, although, even though

Combine the following sentences using the formulas indicated. Rewrite each sentence, adding the correct connecting word and the correct punctuation. You may leave the words in parentheses out of the sentence. *(Answers may vary.)*

Example: Paige enjoys traveling. She visits countries in the Far East.

IC, cc IC. (Formula 1): _Paige enjoys traveling, so she visits countries in the Far East._

(sc DC), IC. (Formula 2): _Since Paige enjoys traveling, she visits countries in the Far East._

IC; ca, IC. (Formula 5): _Paige enjoys traveling; therefore, she visits countries in the Far East._

1. Paige plays golf. (On the other hand,) Reese plays hockey.

IC, cc IC. (Formula 1): **Paige plays golf, but Reese plays hockey.**

(sc DC), IC. (Formula 2): **Although Paige plays golf, Reese plays hockey.**

IC. ca, IC. (Formula 4): **Paige plays golf. However, Reese plays hockey.**

2. Paige may ride her bike to work. (If not,) she will drive to work.

IC, cc IC. (Formula 1): **Paige may ride her bike to work, or she will drive to work.**

IC. ca, IC. (Formula 4): **Paige may ride her bike to work. Otherwise, she will drive to work.**

IC; ca, IC. (Formula 5): **Paige may ride her bike to work; otherwise, she will drive to work.**

Chapter 1: Sentence Patterns

Practice A

Label the sentence patterns in the following sentences. Above each word of the sentence pattern, write its label.

1.   **S**   **TrV**   **DO**
    Some people design their own stationery.

2.   **S** **LV** **PA**
    The embossing process is simple.

3.   **S**   **TrV** **IO**   **DO**
    Embossing gives paper a raised texture.

4.   **S** **LV**   **PA**
    Embossed paper is often very elegant.

5.   **S**   **InV**
    You can emboss with letters or patterns.

Practice B

Label the sentence patterns in the following sentences. Above each word of the sentence pattern, write its label.

6.   **S** **LV**   **PN**
    Cherie is a collector of elegant writing paper and cards.

7.   **S** **TrV**   **IO**   **DO**
    At least once a month, she writes her grandmother a letter about new events at home and at school.

8.   **S** **LV** **PA**
    Cherie is consistent with thank-you notes.

9.   **S** **TrV**   **DO**
    In appreciation for the kindness of others, she sends thank-you notes often.

10.   **S**   **TrV**   **DO**
    Cherie's letters of kindness encourage her friends.

Practice C

Write a sentence for each of the following sentence patterns. *(Answers will vary.)*

11. (S-InV) *Wesley performs better with plenty of sleep.*

12. (S-TrV-DO) *Cherie delivers the student mail in the afternoon.*

13. (S-TrV-IO-DO) *Mom makes Alden and me delicious snacks after school.*

14. (S-LV-PN) *Dan is a reliable friend.*

15. (S-LV-PA) *The drive home through the mountains is beautiful.*

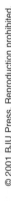

Chapter 1: Phrases and Clauses

Practice A

Identify each italicized group of words as either a phrase *(P)* or a clause *(C)*.

___C___ 1. *An emu is a large Australian bird.*

___P___ 2. *Underneath its thick feathers* lie two small wings.

___P___ 3. The emu, *unable to fly,* runs very swiftly.

___P___ 4. The emu weighs *about one hundred pounds.*

___C___ 5. Emus can be troublesome *because they eat crops.*

Practice B

In each sentence underline any independent clauses once and any dependent clauses twice.

6. Cashmere goats are found mainly in India and Tibet.

7. Although they are found mainly in these areas, cashmere goats have been raised in some European countries.

8. When goats live higher in the mountains, they tend to have darker hair.

9. Cashmere goats are valuable because they have soft, silky wool.

10. Because it is so soft, cashmere wool is used to make fine sweaters and scarves.

Practice C

Identify each italicized group of words as a phrase *(P)*, an independent clause *(IC)*, or a dependent clause *(DC)*.

___P___ 11. *Classified as an amphibian,* a newt is a type of salamander with thin skin and a long tail.

___IC___ 12. *Newts hatch from eggs* that are laid in the spring.

___IC___ 13. Newts generally live in the water, but because they have lungs, *some may live on land.*

___P___ 14. *Having poisonous skin,* newts are not usually disturbed by predators.

___DC___ 15. *If a leg is lost,* a land newt is able to grow another one.

Chapter 1: Sentence Problems

Practice A

Identify each group of words as a sentence *(S)* or a fragment *(F)*.

___F___ 1. Nicholas II, the last czar of Russia, from 1894-1918.

___S___ 2. Aspiring to strengthen Russia's power, he attempted greater military control in the Far East.

___F___ 3. Losing the war, weakening his power and governmental control.

___S___ 4. Reformers and revolutionists forced Nicholas to give up his power.

___F___ 5. The Bolsheviks who shot and killed Nicholas, his wife, his son, and his four daughters.

Practice B

Identify each group of words as a sentence *(S)*, a fragment *(F)*, a fused sentence *(FS)*, or a comma splice *(CS)*.

___CS___ 6. Northern Ireland is one of the four divisions of the United Kingdom, the other three are England, Scotland, and Wales.

___FS___ 7. Northern Ireland separated from Ireland in 1920 now it is often called Ulster.

___F___ 8. Most of the people in Northern Ireland who are largely Protestant.

___S___ 9. Desiring to remain part of Great Britain, they have great contention with the remaining citizens who are mostly Roman Catholic.

___CS___ 10. Catholics desire Northern Ireland to join with the Republic of Ireland, violent disagreement persists between the two parties.

Practice C

Correct the sentence errors by rewriting the sentences correctly in the following blanks.
(Answers may vary.)

11. The Philippine Islands form one country in the Pacific Ocean, more than seven thousand islands make up the Philippines.

    The Philippine Islands form one country in the Pacific Ocean. More than seven thousand islands make up

    the Philippines.

12. Originally, people came to the Philippines from Indonesia and Malaysia these people formed many different communities on different islands.

    Originally, people came to the Philippines from Indonesia and Malaysia, and these people formed many

    different communities on different islands.

13. Spanish explorers colonized the islands in the 1500s, the islands were named for King Philip II.

    Because Spanish explorers colonized the islands in the 1500s, the islands were named for King Philip II.

14. In 1898 Spain gave the United States control of the islands on July 4, 1946, the Philippines were granted independence.

    In 1898 Spain gave the United States control of the islands; on July 4, 1946, the Philippines were

    granted independence.

15. The Japanese temporarily took over the islands in 1941, General Douglas MacArthur regained control for the United States in 1944.

    The Japanese temporarily took over the islands in 1941, but General Douglas MacArthur regained control

    for the United States in 1944.

Chapter 2: Plural Forms of Nouns

Practice A

In the blank write the plural form of the italicized noun.

_____armies_____ 1. Almost every nation has an *army*.

_____branches_____ 2. The United States Army is the *branch* of the armed forces that is responsible for land operations.

_____chiefs_____ 3. The *chief* of staff of the United States Army supervises the members and organizations of the army.

_____radios_____ 4. The development of the *radio* aided military operations.

_____careers_____ 5. Many young people desire a *career* in the army.

Practice B

In the blank write the correct possessive form of the italicized phrase.

6. The army is the oldest branch of *the armed services of the nation*.

    the nation's armed services

7. *The beginning of the army* occurred in 1775 when the Continental Congress created the army to fight in the Revolutionary War.

    The army's beginning

8. Army history records *the heroic acts of many soldiers*.

    many soldiers' heroic acts

9. *The first draft law of Congress* was passed in 1863.

    Congress's first draft law

10. *The first military school of the United States* was opened at West Point in 1802.

    The United States's first military school

Practice C

Underline any errors with plurals or possessives. Rewrite the words correctly on the lines below.

The 1900's were a time of reorganization for the army. In 1903 Congress created the general staff system. Since that time, many chief of staffs have led the army. In 1907 the army's leaders set up an aeronautical division, which became the air force forty years later. The governments' end of the draft occurred in 1973. Afterward, the armed services' began recruiting volunteers. Several reorganizations in the late twentieth century were designed to increase the soldiers's efficiency as well as to cut costs.

1900s, chiefs of staff, government's, services, soldiers'

Chapter 2: Count and Noncount Nouns

Practice A

Label each italicized noun *C* (count) or *NC* (noncount).

__NC__ 1. The air force is responsible for military operations in the air and in *space*.

__C__ 2. Satellites monitor the earth for any *sign* of enemy activity.

__NC__ 3. The air force gives *support* to other branches of the armed services.

__C__ 4. The air force protects ground troops in *battle*.

__C__ 5. A *plane* might deliver fresh troops or supplies.

Practice B

Underline each count noun once and each noncount noun twice.

6. Nuclear weapons have tremendous power for destruction.

7. Therefore, the air force uses advanced technology for many operations.

8. The air force does extensive research throughout the country.

9. Scientists and engineers at universities and in businesses provide great help to the air force.

10. The air force may also help track a hurricane or forecast the weather.

Practice C

Underline each count noun once and each noncount noun twice. (Consider only the common nouns.)

11. During the late 1980s, the Marine Corps had a strength of about 195,000 men and women.

12. Every great nation must have an effective defense.

13. The Marine Corps is trained for amphibious assault.

14. Marines throughout the world are prepared for trouble at any moment.

15. The Marine Corps guards embassies in other countries.

Chapter 2: Functions of Nouns in the Sentence

Practice A

Label each italicized noun *S* (subject), *DO* (direct object), *IO* (indirect object), *OP* (object of the preposition), *PN* (predicate noun), *App* (appositive), or *NA* (noun of direct address).

__DO__ 1. The Continental Congress established a marine *corps* on November 10, 1775.

__PN__ 2. The marines have been a vital *part* of many victories in many wars since that time.

__PN__ 3. During the War of 1812, Captain John Gamble became the only marine *officer* in command of a naval ship.

__OP__ 4. In the Civil War, marines fought in many land and naval *battles*.

__IO__ 5. Marines dealt their *enemies* many lethal blows in both world wars.

Practice B

Label each italicized noun *S* (subject), *DO* (direct object), *IO* (indirect object), *OP* (object of the preposition), *PN* (predicate noun), *App* (appositive), or *NA* (noun of direct address).

__NA__ 6. My father was in the navy, *Orville*.

__App__ 7. The chief of naval operations, an *admiral*, is the highest ranking officer in the navy.

__S__ 8. A nuclear-powered aircraft *carrier* joined the navy's fleet in 1989.

__PN__ 9. Some of the greatest weapons of the navy are undetectable *submarines*.

__DO__ 10. The navy maintains *command* of the sea.

Practice C

Write sentences using each noun in the function that is indicated. *(Answers will vary.)*

11. navy *(predicate noun)* __One of the nation's armed services is the navy.__

12. battleship *(appositive)* __One type of navy ship, a battleship, helps defeat the enemy.__

13. officer *(noun of direct address)* __Officer, may I have a leave of absence?__

14. ship *(object of the preposition)* __All crew members are present on the ship.__

15. crew *(indirect object)* __Please give the crew a day off.__

Chapter 3: Personal Pronoun Usage

Practice A
Underline the correct pronoun from the choices in parentheses.

1. Has *(you, your)* family ever seen a yak?

2. My brother and *(I, me)* learned that the yak is the wild ox of Asia.

3. The cold, dry plateaus of Tibet suit *(they, them)* well.

4. My friend Hiroshi received two tickets to Tibet, so *(he, him)* and I made plans to go.

5. When we visited Tibet, I took some yak pictures of *(my, mine)* own.

Practice B
Underline the correct pronoun from the choices in parentheses.

6. *(Them, Those)* wild Tibetan yaks measure six feet tall at the shoulder.

7. Since this large animal weighs up to twelve hundred pounds, *(who, whom)* do you think could ride one?

8. Sarah told *(we, us)* that a yak carries its head low, with its nose almost touching the ground.

9. *(She, Her)* and Hiroshi recently completed a project about yaks for our biology class.

10. It's *(she, her)* who finds these creatures fascinating.

Practice C
Underline the correct pronoun from the choices in parentheses. In the blank, label the function of the pronoun S (subject), DO (direct object), IO (indirect object), OP (object of the preposition), or PN (predicate noun).

___PN___ 11. Sarah discovered many facts about yaks. It was *(she, her)* who told us that yaks charge furiously at their predators.

___S___ 12. Although yaks look clumsy, *(they, them)* can slide down icy slopes, swim rivers, and climb up steep slopes.

___IO___ 13. Because of the noises domestic yaks make, people gave *(they, them)* the name "grunting ox."

___DO___ 14. Hiroshi also offered some valuable information about yaks. He surprised *(I, me)* with his knowledge of yaks.

___OP___ 15. After class I told him that I would like to learn more about yaks from *(he, him)*.

Chapter 3: Reflexive and Intensive Pronouns

Practice A

Label each italicized pronoun *reflexive* or *intensive*.

_____*intensive*_____ 1. Hiroshi *himself* enjoys photographing the wild animals of foreign countries.

_____*reflexive*_____ 2. He has ventured out to many distant places by *himself.*

_____*intensive*_____ 3. His brother Lee accompanied him on an adventure to Tibet, and they *themselves* took many incredible pictures.

_____*reflexive*_____ 4. Before the trip they researched the country for *themselves.*

_____*intensive*_____ 5. Tibet *itself* is called the Roof of the World because it has the highest plateaus and mountains on earth.

Practice B

In each sentence underline the reflexive pronouns once and the intensive pronouns twice. If the pronoun is reflexive, write its function in the blank. If the pronoun is intensive, write the noun or pronoun it intensifies in the blank.

_____*Mount Everest*_____ 6. Mount Everest, <u>itself</u> one of the world's highest mountains, is located in southern Tibet.

*Hiroshi and his brother* 7. Hiroshi and his brother <u>themselves</u> visited the city Ka-erh in western Tibet, a city which is possibly the highest in the world.

_____*OP*_____ 8. Tibet has been a part of China since 1950, but it once stood by *<u>itself</u>* for several years as an independent state.

_____*Tibet*_____ 9. Large parts of Tibet <u>itself</u> are wastelands.

_____*IO*_____ 10. Through his research Hiroshi taught <u>himself</u> the fact that Tibet has many wild animals besides yaks, animals such as tigers, monkeys, and wild horses.

Practice C

Rewrite each sentence, adding intensive pronouns to emphasize certain elements as suggested.

11. The entire region of Tibet receives less than ten inches of rain annually.
    Emphasize that it is Tibet that receives this amount of rainfall.

    The entire region of Tibet itself receives less than ten inches of rain annually.

    _____

12. The Himalayas block moisture-bearing winds that come sweeping up from India.
    Emphasize that the mountains alone block the winds.

    The Himalayas themselves block moisture-bearing winds that come sweeping up from India.

    _____

13. The climate is very windy, with sudden blizzards and violent winds being very common.
    Emphasize that the typical climate is very windy.

    __The climate itself is very windy, with sudden blizzards and violent winds being very common.__

    _____

14. Tibet's population of two million lives mostly in the southern portion of the country.
    Emphasize that the people live in the country's southern region.

    __Tibet's population of two million lives mostly in the southern portion of the country itself.__

    _____

15. The official language of Tibet is Mandarin Chinese, but the traditional language is Tibetan.
    Emphasize that the traditional language is different from the official language.

    __The official language of Tibet is Mandarin Chinese, but the traditional language itself is Tibetan.__

    _____

Chapter 3: Indefinite Pronouns

Practice A

Underline each indefinite pronoun. In the blank, label the pronoun *singular* or *plural*.

_____singular_____ 1. Barley is <u>one</u> of Tibet's chief crops.

_____singular_____ 2. <u>Most</u> of the food the people eat contains barley flour.

_____singular_____ 3. <u>Everyone</u> understands the importance of the yak as a food source.

_____plural_____ 4. <u>Several</u> of the products made from yaks are milk, cheese, cloth, and shoe leather.

_____plural_____ 5. <u>Many</u> of the yaks are used for transportation.

Practice B

Underline each indefinite pronoun. In the blank, label the pronoun *singular* or *plural*.

_____singular_____ 6. Almost <u>everybody</u> in Tibet wears long robes with high collars and long sleeves.

_____plural_____ 7. While the robes are usually made of wool or sheepskin, <u>some</u> of the wealthy people wear robes made of silk.

_____plural_____ 8. <u>Both</u> of the visitors, Hiroshi and Lee, bought themselves traditional robes while visiting Tibet.

_____singular_____ 9. <u>Each</u> of the households weaves cloth and carpet.

_____singular_____ 10. Exporting wool generates <u>much</u> of their national income.

Practice C

In the blank write an appropriate indefinite pronoun to complete the sentence. Do not use the same pronoun more than once. *(Answers will vary.)*

_____Much_____ 11. _?_ of Hiroshi's time was spent reading articles on Tibet.

_____one_____ 12. Before traveling, _?_ should take the time to learn about the place he will be visiting.

_____something_____ 13. Knowing _?_ about the country's culture and people will enrich your experience.

_____little_____ 14. Learning a _?_ of the language would help a great deal.

_____all_____ 15. Because Hiroshi diligently prepared, _?_ of his trips were fascinating and rewarding.

Chapter 3: Correcting Unclear Reference Problems

Practice A

Label each sentence *clear* or *unclear*.

_____*unclear*_____ 1. When Hiroshi and his brother arrived back home, he became ill with the flu for a week and a half.

_____*clear*_____ 2. Even though he was not feeling well, Hiroshi was still excited about telling his friends about the trip to Tibet.

_____*unclear*_____ 3. Asher told Hiroshi that he was happy he was home.

_____*unclear*_____ 4. Once he felt better, Hiroshi cooked us a Tibetan meal and showed us his photos of the wild animals he saw. It was very good!

_____*clear*_____ 5. After seeing the excitement on Hiroshi's face when he was telling of his adventures, Asher has decided that he wants to visit Tibet for himself.

Practice B

Rewrite each sentence to make the pronoun-antecedent relationship clear. *(Answers will vary.)*

6. Asher told Hiroshi that he wanted to go to Tibet next summer.

   Asher told Hiroshi, "I would like to go to Tibet next summer."

7. Hiroshi and Lee told Asher about their adventures in Tibet and showed him their pictures. He found them fascinating.

   Hiroshi and Lee told Asher about their adventures in Tibet and showed him their pictures. He found the

   pictures fascinating.

8. Hiroshi told us a story about his first ride on a yak. It was hilarious!

   Hiroshi told us a story about his first ride on a yak. The story was hilarious!

9. Yaks were transporting Hiroshi and a guide to a nearby village when they were both stung by huge wasps.

   While transporting Hiroshi and a guide to a nearby village, the yaks were both stung by huge wasps.

10. Hiroshi's yak reared up and then began to run as fast as it could. Finally, it halted abruptly. It frightened Hiroshi.

    Hiroshi's yak reared up and then began to run as fast as it could. Finally, it halted abruptly. The ride

    frightened Hiroshi.

Practice C

Rewrite each sentence to make the pronoun-antecedent relationship clear. *(Answers will vary.)*

11. Although it gave Hiroshi quite a scare, he was not afraid to get back on the rambunctious yak for the ride back into town.

    Although the large creature gave Hiroshi quite a scare, he was not afraid to get back on the rambunctious

    yak for the ride back into town.

12. Lee was seated calmly on another yak while he watched his brother's adventure. The expression on his face was priceless.

    Lee was seated calmly on another yak while he watched his brother's adventure. The expression on

    Hiroshi's face was priceless.

13. Lee quickly reached into his backpack and pulled out his camera to snap a picture of Hiroshi. The careening animal didn't seem to alarm him.

    Lee quickly reached into his backpack and pulled out his camera to snap a picture of Hiroshi. The

    careening animal didn't seem to alarm Lee.

14. Asher told Lee he should have been more concerned for Hiroshi's safety.

    Asher told Lee, "You should have been more concerned for Hiroshi's safety."

15. We all laughed about the story and the picture. Even though Lee embellished the facts for greater dramatic effect, Hiroshi was able to laugh heartily at them.

    We all laughed about the story and the picture. Even though Lee embellished the facts for greater

    dramatic effect, Hiroshi was able to laugh heartily at the story and the picture.

Chapter 4: Principal Parts of Verbs

Practice A

Underline the correct verb from the choices in parentheses. Be sure to check for any auxiliary that may go with the verb you have chosen.

1. Samuel Pepys *(wrote, written)* a famous account of his life in the seventeenth century.

2. His *Diary,* which includes detailed events of his life, was *(gave, given)* to the general public in 1822.

3. Pepys was *(born, borned)* in London in 1633.

4. By 1673 Pepys had *(took, taken)* responsibility for the navy, which he significantly reformed.

5. Through his diaries we have *(got, gotten)* a rich description of England's culture and history.

Practice B

In the blank write the correct past or past participle form of the verb in parentheses.

___*kept*___ 6. The drug penicillin has *(keep)* dangerous bacteria from spreading.

___*killed*___ 7. Sir Alexander Fleming discovered penicillin when he noticed that some mold growing in a laboratory dish had *(kill)* the bacteria in the dish.

___*broken*___ 8. Bacteria cannot survive after the penicillin has *(break)* down their stiff cell walls.

___*known*___ 9. Some types of penicillin have been *(know)* to cause allergic reactions, but most reactions are mild.

___*used*___ 10. Types of penicillin are now commonly *(use)* for the treatment of throat and ear infections.

Practice C

In the blank write the correct past or past participle form of the verb in parentheses.

___*hung*___ 11. Yesterday my father *(hang)* a charming oil portrait over the piano.

___*laid*___ 12. The portrait has been on the table since we *(lay)* it there last week.

___*drunk*___ 13. The kittens have *(drink)* the warm milk and gone to sleep.

___*lain*___ 14. By dinner time the kittens will have *(lie)* in the sun for two hours.

___*sunk*___ 15. The dismantled raft has *(sink)* to the bottom of the lake.

Chapter 4: Perfect Tenses

Name_____

Practice A

Label the tense of each italicized verb *present, present perfect, past, past perfect, future,* or *future perfect.*

___present perfect___ 1. Coral islands *have formed* from rocklike deposits that resist erosion.

___present___ 2. Atolls, coral islands in the shape of rings, *may enclose* an entire lagoon.

___past perfect___ 3. By the time several ocean volcanoes became extinct, a group of coral islands *had formed* around their rims. These islands now make up part of the Tuamotu Archipelago in the South Pacific.

___past___ 4. The islands of the Tuamotu Archipelago *were made* part of French Polynesia.

___future perfect___ 5. By next year the pearl-producing oysters of the lagoons *will have provided* one of the main sources of revenue for the islands.

Practice B

In the blank write the correct form of the verb in parentheses.

___have cultivated___ 6. Numerous oyster farms *(cultivate, present perfect)* the famous black pearls of Tuamotu Archipelago.

___begins___ 7. A pearl *(begin, present)* to form after a foreign object enters the oyster's shell.

___will have begun___ 8. The oyster covers the object with coats of nacre. This process, after some time, *(begin, future perfect)* to form a pearl.

___have produced___ 9. Most of the pearls in the South Pacific are black. However, oysters *(produce, present perfect)* pearls that are green and even white.

___had begun___ 10. Natural pearls were once rare and expensive. Soon after farmers *(begin, past perfect)* to culture them, however, pearls became more available.

Practice C

In the blank write the correct form of the verb in parentheses.

___will collect___ 11. At an oyster farm in French Polynesia, plastic garlands hanging in the water *(collect, future)* the floating larvae of oysters.

___will have placed___ 12. Before the tiny oysters are seven months old, workers *(place, future perfect)* them in hanging baskets for protection under the water.

___had inserted___ 13. Pearl cultivators found that pearls grew bigger and faster after they *(insert, past perfect)* a small bead inside the oyster to start the growth of the pearl.

___harvested___ 14. After three years, the workers *(harvest, past)* the oysters and the black pearls.

___have become___ 15. Black pearls *(become, present perfect)* some of the most expensive pearls in the world.

Chapter 4: Progressive Tenses

Practice A

In the blank, label the tense of the italicized verb.

present progressive   1. China is a type of ceramic that manufacturers *are using* mainly for fine dishes.

past progressive   2. Makers of ceramic *were producing* this type of porcelain first in China; therefore, these products are often called china or chinaware.

future progressive   3. After a fine piece of porcelain china is made, collectors *will be admiring* it for its strength and delicate appearance.

present perfect progressive   4. Since the very first appearance of porcelain, workers *have been making* it from two substances: kaolin and petuntze.

past perfect progressive   5. Before the appearance of porcelain, workers *had been creating* stoneware and earthenware from natural clay fired at high temperatures.

Practice B

In the blank write the progressive form of each italicized verb. Do not change the tense of the verb.

are producing   6. Manufacturers *produce* three main kinds of porcelain china.

have been considering   7. Many collectors *have considered* hard-paste china the best porcelain.

will be firing   8. When he makes the hard-paste china, the manufacturer *will fire* the materials at a much higher temperature because hard-paste china resists melting much better than other types of porcelain.

were attempting   9. Several Europeans developed soft-paste china as they *attempted* to imitate hard-paste china.

have been manufacturing   10. Adding burned animal bones to kaolin and petuntze creates bone china. The English discovered and *have manufactured* most of the world's bone china.

Practice C

In the blank, label the tense of the italicized verb.

past   11. Rulers in China *desired* fine porcelain as far back as A.D. 960.

past perfect   12. By the end of the 1700s, several European countries *had competed* with China in making porcelain.

present perfect   13. The Germans *have decorated* beautiful fine china since the early 1700s.

future perfect   14. This year English manufacturers *will have produced* famous bone china for almost two hundred fifty years.

future   15. Several American and Japanese manufacturers *will continue* to produce several lines of quality porcelain.

Chapter 5: Determiners

Practice A

Underline each adjective. Write *PA* over each predicate adjective. Draw an arrow from each other adjective to the noun it modifies.

1. Hibernation is an inactive state of some animals during winter.
2. These animals have a lower body temperature during hibernation.
3. An animal in this state needs little energy.
4. These animals' bodies adapt to harsh winter conditions.
5. The animals often appear dead. *(PA over dead)*

Practice B

In the blank write an appropriate adjective from the category indicated in parentheses. Try to use a variety of adjectives. (Answers may vary.)

__Many__ 6. _?_ scientists disagree on the hibernation of bears. *(indefinite)*

__Whose__ 7. _?_ opinion is true? *(interrogative)*

__bear's__ 8. Well, a _?_ body temperature does not fall as much as the temperature of other hibernators. *(possessive)*

__These__ 9. _?_ scientists also state that a bear is easily awakened from sleep. *(demonstrative)*

__Some__ 10. _?_ scientists state, however, that a bear's heart rate drops; therefore, bears are true hibernators. *(indefinite)*

Practice C

Label the italicized adjectives *Art* (article), *P* (possessive), *D* (demonstrative), *Int* (interrogative), or *Ind* (indefinite).

__Ind__ 11. *Many* hibernators eat large amounts of food in the fall.

__Int__ 12. *Which* animals are warm-blooded?

__P__ 13. The food is stored in *their* bodies as fat.

__Art__ 14. *The* fat provides energy during hibernation.

__D__ 15. *These* animals alternate periods of hibernation with periods of wakefulness.

Chapter 5: Using Modifiers Correctly

Practice A
Underline the correct adjective or adverb from the choices in parentheses.

1. Bats often scare people *(bad, badly)*.

2. Many times people are afraid because bats appear *(most, mostly)* at night.

3. Bats are valuable because they eat *(large, larger)* numbers of insects.

4. Bats often behave *(timid, timidly)*.

5. Although bats will not intentionally do *(any, no)* harm, they may have rabies.

Practice B
Underline the correct adjective or adverb from the choices in parentheses.

6. People seem *(different, differently)* in their opinions about bats.

7. People in western countries are *(more fearful, most fearful)* of bats than those in European countries are.

8. Most bats are *(real, really)* harmless to people.

9. Bats can probably see as *(good, well)* as human beings.

10. Of flying foxes and brown bats, flying foxes are *(larger, largest)*.

Practice C
Underline the correct adjective or adverb from the choices in parentheses.

11. Compared to those that inhabit exposed areas, bats that live in secluded areas tend to have *(duller, dullest)* markings.

12. Bats that have long, slender wings move the *(fastest, most fastest)* of all.

13. Other bats have *(shorter, more shorter)* wings.

14. Many bats look for a *(good, well)* place to hibernate in the fall or winter.

15. Do some North American bats not eat *(any, no)* food during their hibernation?

Chapter 5: Misplaced Modifiers

Practice A

Label each sentence *C* (clear) or *U* (unclear).

_**C**_ 1. Female bats feed their babies for only a few months.

_**U**_ 2. Bats that perch securely attach themselves to rocks and twigs by their claws.

_**C**_ 3. Not all bats have good night vision.

_**C**_ 4. Bats with poor senses often rely on echoes to locate objects.

_**U**_ 5. Echoes allow even the bat to know how its prey is moving.

Practice B

Rewrite the following sentences, correcting any problems with modifier positions. *(Answers may vary.)*

6. Bats are mammals that can only fly.

   Bats are the only mammals that can fly.

7. All people do not know a lot of facts about bats.

   Not all people know a lot of facts about bats.

8. People who fear bats incorrectly draw conclusions about bats.

   People who fear bats draw incorrect conclusions about bats.

9. All bats are not of the same species.

   Not all bats are of the same species.

10. Some bats have only a wingspan of one foot.

    Some bats have a wingspan of only one foot.

Practice C

Rewrite the following sentences, correcting any problems with modifier positions. *(Answers may vary.)*

11. The Kitti's hog-nosed bat nearly weighs two grams.

    The Kitti's hog-nosed bat weighs nearly two grams.
    _____

12. A bat's digesting its food quickly reduces its superfluous weight.

    A bat's quick digestion of its food reduces its superfluous weight.
    _____

13. Only bats sleep during the day.

    Bats sleep only during the day.
    _____

14. When I was in the woods, I just saw five bats.

    When I was in the woods, I saw just five bats.
    _____

15. I was so frightened that I fainted almost to the ground.

    I was so frightened that I almost fainted to the ground.
    _____

Chapter 6: Functions of Prepositional Phrases

Practice A

Underline the word that each italicized prepositional phrase modifies. Label the phrase either *Adj* (adjectival) or *Adv* (adverbial).

**Adv** 1. *In Woodstock, Oxfordshire, England,* <u>lies</u> Blenheim Palace.

**Adv** 2. Queen Anne <u>rewarded</u> the Duke of Marlborough *with this home.*

**Adj** 3. The Duke's wife, Sarah, was a good <u>friend</u> *of the queen.*

**Adj** 4. An <u>inscription</u> *on the East Gate* tells when the palace was built.

**Adv** 5. Sir John Vanbrugh <u>built</u> the palace *between 1705 and 1722.*

Practice B

Place parentheses around each prepositional phrase. Label the phrase either *Adj* (adjectival) or *Adv* (adverbial).

**Adv** 6. Blenheim was designed(in the English baroque style.)

**Adv** 7. When I visited Blenheim, I toured the palace(with my aunt.)

**Adj** 8. The ceiling(above the Great Hall)is beautiful.

**Adv** 9. It was painted(by Sir James Thornhill.)

**Adj** 10. The painting is a picture(of a triumphant Marlborough.)

Practice C

Place parentheses around each prepositional phrase. Underline the word modified by the prepositional phrase. Label the prepositional phrase either *Adj* (adjectival) or *Adv* (adverbial).

**Adj** 11. My favorite <u>room</u>(in the house)was Sir Winston Churchill's birth room.

**Adv** 12. Blenheim was also the place where Sir Winston Churchill <u>proposed</u>(to his wife.)

**Adv** 13. As we <u>walked</u>(among the rooms,)we saw elegant dishes displayed.

**Adj** 14. I really liked the Meissen <u>tureens</u>(with the lemon-slice handles.)

**Adj** 15. Our guide told us an interesting <u>story</u>(about these particular dishes.)

Chapter 6: Coordinating and Correlative Conjunctions

Practice A

Underline the coordinating and correlative conjunctions in the following sentences.

1. We toured <u>not only</u> the Green Drawing Room <u>but also</u> the Red Drawing Room.

2. The Red Drawing Room houses a portrait of Lady Morton <u>and</u> Mrs. Killigrew.

3. I enjoyed looking at the paintings, <u>but</u> the tapestries on the walls really caught my attention.

4. <u>Neither</u> my aunt <u>nor</u> I could understand why the dog in the tapestry has horse's hooves.

5. Overall, I found the rooms to be elaborate <u>yet</u> delightful.

Practice B

Underline the coordinating and correlative conjunctions in each sentence once. Underline the words or phrases joined by the conjunctions twice.

6. When we toured the grounds of the palace, we visited the <u>Italian Garden</u> <u>and</u> the <u>Great Avenue</u>.

7. <u>Both</u> my <u>aunt</u> <u>and</u> <u>I</u> remarked that we had never seen such lovely sights.

8. <u>I wanted to visit the Grand Bridge</u>, <u>but</u> <u>my aunt said that the walk was too far</u>.

9. <u>Instead, we chose to tour the Rose Garden</u>, <u>for</u> <u>walking among the flowers was less strenuous</u>.

10. My aunt said that we could explore <u>either</u> the <u>Butterfly House</u> <u>or</u> the <u>Marlborough Maze</u> next.

Practice C

Combine a word or phrase from the first sentence with a word or phrase from the second sentence to make a compound sentence element joined by the type of conjunction indicated in parentheses. Use a variety of conjunctions. In the blank write the new sentence. (Answers will vary.)

11. We saw butterflies in the Butterfly House. We also saw moths. *(correlative)*

   We saw both butterflies and moths in the Butterfly House.

12. The Butterfly House accommodates Owl butterflies. The Butterfly House accommodates Heliconius butterflies. *(coordinating)*

   The Butterfly House accommodates Owl butterflies and Heliconius butterflies.

13. My aunt did not see any Monarch butterflies. I did not see any Monarch butterflies. *(correlative)*

   Neither my aunt nor I saw any Monarch butterflies.

14. I ventured through the Marlborough Maze. My aunt did not. *(coordinating)*

   I ventured through the Marlborough Maze, but my aunt did not.

15. Surprisingly, I did not make any incorrect turns in the maze. I also did not get lost. *(coordinating)*

   Surprisingly, I did not make any incorrect turns in the maze, nor did I get lost.

Chapter 6: Subordinating Conjunctions

Practice A

Underline the subordinating conjunctions in the following sentences.

1. <u>After</u> I made it through the maze, I rested with my aunt on a bench.

2. <u>Although</u> my aunt was tired, she still wanted to see more sights at the palace.

3. We decided to take a ride on the Blenheim's railway <u>so that</u> our feet could take a break.

4. <u>Once</u> we arrived back at the palace, we felt much better.

5. We visited the Grand Cascade <u>since</u> our strength was renewed.

Practice B

Place parentheses around the dependent clauses. Underline the subordinating conjunction that begins each clause.

6. (<u>When</u> we finished admiring the falls,) we walked along the lake.

7. My aunt told me then (<u>that</u> she would like to walk across the Grand Bridge.)

8. (<u>As</u> we made our way across the bridge,) we noticed many people taking photographs of the scenery.

9. (<u>While</u> they took their photographs,) my aunt and I looked at the view of the palace with our binoculars.

10. I wanted to learn more about the palace (<u>because</u> it had intrigued me so much.)

Practice C

Use a subordinating conjunction to combine the two sentences by making one a dependent clause. Try to represent the relationship between the two ideas. In the blank write the new sentence.
(Answers will vary.)

11. We toured the interior of the palace one more time. We returned home.

    We toured the interior of the palace one more time before we returned home.

12. We wanted to see the rooms again. There were a couple of rooms that we had missed.

    We wanted to see the rooms again since there were a couple of rooms that we had missed.

13. I didn't realize how much I had missed. We went on our second tour.

    I didn't realize how much I had missed until we went on our second tour.

14. Our second tour was better than our first. We learned more facts about the palace.

    Our second tour was better than our first because we learned more facts about the palace.

15. I will visit Blenheim Palace again. I have the opportunity.

    I will visit Blenheim Palace again if I have the opportunity.

Chapter 7: Participles

Practice A

Underline the present and past participles. Draw an arrow from each underlined participle to the noun it modifies.

1. Color enhances beauty, and <u>varied</u> colors often change moods and atmospheres.

2. Several shades of green can create a calm, <u>relaxing</u> atmosphere.

3. A <u>subdued</u> blue can be peaceful as well, or it can indicate a feeling of melancholy.

4. Red is associated with <u>building</u> excitement and even <u>increased</u> anger.

5. A vibrant yellow appears sunny and cheerful; decorating with yellow promotes a pleasant, <u>inviting</u> atmosphere.

Practice B

Underline the participial phrases. Draw an arrow from each underlined participial phrase to the noun it modifies. In the blank, label each underlined participial phrase present or past.

___*present*___ 6. Color actually begins as light waves <u>differing in length</u>.

___*past*___ 7. Our eyes perceive the various lengths as <u>differently colored</u> waves of light.

___*present*___ 8. Red, <u>having the longest wavelengths</u>, appears at one end of the spectrum.

___*present*___ 9. <u>Appearing at the opposite end</u>, the color violet has the shortest wavelengths.

___*past*___ 10. The long yellow wavelengths <u>combined with short blue wavelengths</u> are reflected as medium wavelengths and appear green.

Practice C

A. Underline each participle and place parentheses around each participial phrase.
B. Draw an arrow from each participle to the word it modifies.
C. In the blank, label each participial phrase present or past.
D. Label the sentence patterns. Above each word of the sentence pattern write its label.

___*past*___ 11. White waves of light(<u>bent</u> by a prism)display all the colors of the rainbow.

___*past*___ 12. Light waves,(not actually <u>colored</u> themselves,)create the sense of color in the brain.

___*present*___ 13. The eye contains three(color-<u>sensing</u>)cones.

___*present*___ 14. (<u>Affecting</u> more men than women,)colorblindness is an inherited disorder.

___*past*___ 15. People(<u>blinded</u> to all color)have achromatic vision.

Chapter 7: Gerunds

Practice A

Underline the gerunds. In the blank, label each underlined gerund *S* (subject), *DO* (direct object), *IO* (indirect object), *OP* (object of the preposition), or *PN* (predicate noun).

__S__ 1. <u>Cooking</u> prepares food and usually makes it taste better.

__OP__ 2. Creative meals result from <u>obtaining</u> new ideas and recipes.

__IO__ 3. If you give meal <u>planning</u> enough time, you can make meals much more efficiently.

__PN__ 4. One beneficial activity to ensure a healthful diet is <u>planning</u> the basics of nutrition.

__DO__ 5. If you include <u>meeting</u> basic nutrition requirements in your meals, your dinner time can be both healthful and delicious.

Practice B

Label each italicized word *G* (gerund) or *P* (participle).

__G__ 6. *Baking* requires the placement of food in an oven. Bread, cookies, and pastries are foods that are usually baked.

__P__ 7. Many people enjoy the aroma of *baking* bread.

__G__ 8. When you are frying meat or vegetables, you will begin by *heating* an amount of fat in a pan or skillet.

__G__ 9. *Boiling* requires that the food, usually vegetables, be kept in water at least 212°F.

__P__ 10. Pasta also is often cooked in *boiling* water.

Practice C

Place parentheses around the gerund or gerund phrase. In the blank, label the gerund or gerund phrase *S* (subject), *DO* (direct object), *IO* (indirect object), *OP* (object of the preposition), or *PN* (predicate noun).

__OP__ 11. An appealing meal results from(combining foods with variety in color, temperature, texture, and)taste.

__S__ 12. (The coloring of food)should be diverse. For example, a brightly colored fruit or vegetable adds variety to a meal.

__DO__ 13. Most cooks prefer(including at least one hot food and one cold food in the menu.)

__PN__ 14. Another creative idea is(incorporating a theme into the menu.)

__IO__ 15. Some favorite recipes and a little creativity give(dining)double pleasure and create an enjoyable atmosphere for friends, family, or guests.

Chapter 7: Infinitives

Practice A

Underline the infinitives. Not every sentence contains an infinitive.

1. The country of Congo happens <u>to lie</u> along the equator in west-central Africa.

2. Visitors from cooler, drier climates are likely <u>to swelter</u> in the heat and humidity.

3. Farming, hunting, and fishing have traditionally been the most common occupations of the people, but today many more have begun <u>to acquire</u> office and technical positions.

4. Trees and vegetation cover the northern region, and wild animals are known <u>to inhabit</u> the forests.

5. The Congo River, the world's fifth longest river, flows through Congo to the Atlantic Ocean.

Practice B

Underline the infinitives. Label the function of each infinitive *N* (noun), *Adj* (adjective), or *Adv* (adverb).

_N_ 6. I decided <u>to learn</u> more about rural life in Africa.

_N_ 7. <u>To hunt</u> is an activity that many people enjoy.

Adv 8. <u>To kill</u> their prey, hunters may use a bow and arrows.

Adj 9. Leaves and berries <u>to supplement</u> any game are often collected by some of the women.

Adj 10. The privilege <u>to collect</u> fruit and plants from farmers' fields is given to those who help farmers with their crops.

Practice C

Underline the infinitive phrases. Label the function of each infinitive phrase *N* (noun), *Adj* (adjective), or *Adv* (adverb).

_N_ 11. Would you like <u>to know the reason for the twenty-four-second shot clock in the National Basketball Association</u>?

_N_ 12. During the 1953–54 season, many NBA teams were in financial trouble. <u>To go to a game</u> was boring because the game moved very slowly.

Adj 13. At that time a team in the lead had no incentive <u>to shoot the ball</u>.

Adv 14. <u>To save the game</u>, Danny Biasone, owner of the Syracuse Nationals, proposed the twenty-four-second rule, which requires the shooting of a basket within twenty-four seconds after acquiring possession of the ball.

_N_ 15. The rule went into effect at the beginning of the 1954–55 season. Scoring began <u>to rise an average of fourteen points per game that year</u>, and fans quickly responded to the increased excitement of the game.

Chapter 8: Independent and Dependent Clauses

Practice A

Label each italicized group of words *P* (phrase) or *C* (clause).

___C___   1. *Volcanoes are very interesting.*

___P___   2. There are three types *of volcanoes.*

___C___   3. Volcanoes are classified by the way *that they are formed.*

___C___   4. A person *who studies volcanoes* must be familiar with several terms.

___P___   5. Magma is melted rock found *under the earth's surface.*

Practice B

Label each italicized group of words *P* (phrase), *IC* (independent clause), or *DC* (dependent clause).

___DC___   6. *Once magma has come to the earth's surface,* it is called lava.

___IC___   7. Lava that is very fluid moves quickly, but *sticky lava does not move as fast.*

___IC___   8. *Volcanoes also erupt rock fragments.*

___P___   9. These rock fragments range in size; they can be grains *of volcanic dust* or volcanic bombs.

___DC___   10. *Since volcanic ash sometimes helps to create a mudflow,* it can be a harmful substance.

Practice C

Place parentheses around each dependent clause.

11. (Whereas a shield volcano is formed by lava,)cinder-cone volcanoes are formed by rock fragments.

12. Composite volcanoes received their name(because they are formed by lava and rock fragments.)

13. (Although they may erupt sometime in the future,)dormant volcanoes are considered inactive.

14. (If a volcano erupts repeatedly,)it is called an active volcano.

15. (Once a volcano erupts on a regular basis,)it is considered an intermittent volcano.

Chapter 8: Using Independent and Dependent Clauses

Practice A

Underline the coordinating conjunctions. Label each sentence S (simple) or Cd (compound). Not every sentence contains a coordinating conjunction.

__S__ 1. There are four types of volcanic eruptions: Strombolian, Hawaiian, Peléean, <u>and</u> vulcanian.

__Cd__ 2. Hawaiian volcanic eruptions are the least dangerous, <u>but</u> Peléean are the most destructive.

__Cd__ 3. A volcano erupted on Mount Pelée in 1902, <u>and</u> it killed almost thirty-eight thousand people.

__Cd__ 4. Mauna Loa is located in Hawaii; it is the world's largest active volcano.

__S__ 5. Kilauea is also a Hawaiian volcano <u>and</u> is active.

Practice B

Label each sentence S (simple), Cd (compound), or Cx (complex).

__Cx__ 6. Although many people think of volcanoes as devastating, volcanoes also have positive effects.

__Cd__ 7. People use lava to make roads, and they use pumice as an abrasive.

__S__ 8. In Iceland people use water from volcanic hot springs to heat their homes.

__Cx__ 9. People from other countries are able to use geothermal energy since volcanoes produce underground steam.

__Cx__ 10. Volcanoes are also helpful because they allow scientists to learn more about the earth.

Practice C

Label each sentence S (simple), Cd (compound), Cx (complex), or Cd-Cx (compound-complex).

__S__ 11. Mexico City is the home of two volcanoes: Popocatépetl and Ixtacihuatl.

__Cd__ 12. Popocatépetl is also called "Smoking Mountain," and it reaches 17,883 feet.

__Cx__ 13. Did Popocatépetl receive its name because it is always emitting sulfur?

__Cd-Cx__ 14. When my friends visited Mexico City last summer, they saw Popocatépetl; they were also able to see Ixtacihuatl.

__Cd-Cx__ 15. After they returned home, I looked at their photographs, and I asked them whether they saw any other volcanoes.

Chapter 8: Kinds of Dependent Clauses

Practice A

In the blank write the word that the italicized clause modifies.

___country___ 1. El Salvador is a country *that is well known for its volcanoes.*

___Izalco___ 2. Izalco, *which is one of El Salvador's volcanoes,* is called the Lighthouse of the Pacific.

___should visit___ 3. I should visit El Salvador *when Izalco is not active.*

___island___ 4. Iceland is an island *where there are two hundred volcanoes.*

___fascinate___ 5. Volcanoes fascinate me *because they are so powerful.*

Practice B

In the blank, label the italicized clause *Adj* (adjective) or *Adv* (adverb).

___Adj___ 6. Mount St. Helens is a volcano *that is located in Washington.*

___Adv___ 7. Many acres of forest were destroyed *when Mount St. Helens erupted.*

___Adj___ 8. A volcanologist is a person *who studies why volcanoes erupt.*

___Adv___ 9. *As a volcano threatens to erupt* volcanologists try to study the volcanic activity.

___Adj___ 10. Earthquakes, *which often occur before an eruption,* are good precursory warnings that a volcano is going to erupt.

Practice C

Place parentheses around the dependent clauses. In the blank, label the clause *Adj* (adjective) or *Adv* (adverb).

___Adv___ 11. (Whenever a volcanologist wants to measure a volcano's expansion,)he uses a tiltmeter.

___Adv___ 12. A seismograph also aids a scientist(because it is an earthquake identifier.)

___Adj___ 13. Mount Shasta is a volcano(that has a smaller volcano located on its western slopes.)

___Adj___ 14. Mount Etna,(which is located in Sicily,)first erupted around 700 B.C.

___Adj___ 15. Hawaii is the state(where the largest volcano in the world is located.)

Chapter 9: Simple and Compound Subjects

Practice A

Underline the verb in parentheses that agrees with the subject.

1. Birte *(visits, visit)* Denmark every year.

2. Her parents *(sails, sail)* to Denmark each spring.

3. Water *(surrounds, surround)* Denmark.

4. Many islands *(is located, are located)* near Denmark.

5. Denmark *(borders, border)* Germany.

Practice B

Questions 6-10: Proofread the following paragraph for errors in subject-verb agreement. Cross out each incorrect verb and write the correct verb above it.

This summer Thore and I ~~plans~~ *plan* to visit Denmark. Neither he nor I ~~has~~ *have* ever been there before, so we are looking forward to our trip. While we are there, I hope to see the Royal Library or the National Museum. Thore's aunt and uncle ~~says~~ *say* that they visited these sights a few years ago. Both his aunt and his uncle ~~wishes~~ *wish* that they could return to Denmark, but unfortunately they don't have the time or the money to go. Either my parents or my grandmother ~~are~~ *is* giving me some spending money for the trip, so neither Thore nor I will have to worry about finances. I'm so thankful for their generosity!

Practice C

Combine the two sentences using a compound subject. Use the verb that agrees with the subject of your new sentence. *(Answers will vary.)*

11. Norway is a Scandinavian country.
    Denmark is a Scandinavian country.

    Both Norway and Denmark are Scandinavian countries.

12. Norway lies closer to Denmark.
    Sweden lies closer to Denmark.

    Either Norway or Sweden lies closer to Denmark.

13. Poland does not border Denmark.
    Finland does not border Denmark.

    Neither Poland nor Finland borders Denmark.

14. Ålborg is a city in Denmark.
    Århus is a city in Denmark.

    Ålborg and Århus are cities in Denmark.

15. Afua does not speak Danish.
    Wilhelm does not speak Danish.

    Neither Afua nor Wilhelm speaks Danish.

Chapter 9: Finding the Subject

Practice A

Underline the subject of each sentence. Then underline the verb in parentheses that agrees with the subject.

1. <u>Copenhagen</u> and <u>Odense</u>, not Helsinki, *(is, <u>are</u>)* cities in Denmark.

2. The <u>people</u> of Denmark *(is called, <u>are called</u>)* Danes.

3. There *(is, <u>are</u>)* over five million <u>inhabitants</u> who live in Denmark.

4. Who *(<u>is</u>, are)* a famous <u>writer</u> from Denmark?

5. <u>Grundtvig</u>, not Oehlenschläger, *(<u>was</u>, were)* a Danish hymn writer.

Practice B

Write in the blank the correct form of the verb in parentheses.

_____*is*_____ 6. One of Denmark's most famous composers _?_ Carl A. Nielsen. *(be)*

_____*listens*_____ 7. My sister, not my brothers, _?_ to his symphonies. *(listen)*

_____*are*_____ 8. There _?_ five areas of land in Denmark. *(be)*

_____*stretch*_____ 9. The beaches of the Western Dune Coast _?_ along the upper western coast of Jutland. *(stretch)*

_____*lies*_____ 10. Bornholm, not the Northern Flat Plains, _?_ near the southern part of Sweden. *(lie)*

Practice C

Questions 11–15: Proofread the following paragraph for errors in subject-verb agreement. Cross out each incorrect verb and write the correct verb above it.

     Hans Christian Andersen's greatest gift to Denmark ~~were~~ *was* his fairy tales. His collection ~~are~~ *is* stories for children and adults alike. Andersen also wrote plays and novels. However, his fairy tales, not his greatest novel, ~~is~~ *are* still read outside of Scandinavia. In Andersen's collection there ~~is~~ *are* fairy tales about both people and animals. His tales about human nature ~~has~~ *have* entertained many generations.

Chapter 9: Indefinite Pronouns and Problem Nouns as Subjects

Practice A
Underline the verb in parentheses that agrees with the subject.

1. Each of Tia's brothers *(owns, own)* a book of fairy tales by Hans Christian Andersen.

2. "The Emperor's New Clothes" *(is, are)* one of his famous stories.

3. Neither of the girls *(has read, have read)* "The Ugly Duckling."

4. *(Was, Were)* "Little Ida's Flowers" also authored by Andersen?

5. A group of children always *(crowds, crowd)* around the librarian whenever she starts to read one of Andersen's tales.

Practice B
Underline the verb in parentheses that agrees with the subject.

6. Today I read that seven dollars and sixty-eight cents *(is, are)* equal to one Danish krone.

7. None of Denmark *(is, are)* bordered by another Scandinavian country.

8. All of the country *(experiences, experience)* similar weather.

9. *(Does, Do)* some of the Danish people play board games?

10. I wonder if checkers *(is, are)* popular in Denmark.

Practice C
Underline the verb in parentheses that agrees with the subject.

11. My soccer team *(is, are)* taking a tour of Denmark next June.

12. Do you think athletics *(is, are)* important to the Danish people?

13. *(Does, Do)* any of you know about the educational system in Denmark?

14. I have read that most of the Danish people *(is, are)* literate.

15. Five years of high school education *(allows, allow)* a Danish student to be qualified for higher education.

Chapter 9: Pronoun-Antecedent Agreement

Practice A

Underline the pronoun in parentheses that agrees with the antecedent.

1. Neither Kirk nor his friend Thurston has taken *(his, their)* family to Tivoli Gardens.

2. Kristen and Ingrid took *(her, their)* American exchange student there last year.

3. Many like to take *(its, their)* friends to Tivoli Gardens at night.

4. Do all of the rides have *(its, their)* lights on at night?

5. One of the clowns gave me *(his, their)* blue balloon.

Practice B

In the blank write the pronoun that agrees with the antecedent.

_____*her*_____ 6. I wish that my aunt would give me _?_ recipe for Danish kringle.

_____*their*_____ 7. Most of my relatives enjoy coffee with _?_ Danish pastries.

_____*his*_____ 8. Someone in the class remembered that _?_ mother used to make kringle at Christmastime.

_____*his*_____ 9. Stanley hopes to visit _?_ great uncle who lives in Denmark.

_____*she*_____ 10. Either Jayne or Krischa will buy a Danish flag when _?_ is in Denmark.

Practice C

Underline the antecedent of the pronoun in parentheses. Then underline the pronoun in the parentheses that agrees with the antecedent.

11. Denmark is a land with beaches, lakes, and farms. Many believe *(its, their)* countryside is beautiful.

12. Both of Kaysa's Danish grandfathers spent *(his, their)* lives on a farm.

13. One of her grandmothers lived *(her, their)* early life in the city.

14. As far as he knows, none of Kaleb's family members are Danish. *(It, They)* are Norwegian.

15. If anyone has an opportunity to visit Denmark, *(he, they)* should not let the opportunity pass him by.

Chapter 10: Spelling

Practice A

Label the italicized words *C* (correct) or *I* (incorrect).

___*I*___ 1. Spelling words incorrectly has always caused me much *greif.*

___*I*___ 2. Even my two *sister-in-laws* have tried to help me with my spelling.

___*C*___ 3. Yesterday two unusual *events* occurred.

___*C*___ 4. I spelled both *"nachos"* and "tomatoes" correctly.

___*C*___ 5. A great *achievement* for me is spelling words correctly.

Practice B

Underline the correct word from the choices in parentheses.

6. I've tried to improve my spelling by *(keepping, keeping)* a list of words that I often misspell.

7. *(Recieve, Receive)* is one of the words that appears on my list.

8. I hope that this practice will be a good *(deterrent, deterent)* for some of my spelling problems.

9. Now I am *(beginning, begining)* to be a better speller.

10. I have also worked on *(memorizing, memorizeing)* specific spelling rules.

Practice C

Underline any misspelled words and write the corrections in the blanks.

___*"Obedience"*___ 11. Sometimes even a children's song like "Obedeince" can help a person with spelling.

___*deceiving*___ 12. Some words are decieving to the eye.

___*inaccurately*___ 13. Often I believe that I have spelled a word inaccuratly.

___*weird*___ 14. However, I remember that even though some words look wierd, they are still spelled correctly.

___*easier*___ 15. It's great to know that spelling is becoming easyer for me!

Chapter 10: Troublesome Verbs

Practice A

Underline the correct verb from the choices in parentheses.

1. I am determined that I *(shall, <u>will</u>)* learn to spell troublesome verbs correctly.

2. I have found that there are several ways that I *(may, <u>can</u>)* accomplish this task.

3. First, I can *(<u>sit</u>, set)* down to study the differences between the words.

4. I can also *(rise, <u>raise</u>)* my hand to ask my teacher a question about a word that I'm unsure of.

5. If I *(lie, <u>lay</u>)* a dictionary next to my desk, I will be able to double-check my spelling easily.

Practice B

Questions 6-10: Proofread the following paragraph for errors with troublesome verbs. Cross out each incorrect verb and write the correct verb above it.

Shall I tell you more tips about how you ~~may~~ *can* remember to spell troublesome verbs correctly? One thing to remember is that some verbs ~~shall~~ *will* have a direct object. Other verbs are used for preference or for permission. Some of these words seem tricky, but ~~sit~~ *set* your mind at ease and ~~lie~~ *lay* your worries aside. These difficult words can be conquered. Are you ready to ~~raise~~ *rise* to the challenge?

Practice C

Write five sentences using the following italicized words correctly. *(Answers will vary.)*

11. *rise* **My grandparents rise early every morning.**

12. past of *lay* **Yesterday one of their hens laid several eggs.**

13. *will* **When will Grandpa and Grandma buy a new rooster?**

14. *may* **May we see the hen house?**

15. *sit* **How long will that hen sit on her eggs?**

Chapter 10: Other Troublesome Words

Practice A

Label the italicized word *C* (correct) or *I* (incorrect).

___*I*___ 1. The more spelling words I memorize, the *less* I have to look up in the dictionary.

___*I*___ 2. My grandparents are *real* good spellers.

___*C*___ 3. They think that *it's* fun to do crossword puzzles.

___*I*___ 4. I think that they consider doing crossword puzzles to be *they're* hobby.

___*C*___ 5. While they work on the puzzles, Grandpa always asks Grandma if she will *lend* him her reading glasses.

Practice B

Underline the correct word from the choices in parentheses.

6. On Saturday I bought some new *(stationary, stationery)*.

7. I plan to write to Grandpa and Grandma to ask for some wise *(council, counsel)*.

8. I respect my grandparents because they have had such a great *(affect, effect)* on my life.

9. Grandpa and Grandma wrote back and gave me several *(principals, principles)* to follow.

10. They also said that they would *(pray, prey)* for me.

Practice C

Questions 11-15: Proofread the following paragraph for errors with troublesome words. Cross out each error and write the correct word above it.

It was Grandpa's ~~prophesy~~ *prophecy* that I would receive an A on my next spelling test. I studied harder than I've ever studied before, so I was ~~real~~ *really* pleased when my teacher passed back my test. I spelled every word correctly ~~accept~~ *except* for one. I forgot how to spell the ~~capitol~~ *capital* of Florida. I'm still thankful that I was able to spell all of the other words correctly, though. As a reward for my hard work, Grandpa and Grandma are going to take me out for ~~desert~~ *dessert*.

Name_____

Chapter 11: Personal Names, Religions, Nationalities

Practice A

Underline each word that contains a capitalization error.

1. I asked <u>pastor</u> Dryer if he could tell me anything about <u>buddhism</u>.

2. He told me that it is an <u>asian</u> religion.

3. The <u>Founder</u> of this religion is known as the <u>enlightened one</u>.

4. Instead of following the Bible, many <u>buddhists</u> follow what is written in the <u>tipitaka</u>.

5. After hearing about this religion, I am thankful that my <u>father</u> in heaven has led me to the truth of <u>his word</u>.

Practice B

Underline each word that contains a capitalization error and write the correction in the blank. If the sentence is correct, write *C* in the blank.

_____*C*_____ 6. My British literature teacher is Dr. Geoffrey A. Klein.

____*Spenserian*____ 7. This week Dr. Klein is teaching us about <u>spenserian</u> stanza.

_____*Scots*_____ 8. Robert Burns, who often wrote in <u>scots</u>, used this stanza form in some of his poems.

_____*British*_____ 9. John Keats, a <u>british</u> poet, also used this poetic form in his poem "The Eve of St. Agnes."

_____*C*_____ 10. "She dwells with Beauty—Beauty that must die" is a line from Keats's "Ode on Melancholy."

Practice C

Questions 11-15: Proofread the following paragraph for errors in capitalization. Cross out each error and write the correct letter above it.

Today my ~~D~~*d*ad told me about the ~~s~~*S*wiss reformer Ulrich Zwingli. In the early 1500s, Zwingli read Erasmus's translation of the ~~n~~*N*ew ~~t~~*T*estament, and he was greatly influenced by Erasmus. Zwingli preached against Roman ~~c~~*C*atholicism. He believed that a person is saved by faith and not by works. In addition, Zwingli believed in the individual priesthood of the believer.

Chapter 11: Place Names, Transportation, Astronomical Terms

Practice A

Label the italicized terms C (correctly capitalized) or I (incorrectly capitalized).

___*I*___ 1. Neptune is the eighth planet from the *sun*.

___*C*___ 2. Have you ever heard of the *Galaxy,* a large military jet?

___*I*___ 3. Its steam exhaust system and its multitube boiler made the *rocket* a profitable steam loco-motive in 1829.

___*I*___ 4. The Jacobsens' address is 285 *starburst lane.*

___*C*___ 5. The *state flag* of South Carolina has a crescent moon and a palmetto tree.

Practice B

In the blank write the letter of the choice that is capitalized correctly.

___*C*___ 6. A. the southeast
B. the Far east
C. the Middle East

___*B*___ 7. A. a Mountain Lake
B. Lake Oswego
C. a freshwater Lake

___*C*___ 8. A. Auckland, new Zealand
B. Cape town, South Africa
C. Riyadh, Saudi Arabia

___*A*___ 9. A. Mount Kilimanjaro
B. carlsbad caverns
C. a deep Valley

___*C*___ 10. A. the capital of north Dakota
B. a river in New mexico
C. a bridge in West Virginia

Practice C

Underline each word that contains a capitalization error and write the correction in the blank. If the sentence is correct, write C in the blank.

_____*New*_____ 11. William Driver was originally from <u>new</u> England.

_____*Salem*_____ 12. He was born in <u>salem</u>, Massachusetts, in 1803.

_____*Doggett*_____ 13. When he was twenty-one, he commanded his first ship, the *Charles* <u>*doggett*</u>.

_____*Old*_____ 14. Driver flew the American flag on his ship; he called the flag <u>old</u> Glory.

_____*Tennessee*_____ 15. When Driver lived in <u>tennessee</u> in the mid-1860s, he hid his flag in a blanket.

Chapter 11: Businesses and Organizations,
Cultural and Historical Terms, Titles and First Words

Practice A

In the blank write the letter of the choice that is capitalized correctly.

___C___   1.   A. Levi's Blue jeans
                 B. Middle school
                 C. the Korean War

___B___   2.   A. Father's day
                 B. Nobel Prize
                 C. Parent teacher Association

___B___   3.   A. the school's Chess Club
                 B. Socialist
                 C. the colosseum in rome

___A___   4.   A. Republican Party
                 B. the house of Representatives
                 C. Reform bill of 1832

___B___   5.   A. the *San Francisco examiner*
                 B. a U-boat
                 C. a difficult Science quiz

Practice B

Underline each word that contains a capitalization error and write the correction in the blank. If the sentence is correct, write *C* in the blank.

_____C_____   6.   Willis asked, "Would you like to go to a concert for your birthday?"

_____but_____   7.   "I'd enjoy that," said Adrienne, "<u>But</u> what concert shall we attend?"

_____College_____   8.   "There's a concert going on at Lake Erie <u>college</u> this weekend," answered Willis.

_____Four_____   9.   "I believe you're right," said Adrienne. "Aren't they playing Vivaldi's *The <u>four</u> Seasons?"*

_____Bank_____   10.   "Yes, they are," replied Willis. "I think we can purchase tickets at Society <u>bank</u>."

Practice C

Questions 11-15: Rewrite the following letter on the blanks below, correcting any capitalization errors.

Dear Mr. and Mrs. Gamboe and family,

Thank you for inviting me to the singspiration at your home last night. I am so glad that we were able to sing my favorite hymn, "Be Thou my Vision." I think my favorite lines are "Heart of my own heart, whatever befall, / still be my Vision, o Ruler of all." These words encourage me to have God as my focus no matter what happens in my life. Overall, I thought the evening was very spiritually uplifting, and once again, I appreciate your hospitality.

sincerely,

Omari Gress

Dear Mr. and Mrs. Gamboe and Family,

Thank you for inviting me to the singspiration at your home last night. I am so glad that we were able to sing my favorite hymn, "Be Thou My Vision." I think my favorite lines are "Heart of my own heart, whatever befall, / Still be my Vision, O Ruler of all." These words encourage me to have God as my focus no matter what happens in my life. Overall, I thought the evening was very spiritually uplifting, and once again, I appreciate your hospitality.

Sincerely,

Omari Gress

NOTE: Some students may identify Vision *in the third line as a capitalization error. Explain that the translators of this ancient Irish hymn capitalized* Vision *in this line because this word refers to God.*

Chapter 12: Commas

Practice A

Label the following sentences *C* (correct) or *I* (incorrect).

___I___ 1. A plant, that is a nuisance, is a weed.

___C___ 2. Uncle Ralph, who enjoys gardening, is constantly ridding his garden of weeds.

___I___ 3. The weed, with which he struggles the most, is the dandelion.

___C___ 4. A weed, which grows in a garden, can often be a pretty flower.

___C___ 5. This flower, which appears attractive, can actually be deadly.

Practice B

Identify the sentence that is punctuated correctly. In the blank write the letter of the choice that corresponds to the correct answer.

___B___ 6. A. A dandelion is yellow, and grows in fields and yards.
B. A dandelion is yellow and grows in fields and yards.

___A___ 7. A. The dandelion came from Europe, and it has a French name.
B. The dandelion came from Europe, and, it has a French name.

___A___ 8. A. My little sister puts dandelions in a vase or a small glass pitcher.
B. My little sister puts dandelions in a vase, or a small glass pitcher.

___B___ 9. A. The advertisement on the bag of weed killer is, "Destroy those dandelions!"
B. The advertisement on the bag of weed killer is "Destroy those dandelions!"

___B___ 10. A. This weed killer should last us until August, 2006.
B. This weed killer should last us until August 2006.

Practice C

Insert any missing commas into the following sentences. If the sentence is correct, write *C* in the blank.

___C___ 11. People who like dandelion leaves eat them cooked in some dishes or raw in a salad.

___C___ 12. Dandelion leaves that are the tastiest are young leaves.

_____ 13. A dandelion's root,which has hairlike branches,grows to about three feet long.

_____ 14. Jacques,who likes blowing on dandelions,does not realize that he is actually spreading dandelion seeds.

___C___ 15. Gardeners not only want to kill dandelions but also want to preserve the grass.

Chapter 12: Quotation Marks, Ellipses, and Underlining for Italics

Practice A

Label the following sentences *C* (correct) or *I* (incorrect).

_____*I*_____ 1. "How are we going to get rid of all these weeds in our back yard? asked Yolanda."

_____*C*_____ 2. "Well," answered Dee, "I don't know, but . . ."

_____*I*_____ 3. "I was thinking, said Yolanda, that we should purchase a pesticide."

_____*C*_____ 4. Dee thought that Yolanda had made a good suggestion.

_____*I*_____ 5. The dictionary defines the word weed as "a plant considered undesirable . . . or troublesome."

Practice B

Insert any missing quotation marks into the following sentences.

6. The nursery rhyme says,"A man of words and not of deeds / Is like a garden full of weeds."

7. According to St. Augustine,"Anger is a weed; hate is the tree."

8. "Isn't it interesting,"said Philippe,"how people associate weeds with vice?"

9. "I suppose,"added Kassandra,"that people dislike weeds just as much as they dislike evil deeds."

10. "I think you're right,"answered Philippe."Weeds damage plants just like sin damages people's lives."

Practice C

In the following sentences place quotation marks around the terms that require quotation marks and underline the terms that should be italicized.

11. The word <u>gardening</u> has two <u>n</u>'s.

12. "Thy Word Is like a Garden, Lord"is a hymn I learned as a child.

13. Does Peg subscribe to <u>Better Homes and Gardens</u>?

14. Robert Louis Stevenson's <u>A Child's Garden of Verses</u> is a book of poetry for children.

15. Andrew Marvell wrote a poem entitled"The Garden."

Chapter 12: Apostrophes

Practice A

Underline the word that is punctuated correctly from the choices in parentheses.

1. I hope *(its, <u>it's</u>)* going to rain.

2. The *(<u>vegetables</u>, vegetable's)* in our garden really need the rain.

3. *(<u>Mom's</u>, Moms')* carrots are growing fast.

4. *(Dads, <u>Dad's</u>)* allowing Emily and Erik to grow a tomato plant.

5. So far, *(<u>Emily and Erik's</u>, Emily's and Erik's)* plant does not have any tomatoes.

Practice B

Insert any missing apostrophes into the following sentences.

6. Wouldn't it be fun to grow watermelons?

7. Grandpa told me that he used to grow watermelons back in '44.

8. Aunt Francine's string beans are ready to be picked.

9. I hope that my potatoes taste as good as Percy's do.

10. The Lloyds' garden is full of delicious vegetables.

Practice C

Questions 11-15: Insert any missing apostrophes into the following paragraph. Underline any words that have misplaced apostrophes.

<u>Renee's</u> and Larry's garden always produces beautiful squash. Larry says that there are two types of squash: summer squash and winter squash. Renee says that they've never grown winter squash, although the Williamses, their next-door neighbors, have grown winter squash since '95. Last year Larry and Renee grew zucchini. It's strange how people vary in their taste for vegetables. Larry likes his zucchini raw, but Renee likes <u>her's</u> fried. Summer is almost here, so they'll be enjoying more squash soon.

Chapter 12: Other Punctuation

Practice A

Identify the punctuation missing from each sentence. In the blank write the letter that corresponds to the correct answer.

> A. semicolon
> B. colon

___A___ 1. Yellow crookneck is a summer squash banana squash is a winter squash.

___B___ 2. You may start cooking the squash at 630 P.M.

___B___ 3. Several states are important squash producers Texas, Florida, California, New Jersey, and New York.

___B___ 4. There's only one way I like my squash prepared steamed

___A___ 5. Squash is a healthy vegetable it is a low-calorie food.

Practice B

Identify the punctuation missing from each sentence. In the blank write the letter that corresponds to the correct answer.

> A. hyphen
> B. dash
> C. parentheses

___A___ 6. Corrina planted twenty four tomato plants.

___C___ 7. She is growing three kinds of tomatoes: 1 cherry tomatoes, 2 Big Boy Hybrid tomatoes, and 3 Ponderosa tomatoes.

___C___ 8. Solar Set another kind of tomato is grown in high temperatures at high levels of humidity.

___B___ 9. The tomato although many consider it a vegetable is really a fruit.

___B___ 10. People use tomatoes in ketchup, tomato sauce, and did you remember to pick up some tomato soup at the grocery store?

Practice C

Identify the punctuation missing from each sentence. In the blank write the letter that corresponds to the correct answer.

    A. semicolon
    B. colon
    C. hyphen
    D. dash
    E. parentheses

_____A_____ 11. The tomato plant has hairy stems it also has yellow flowers.

_____D or E_____ 12. Tomatoes they can grow in just about any type of soil are green before they ripen.

_____B_____ 13. Tomatoes ripen into various colors red, orange, or yellow.

_____C_____ 14. My sister in law likes to eat bacon, lettuce, and tomato sandwiches.

_____D or E_____ 15. Ponderosa tomatoes a large variety are Dad's favorite.

Working Together

Whether you have been teaching for many years or are just getting started, your comments are vital in helping us maintain our standard of excellence. In fact, most of the improvements in our materials started with good advice from consumers. So after you have put our products to the test, please give us your thoughtful comments and honest assessment.

And thanks for your valuable help!

Book Title _____ Grade level _____

Material was ☐ used in classroom. ☐ used in home school. ☐ examined only.

How did you hear about us?

_____
_____
_____

I liked

_____
_____
_____

I'd like it better if

_____
_____
_____

How did our material compare with other publishers' materials?

_____
_____
_____

Other comments?

_____
_____
_____

(OPTIONAL)
☐ Dr. ☐ Miss ☐ Mrs. ☐ Mr. _____

School_____

Street_____

City_____State_____ZIP_____

Phone(___)_____

Fold and tape. DO NOT STAPLE.
Mailing address on the other side.

BJU PRESS

Greenville, SC 29614

TAPE SHUT — <u>DO NOT STAPLE</u>

BUSINESS REPLY MAIL
FIRST-CLASS MAIL   PERMIT NO. 344   GREENVILLE, SC

POSTAGE WILL BE PAID BY ADDRESSEE

BJU PRESS
TEXTBOOK DIVISION
1700 WADE HAMPTON BLVD.
GREENVILLE, SC 29609-9971

- - - - - Fold here -

- - - - - Fold here -